Adapting to European Integration

Small States and the European Union

edited by

KENNETH HANF and BEN SOETENDORP

Longman
London and New York

Addison Wesley Longman Limited
Edinburgh Gate
Harlow, Essex CM20 2JE, United Kingdom
and Associated Companies throughout the world.

*Published in the United States of America
by Addison Wesley Longman, New York*

First published 1998

ISBN 0 582-28699-9

British Library Cataloguing-in-Publication Data

A catalogue record for this book is available from the British Library

Library of Congress Cataloging-in-Publication Data

Adapting to European integration : small states and the European Union
  / edited by Kenneth Hanf and Ben Soetendorp.
        p.   cm.
    Includes bibliographical references and index.
    ISBN 0-582-28699-9 (PPR)
      1. European Union Countries–Politics and government.   2. European
  Union.   I. Hanf, Kenneth.   II. Soetendorp, Ben, 1944–
  D1060.A28   1997
  337.1'42–dc21   97–10486
                                                                         CIP

Set by 35 in 10/12pt Times
Produced through Longman Malaysia, PP

Contents

Contributors

Jan Beyers graduated in political science from the University of Antwerp and has done research on the participation of Belgian officials in negotiations of the Council of Ministers and on Belgian foreign policy-making. He has published on these topics in the *Journal of Regional and Federal Studies, The International Spectator* and *Res Publica*. Presently he is engaged in research at the University of Antwerp on the social basis of European policy in Belgium.

Michael Christakis is presently International Relations Advisor in the Foundation for Mediterranean Studies and Lecturer in the National School of Public Administration in Athens, Greece. From July 1988 to January 1990 he served as Chief Editor of *PARADIGMS*, the University of Kent's Journal of International Relations.

Since 1994, **Søren Z. von Dosenrode** has held a Jean Monnet Professorship in Political Science at the University of Aalborg in Denmark. His main research area is the analysis of European politics. Recent publications include 'Networks in Danish EU-Policy Making' (Aalborg University, 1997) and 'Danish EU-Policy Making – The Interplay of Government, Administration and Parliament' in H. Branner and M. Kelstruup, eds., *The Formulation of Danish European Policies* (forthcoming).

Magnus Ekengren is working at the Swedish Ministry for Foreign Affairs, and is a PhD candidate at the Department of Political Science of the Stockholm University. He is writing a dissertation on 'The Time of European Governance'. He was previously a Research Assistant at the Swedish Institute of International Affairs.

Kenneth Hanf is Senior Lecturer in Public Administration in the Department of Public Administration of the Erasmus University in Rotterdam, The Netherlands. His research has focused on questions of multi-actor and multi-level implementation of environmental policy at both the national and international levels. Recent publications include 'Implementing International Environmental Agreements: Translating Good Intentions into Concrete Actions' in A. Blowers and P. Glasbergen, eds., *Environmental Policy in an International Context* (1996) and, together with A. Underdal, 'Domesticating International Agreements: The Problem of Implementation and Compliance' in A. Underdal, ed., *The International Politics of Environmental Management* (1997).

Bart Kerremans is currently an Assistant Professor in International Relations and a Senior Research Fellow of the Scientific Fund Flanders at the Katholieke Universiteit in Leuven, Belgium. He is engaged in research on EU decision-making and on the external economic relations of the European Union. Recent publications include *Besluitvorming en integratie in de externe economische betrekkingen van de Europese Unie* (1996) and *Internationale economische organisaties* (1997), co-authored with L. Cuyvers.

Stephan Kux is a senior lecturer at the Europainstitut of the University of Basel in Switzerland. His main research interests are decision-making in the EU, multi-level governance, federalism and subsidiarity in the EU, and environmental policy and administration. Recent publications include *Zukunft Neutralität?* (1994), *Die neue Welthandelsordnung* (1995) and *Aufbruch der Kantone nach Europa (1997)*.

Brigid Laffan is Jean Monnet Professor of European Politics at University College, Dublin. She is the author of *Integration and Co-operation in Europe* (1992), *Constitutions-Building in the Union* (1996) and *The Finances of the Union* (1997).

Since 1980, **Paul Luif** has been member of the scientific staff of the Austrian Institute for International Affairs in Laxenburg near Vienna. His research is on foreign policies of neutral states in Europe, European Integration, Common Foreign and Security Policy, and the enlargement of the European Union. His publications include *On the Road to Brussels: The Political Dimension of Austria's, Finland's and Sweden's Accession to the European Union* (1995) and 'Enlargement as a Challenge and Incentive for Reform' in E. Regelsberger *et al.*, eds, *Foreign Policy of the European Union: From ECP to CFSP and Beyond* (1997).

Francesc Morata is Professor of Political Science and Public Administration at the Autonomous University of Barcelona. His research fields include the analysis of public policy, intergovernmental relations and European integration. He has published extensively on questions of regional government in Spain and the impact of the EU on Spanish policy ('Vying for European Funds: Territorial Restructuring in Spain' in L. Hooghe, ed., *Cohesion Policy and European Integration* (1996) and 'Spanish Regions in the EU' in B. Jones and M. Keating, eds., *The European Union and the Regions* (1995)). He has also written on environmental policy and administration in Spain.

Ben Soetendorp is Associate Professor in International Relations at Leiden University. He has written extensively on foreign policy-making in Western Europe in a comparative perspective, focusing on the interaction between the European Union and the member states. Among others, his recent publications include 'The Evolution of the EC/EU as a Single Foreign Policy Actor' in W. Carlsnaes and S. Smith, eds., *European Foreign Policy* (1994).

Bengt Sundelius is Senior Lecturer in European Political Studies with the Swedish Research Council for the Humanities and Social Sciences, posted at Uppsala University.

Ulf Sverdrup is a Research Fellow at ARENA (Advanced Research on the Europeanisation of the Nation State) at the University of Oslo in Norway. He is currently writing his PhD dissertation on the topic of Europeanisation of the national budgeting systems. He has a broad research interest in questions of European integration and issues of institutional theory. He has published an analysis of the institutional changes in the Norwegian Ministry of Finance and, together with A. Farsund, has co-written an article on institutional adaptation.

Etain Tannam is a lecturer in politics at University College, Galway. She has recently completed a book on the topic of the European Union and the relationship between Northern Ireland and the Republic of Ireland. Other publications include articles in *Governance, Ethnic and Racial Studies* and *Regional and Federal Studies*.

Preface

In theory, edited volumes appear to be an easy way to make interesting information on important topics available to a broad audience in a relatively short time. In practice, they turn out to take much more time and energy than initially foreseen. For the authors, there is always just one more request for another change or addition to the text – after they had assumed that the manuscript had long since been sent to the publisher. For the editors there is often the frustrating wait for the last revisions to reach their desk. Then, too, there are the agonizing decisions to be made as to whether to ask for a last rewrite or to carry out the final revision of a chapter themselves. And of course there is the perennial problem of finding a sufficiently large block of unencumbered time to work efficiently on finally writing the conclusions.

And yet, somehow the day arrives when the manuscript is sent off to the publisher. But that point would not have come, in this case, if the European Consortium for Political Research (ECPR) had not funded a research planning session in Uppsala, Sweden, where the initial 'hard core' of the contributors to this volume first met to discuss the project of small states and European integration. This support was followed by the successful effort of Michael Christakis, one of the contributors to the book, in introducing us to secrets of the local politics and hospitality of Crete, where we held our second working session to discuss the first drafts of the chapters. We also owe a debt of gratitude to the municipal government of Heraklion for receiving us so cordially during this visit. And of course, our thanks are due to Chris Harrison of Addison Wesley Longman, who so patiently waited for the publishable outcome of all this activity, often wondering, we are sure, why deadlines are included in contracts if they are regularly exceeded.

Kenneth Hanf and Ben Soetendorp
January 1997

Abbreviations

AJI	
ARE	(Spanish) Assembly of European Regions
AUNS	(Swiss) Action for an Independent and Neutral Switzerland
BNC	(Dutch) Interministerial Working Group to Assess New Commission Proposals
CAP	Common Agricultural Policy
CDGAE	(Spanish) Committee on Economic Affairs
CEI	Interministerial Economic Committee
CFSP	Common Foreign and Security Policy
CIEA-CE	(Spanish) Interministerial Committee for Economic Affairs related to the EC
CiU	(Spanish) Catalan Nationalists
CMRE	Council of Municipalities and Regions and Europe
Co-Co	(Dutch) Coordination Committee for European Integration and Association Issues
COREPER	Committee of Permanent Representatives
COREU	Correspondant Européen
CVP	(Swiss) Christian People's Democratic Party
DG2	Direction for the Agricultural Policy
EBS	(Swiss) European Movement Switzerland
EC	European Community
ECJ	European Court of Justice
ECOFIN	Council of Financial and Economics Ministers
ECSC	European Coal and Steel Community
ECU	European Currency Unit
EEA	European Economic Area
EEC	European Economic Community
EFTA	European Free Trade Association
EMS	European Monetary System
EMU	Economic and Monetary Union
ENYEK	Special Legal Service for the European Communities
EP	European Parliament

ERDF	European Regional Development Fund
ERM	Exchange Rate Mechanism
ESA	European Surveillance Authority
ESF	European Social Fund
EU	European Union
FDP	(Swiss) Radical Democratic Party
FPÖ	(Austria) Freedom Party
GATT	General Agreement on Tariffs and Trade
GDP	Gross Domestic Product
GNP	Gross National Product
IBEC	Irish Business Employers Confederation
ICMSA	Irish Creamery Milk Suppliers Association
ICTU	Irish Congress of Trade Unions
IEA	Institute of European Affairs
IFA	Irish Farmers Association
IGC	Intergovernmental Conference
IMP	Integrated Mediterranean Programme
IO	Interest Organization
KKE	(Greek) Communist Party
MEP	Member of the European Parliament
NATO	North Atlantic Treaty Organization
NDP	National Development Plan
NEAT	(Swiss) New Alpine Transit Route
N + N	neutral and non-aligned
OECD	Organization for Economic Cooperation and Development
ÖVP	(Austrian) Christian Democratic People's Party
PASOK	(Greek) Panhellenic Socialist Movement
PMO	Prime Minister's Office
PR	Permanent Representation
PSOE	(Spanish) Socialist Party
REA	(Dutch) Council for European Affairs
SEA	Single European Act
SECE	(Spanish) Secretariat of State for the EC
SGB	(Swiss) Swiss Federation of Trade Unions
SPÖ	(Austrian) Social Democratic Party of Austria
SPS	(Swiss) Social Democratic Party
SVP	(Swiss) Swiss People's Party
TD	(Ireland) Member of Parliament
TEU	Treaty on European Union (Maastricht Treaty)
UN	United Nations
WEU	West European Union
WTO	World Trade Organization

Chapter 1

Small States and the Europeanization of Public Policy

KENNETH HANF AND BEN SOETENDORP

Introduction: the Europeanization of public policy

Decision-making in the western European states is becoming more Europeanized in the sense that what happens now at the level of the European Union (EU) penetrates more and more areas of national policy-making. Interactions with Brussels as well as bilateral contacts with partners in the member-states lead to a Europeanization of public policy-making within the different countries. The Europeanization in and through the EU, as Wessels (1995) has pointed out, is an 'essential tendency' of the evolution of the post-war state in western Europe. The term 'Europeanization' is understood as a process in which Europe, and especially the EU, become an increasingly more relevant and important point of political reference for the actors at the level of the member-states. Laffan and Tannam note in Chapter 5 that more and more decisions with regard to different policy sectors are taken through 'intergovernmental and transgovernmental policy networks that reach from Brussels into subnational government in the member-states'. Consequently, they observe further, politicians and officials participate now in an evolving polity which provides opportunities for political action but also imposes constraints on their freedom of action. Therefore, if they are to respond effectively to the needs and demands of the citizens of their countries, they will need to learn to work in a system of public policy-making that involves complex games in multiple arenas.

Still, member-states have not been inclined to give up their central position. Even in those policy sectors where this process has proceeded the farthest, the member-states are still the central actors, although they are now deeply embedded in the Euro-level policy-making process (Richardson, 1996: x). In the coming years, through both the constitutional decisions based on the work on the pending intergovernmental conference and the legislative decisions through which these are worked out, a balance will be sought between 'continued integration and continued national sovereignty' (ibid.: xi). Wessels notes that up until now this has meant trading de facto sovereignty for access to and influence on the policy decisions made jointly through the policy process of the EU. By means of the Council working groups and other familiar consultative committees, national representatives sit on the committees that control the formation of EU policy (Wessels, 1995).

Most frequently these developments are examined in terms of how policy-making is organized at the EU level, and how the interaction of national and European-level actors affects the definition of national interest, the resources available for pursuing it, the exercise of influence and the legitimacy of the decisions reached at the EU level. Likewise, interest is focused on the organizational alternatives for organizing the relations between the different institutional actors of the EU. But equally important are the kinds of adjustments made at national level – in the way that politics is organized and policy is made – in order to accommodate new situations and participate effectively in EU-level game. This Europeanization has had, as Richardson has pointed out, 'a major impact on the policy processes at the national level, on the behaviour of different policy actors, both public and private, and on the institutions of the member states' (Richardson, 1996: x). As a result of the intermingling of EU and national levels, 'the national political system will become progressively permeated by environmental inputs from "outside" which, over time, become internalized in politics and policy making' (Ladrech, 1994). Therefore, while the result at the macro European level may well be some kind of 'co-operative federalism without a state' (Richardson, 1996), important changes will be introduced at the level of the individual member-states themselves as well. Laffan and Tannam also remind us that 'EU membership is not just about involvement in Brussels-level decision-making because the EU can and does act as an agent of change in the member-states'. Viewed in these terms, Europeanization involves 'an incremental process reorienting the direction and shape of politics to the degree that EC political and economic dynamics become part of the organisational logic of national politics and policy-making' (Ladrech, 1994: 69).

In this connection we can also refer to the observation of Albert Weale that 'Participation in international regimes of environmental protection cannot be understood without examining the changing patterns of domestic politics' (Weale, 1992: 200). In our view, this applies to other policy areas as well. As Weale further points out, '[t]he internationalisation of political life does not simply mean that domestic policy is constrained by international factors; it also means that foreign policy-making is constrained by domestic factors' (*ibid.*: 200). However, this mutual restraint does not occur in the form of two levels of action confronting each other but rather in the form of interrelated actors in a multi-level set of linked games, where some of the interactions are 'mediated' through a more 'central' actor that aggregates inputs from other participants. In turn, these other actors can themselves, either directly or again via another intermediary actor 'specialized' in their interest sector (at both national and international levels), seek to gain access to and influence over authoritative decision-makers with regard to a particular phase of the policy process.

Each member-state tries to ensure that European outcomes are as close as possible to the national interest, yet these national interests themselves are now defined in the context of the EU. In this sense, national interests are not formed in a (domestic) vacuum and 'brought to Brussels' to be 'defended' or 'realized'. Again, we have here to do with nested games: the outcomes of the games in national capitals are influenced by what is decided in Brussels; at the same time, however, what is decided in Brussels depends on or is influenced by the outcomes of the games within each member-state. This does not only occur sequentially, but simultaneously through the various structures and processes that join national and EU actors in the formulation and implementation of policy decisions.

Of course, the role of domestic institutional structures in the formulation and implementation of EU policies has long been recognized. Quite often, however, the analysts have been more interested in the emergence of transnational subsystems in the EU than in the relationships between existing sectoral arrangements at national-level and EU policy-making. For example, Bulmer states that 'the pattern of negotiations in each policy sub-structure sets the key in which the relevant national ministers (and interest groups) will behave in the upper decisional tier' (Bulmer, 1983). In trying to account for the way in which national interests are defended in Brussels, it can be argued that the characteristics of domestic policy networks will constrain the ways in which national interests are promoted in the negotiation of a European directive or other decisions. In this sense, the leeway for action at the European level will be determined by the constellation of political forces on the issue at home. Other studies also stress the relationship between the behaviour of the member-state in the EU and the degree of its domestic adaptation to the external environment of the EU. In their study of the Federal Republic of Germany and the EU, Bulmer and Paterson argued that the internal policy-making style and the priority given by political parties, public opinion and socio-economic interest groups to domestic issues over European integration, were significant barriers to a leading role by Germany in the EC (Bulmer and Paterson, 1987). George and his colleagues propose that the position of Britain as a semi-detached member is a result of the gap between steady governmental adjustment to working within the EU on the one hand and slow political adaptation on the other (George, 1992).

What we want to examine is the extent to which there has been, as a result of the impact of Europeanization of public policy and, more specifically, as a result of membership in the EU, a reorientation of 'the organisational logic of national politics and policy-making', as Ladrech calls it (Ladrech, 1994: 69). This means that the country studies that follow seek to describe and understand the 'redefinition of political activity' as a result of EC membership – the 'reorientation of national politics by way of organisational change' (*ibid.*). It is assumed, therefore, that joining the EC has affected the political and administrative institutions of the member-states of the EC/EU in many ways, as the political leadership and the bureaucracy seek to cope with a considerably larger and more complex political environment.

The focus on small states

But why look at smaller states? A simple answer would be that the literature on the relationship between the EU and its member-states is most concerned with explaining the role of the larger states: France, Germany and Britain. Few scholars have focused on the relationship between the behaviour of the smaller members in the EU and the degree of their domestic adaptation to the external environment of the Union. This granted, what is a 'small state'? People seem to have an intuitively accurate idea about the nature of small states. For example, we almost automatically think of such characteristics as small territory, small population, little military strength, limited raw materials or resources, etc. Nevertheless, it remains difficult to come up with some kind of clear-cut definition of smallness. The observations made by Amstrup and Handel in their survey of research efforts on small states some years ago, saying that no definition of a small state is completely satisfactory, is still valid (Amstrup, 1976; Handel, 1981). Since a great part of the literature on small states deals with security problems, they have taken as their point of departure the perceptions of the state itself with regard to its capabilities for defending its security and asserting its national interests. In this sense a small state, or a weak state as some authors refer to it, is one that itself recognizes that it cannot obtain security primarily by use of its own capabilities. However, small states may have a problem of survival not only in their security policy but also in their trade policy. Handel therefore argues that weak states may be defined in economic terms as well. A small state may be defined as one that depends comparatively heavily upon foreign trade, both for supplies and sales markets (cf. Handel, 1981: 46).

In light of the difficulties encountered with the development of a concrete, scientific definition of a small state, some scholars who work on small-states theory avoid the entire problem of definition, either because it seems irrelevant to them or because it seems impossible to solve. Smallness is, in this conception, a comparative and not an absolute idea. 'Whatever scales of magnitude are employed seem arbitrary and it is difficult to pick out on them where smallness begins or ends' (Amstrup, 1976: 165–6). We are inclined, for the reasons mentioned, to follow the same approach to the problem of a definition. In our view, irrespective of the difference in their relative size, both Spain and the Netherlands are treated in this volume as small states. Spain forms a kind of hybrid in this regard: while it is formally counted under the large-state category (the number of votes, Commissioners), in many ways it is still in the category of a small state (cf. Handel, 1981: 31). The case of Spain underlines how problematic such distinctions of role and weight are in terms of physical size, i.e. land mass and population. With regard to some 'objective' criteria of economic development, the Netherlands is larger than other countries that surpass it in the usual measures of 'largeness'. It is not our intention to make a contribution to this discussion, nor do we necessarily take it as our point of departure. We feel that it is justification enough for a focus on these states that there is, relatively speaking, an information gap since discussions of the member-states within the EU usually focus on the larger member-states. Ironically, there are at present more smaller member-states than there are large ones; further expansion of the EU eastward will also increase the number of small states.

Since, in any case, small states can only be 'effective' at the international level if they are well organized in preparing and presenting their position on issues – relying on the 'force' of persuasion and argument – we would expect to find a self-conscious and systematic effort to ensure that institutional adjustments are appropriate, are carried out and function as intended. In this sense, efforts to adapt governmental and administrative structures and procedures to changes in the international environment would be centralized to ensure a well-functioning system of management with regard to EU affairs. Furthermore, and in this connection, it would seem plausible to assume that the political leadership in the smaller states, at least the cabinet and in particular the prime minister, would take direct interest in these adjustments and in European affairs. Therefore, in the chapters that follow, we will be interested in seeing to what extent explicit adaptation was sought in setting up EU-specific structures and processes, and to what extent countries built further on already existing structures or absorbed EU affairs into the 'normal order' of governmental business in other ways.

The countries discussed in the following chapters have been selected in 'historical pairs', that is couples of member-states which can be located at different points in the process of enlargement and deepening of the EU. The first pair consists of Belgium and the Netherlands, two of the original six members of the European Economic Community (EEC). These countries have participated in the initial efforts to design and put into operation the institutions and processes for joint decision-making. Denmark and Ireland entered an ongoing policy game. Instead of gradually growing with the EC, there was already something to which these two countries had to adjust upon becoming members. This was, of course, even more so the case with the accession of Greece (1981) and Spain (1986). Not only were numerous policies already in place, to which national legislation had to be harmonized, but also the very definite procedural moves, negotiating traditions and policy style of the EC had to be learned. The abrupt immersion into the realities of a highly developed and self-conscious political system was even more abrupt and dislocating for the most recent member pair in our sample, Austria and Sweden. Norway and Switzerland have been included as two countries where the political leadership had begun the preparations for membership only to see their efforts frustrated by the rejection of this membership by the broader public. Nevertheless, both foreign and domestic policy of these countries continue to be affected by developments within the EU. In this sense, these countries will also have to adjust to the impacts of this form of indirect Europeanization.

Irrespective of size, it could be argued that the impact of EU membership will depend on the point in time, with regard to the stage or degree of integration, at which a country becomes a member. Normally, international cooperation is an extended process which moves from an initial general commitment to deal jointly with a particular problem to the gradual expanding of the scope of the obligations and the filling in of the broad programmatic agreement with more concrete obligations. Under such conditions, there is a chance, over time, to become accustomed to working with other countries and, in some cases, through an international bureaucracy; to having national policy and policy-making processes 'interfered' with by actors and decisions from 'outside'. At the same time, regular contacts and interactions lead to familiarity, which in turn can breed trust and confidence in one's partners, mutual understanding of one another's situation and appreciation of new possibilities for action. In particular, Greece, Portugal and Spain and, most recently, Sweden, Finland and Austria, are countries that entered into an advanced form of cooperation and integration and had to swallow the whole ball of wax in one gulp. They were forced to move from a situation of relatively limited effects or impacts from European integration on domestic policy and politics (even though we will see that the EU had consequences for non-members long before they formally applied for membership) to a position where they were expected to take on a full set of obligations and to adjust quickly to the way in which things are done at the EU level.

What are we looking at?

In this book we examine the process of Europeanization of the smaller member-states of the EU, that is the impact of their membership on the domestic politics and institutions of these countries. Our aim is to describe and analyse how the political institutions in eight small member-states and two non-members responded to the internal and external demands springing from EC/EU membership. Most recently, two significant events in the recent history of European integration have occurred: the signing of the Single European Act (SEA) in 1986 and of the Treaty on European Union (TEU) in 1992, which at first glance could be expected to have had significant institutional implications for the member-states. The SEA and TEU extended EC/EU policy-making to new policy areas and established the more frequent use of qualified majority voting. At the same time, the most recent expansion of membership has brought new member-states into the fold, while further enlargement is on the agenda. As a consequence, the volume of EC/EU regulations that the member-states have had to deal with has increased, and the number of actors involved in the European policy-making process has enlarged. The intensification of the decision-making process, in terms of both deepening and extending the range of European policy, has confronted the member-states with the necessity to respond to the changes in the European environment.

The drawn-out political battles preceding the ratification of the TEU in several member-states made it obvious that while institutional adjustment to the additional European level of decision-making has taken place at the level of central government, there appears to be a wide variety of ways in which the various political actors in the different countries have internalized EC membership. Yet there are also similarities in the general strategies of response.

The analysis starts from the assumption that the policy and institutional consequences of the SEA and the Maastricht Treaty, for heuristic purposes, can be translated into a number of 'functional imperatives' regarding the capacities of the member-states to manage their 'European affairs' both in Brussels and at home. In the first place, member-states are required to engage in a wider range of activity with regard to the EU and at the European level. Preparation for the completion of the internal market and activities in new areas of policy competence have provided new opportunities for pursuing national objectives as well as contributing to a deepening of the integration process. In order to participate effectively in these decisions, member-states need to be in a position to organize and present their national positions effectively. The successful promotion of national interests within the context of European cooperation, in turn, presupposes the development of appropriate structures and processes for mobilizing domestic support as well as for coordinating the activities through which these national inputs are developed. It can, therefore, be assumed that membership of the EU will entail significant impacts not only on the substantive policies of the member-states but on their polity and domestic politics as well, that is, the way in which the national political game is played, the players involved and the way in which political decision-making within the separate countries, between different member-states and at the European level are linked together. If a given member-state is to 'manage its participation in Europe' effectively, it is to be assumed that adjustments will have to be made in its political and administrative institutions, and in the strategies that shape its international relations. Whether and to what extent a country in fact adapts to the various institutional challenges posed by advancing European integration – and the form that these responses take – is the empirical focus of this book.

An analysis of institutional adaptation should, of course, make clear what the authors understand by this concept. To describe and analyse such a process of change we will use the concept of adaptation borrowed from Ernst Haas (1990). Haas defines adaptation as the ability of a political actor to change its behaviour so as to meet challenges in the form of new demands by altering the means of action. As Haas points out, insofar as the ultimate ends are not questioned, the change in behaviour takes the form of a search for more adequate means to meet the new demands. Although institutional adaptation can be viewed, in the first instance, as a process of conscious choice, it is not necessarily a process of rational analysis of the challenge posed to existing arrangements in order to find the adjustment that would seem to be the most effective response to the particular challenge of 'managing European membership' effectively. It cannot, of course, be assumed that political actors adapt to changes in their environment automatically, and with success. Adjustment to external developments is not simply a stimulus–response reaction.

How a particular challenge is perceived and understood, the range of potential adjustments that come under consideration and the selection of one particular institutional response will depend on a number of country-specific factors. Obviously, the extent to which such adaptation occurs will depend on such things as prevailing institutional traditions, the balance of political power, the configuration of interests affected by European membership and the more general political culture of the country. Furthermore, even if adjustments are made, there is no guarantee that they will be appropriate or effective. Whether the new institutions will operate as intended, and with the expected results, will depend on the interplay of formal structures and the political dynamics of the domestic political process. Clearly, the adjustments chosen and the degree to which they have facilitated effective participation within the EC will vary from country to country. Such variety provides a rich opportunity for comparing specific national responses to a set of generally similar challenges to the 'organizational logic' of policy-making in the selected member-states. The chapters in this book describe and analyse the choices made and examine the factors, unique to each country, that have shaped the patterns of institutional adaptation that have emerged.

What has changed?

With Ladrech, we have used the notion of changes in the 'organisational logic of politics and policy-making' to refer to the 'adaptive processes of organisations to a changed or changing environment' (Ladrech, 1994: 71). But what has, in fact, been changed? Which impacts of Europeanization are of interest here? Perhaps the most obvious classification of types of impact is that which looks at the three 'Ps': policy, politics and polity. Clearly, membership in the EU has direct and intended consequences for the substantive policy that a country can and does pursue. Upon joining the EU – as a 'going concern' – one of the first things that must be done is to 'harmonize' existing national legislation to bring it into line with EU policy. Thereafter, efforts will be made to get national preferences, objectives and strategies incorporated into new European legislation. Member-states also have responsibility for the implementation of EU policy by means of national programmes and administrative action. As we have seen, the introduction of a new level of policy-making also changes both the substantive targets of political activity and the institutional arrangements through which societal interests seek to exert influence and shape policy decisions. Policy decisions of the EU define losers and winners in the political game; EU decisions become part of the national political struggle; and Brussels becomes an alternative arena for achieving the objectives of national actors.

However, while all this is important for defining the issues and stakes of the political game within the member-states, and for shaping the constellation and dynamics of the political forces involved, these impacts are not the focus of the studies in this book. It is the consequences of Europeanization for the 'polity' that are the central issue in the following chapters. It is assumed that changes can run from modifications of the constitutional order, in order to accommodate formal membership, to the introduction of new decision-making structures and procedures to structure the process by which member-states organize their participation in the EU. The country chapters contained in this book are organized around an examination of three dimensions of adaptation with regard to central government: governmental adaptation, political adaptation and strategic adaptation. Restricting our focus to changes that have taken place at the national level means that a number of other interesting institutional and political adjustments taking place in member-states are not examined. For example, the response of political parties and interest groups, subnational implementation of European legislation, the changing role (in detail) of subnational actors, especially regions, and the shifting balance between them and national government are not treated, except to the extent that these have affected the relationships between national governmental and administrative actors and these other participants in the policy process.

Governmental adaptation focuses, in the first instance, on the responses at the level of central government and refers to organizational adjustments and the changes in institutional capacity to meet the new challenges. Emphasis is laid on factors related to the national policy-making style such as departmental autonomy or the extent of centralization which are unique to each country and which have shaped the patterns of adaptation that have emerged. Here we look at the extent to which new actors have appeared on the scene with regard to European policy; the extent to which new institutional arrangements and procedures have been introduced to structure the relevant decision-making; and the kinds of mechanisms that have been set up to coordinate the participation of this extended set of actors. Although the focus here is initially that of the central level of decision-making, we will also explore the consequences of EU membership for the involvement of subnational actors in the processes of policy formulation and implementation, whenever this would seem relevant.

For each country we will look at what, if anything, has been done at the domestic level to change the way of doing government business in order to accommodate the consequences of membership of the EU (or changes in the way in which the EU functions as a result of modifications in the treaties). Furthermore, we want to examine the extent to which decision-making responsibilities and powers regarding the country's participation in EU policy process have been reallocated.

Since Europeanization entails an 'internationalization' of traditional domestically orientated actors, it is interesting to note the occasion for and the point in time that sectoral ministries become involved in European decision-making. Have standard operating procedures been developed to organize this participation, both within the individual ministries and between them? Of particular interest in this regard are changes in the relations between the foreign office and the sectoral ministries as a consequence of extension of EU policy-making to additional policy sectors and participation of sectoral ministers in sectoral councils of ministers. To what extent does the foreign office play a role as policy-maker, gate-keeper, respected 'honest broker' or simply postmaster? Again, given the importance to small states of managing their 'foreign' affairs effectively, it could be expected that the prime minister would seek to introduce some kind of systematic central political control over both the process of adaptation and the management of European affairs. In this regard, has the degree and form of the prime minister's involvement in policy-making and/or policy coordination changed? Are there any new coordinating units at the Cabinet level or in the prime minister's office?

Posing these questions in this way runs the risk of assuming that these countries have made significant changes in the organization, procedures and style of policy-making and implementation in response to the Europeanization of public policy. Yet exactly this remains to be seen. It is equally possible that there has been no radical response to Europeanization in the form of new solutions to apparently new problems. Existing routines and capabilities can be judged to be adequate and appropriate for coping with new challenges, requiring only incremental adjustments to accommodate the demands of EU membership. Moreover, institutional changes may more strongly reflect the historical experience and traditions of the country, and be shaped more directly by the pattern of constraints and possibilities defined by the endogenous dynamics of the country's political system. In this sense, although it may be tempting to assume that there will be some kind of convergence in the responses of different countries, by virtue of the shared status of smallness, it is equally possible that the variation in endogenous factors will lead to significant variation in the country-specific responses to common 'imperatives' of membership.

These observations should make us beware of exaggerating the 'rationalistic' features of the process of adaptation. In the first place, it cannot be assumed that there is some kind of centralized systematic planning and execution of adjustment to the perceived exigencies of Europeanization. Even though this would seem consistent with the self-conscious status of a small state, some features of the country, for example the strong emphasis on consensus politics through corporatist structures, may make adjustment to the EU policy style difficult; and other domestic political factors can set effective limits to the room available for change. At the domestic level, then, Europeanization may very well be more a process of gradual adaptation instead of a dramatic break with the past. Incremental adaptation to existing proced- ures and structures may have occurred, resulting in a gradual development of the requisite variety needed to handle new challenges from the environment.

Political adaptation concentrates on the response at the political level and has to do with the willingness of the political decision-makers to change their behaviour to meet the new demands. It refers basically to the extent that the EC/EU dimension has been internalized in domestic policy-making and the way in which the country's own history as well as the attitudes towards European integration facilitate or hinder such a commitment to the objectives of integration and the concrete legislative measures forthcoming from the joint policy process.

There are a number of aspects to this dimension of adaptation. The first has to do with the general pattern of support for or opposition to the goal of political integration. To what extent is there, in a given country, a general commitment to the value and institutionalization of European integration as such, as contrasted with a more instrumental approach which sees the EU, in the first instance, as a means for achieving concrete national objectives? To what extent do the political leadership and the general public, or key elements of society, differ in this regard? Is there a broad political consensus carrying the country's participation, and obligations, as a member of the EU? What is the position of the key social groups and the political parties on this point, i.e. the value of and the justification for the country's involve- ment in Europe? Is there an awareness that Europeanization, whether one likes it or not, is a given fact of contemporary political life, defining the context and the possibilities for the pursuance of national policy objectives? In this connection we would need to know to what extent (and among which groups of actors and interests) there was support for or opposition to the countries' membership or acceptance of changes in the EU. Which kinds of demands were made for what kinds of actions (responses) by which (societal) groups to which parts of the politico-administrative 'establishment'?

Another aspect has to do with the extent to which the EU is consciously seen as a means for promoting national objectives. Do we see a loosening of the traditional 'fixation' on national decision-making and policy, which is no longer adequate in the interdependent policy world driving the Europeanization process? Do we find attempts to use the European arena to achieve what some are unable to reach in the national context? Are actors within the member-states beginning to use the EU system to process problems of their own? To the extent that this is happening, the country in question is not only reacting to measures coming from Europe but also trying to work through the European policy process to seek solutions to national problems. In the process, the country's 'national interest' comes to be (co-)defined by European policy and context (and not as something that is brought to EU deliberations from 'the outside'). Has the EU, in this sense, become an 'alternative arena' for pursuing national objectives?

Of course, with regard to the EU the proof of the pudding is also in the imple- menting. Do the member-states attempt to win back the leeway for national policy surrendered during the formulation of joint policy during the implementation of the same measures, which is more directly under national control? What are the implementation records of the individual member-states and what measures have been taken, at the national level, in order to improve the implementation of EU policy? The faithful as well as effective execution of European legislation also makes demands on the administrative system of the member-states which require the necessary changes in organization and procedure. How do the different countries view the 'legitimacy' and urgency of EU legislation and how is the implementation of this policy organized?

Of particular interest is the question of whether there is a discrepancy or 'gap' between the political will to adapt and the institutional capacity to adapt – important because of the need for support and legitimation for participation in the process of further political integration and functioning of the EU. Here it is a question of some rather straightforward calculations of the consequences of events and policies at the EU level for domestic political support and the survival of the present government. In this connection, a country's attitude toward the EU policy process, as well as with regard to the process of political integration as such, will be shaped by the constellation of domestic political forces. The relative weight of the pros and cons for European integration and the priorities and distribution of costs and benefits among groups within the member-state concerning the issues under discussion in Brussels will be important factors determining the constraints and 'permissive consensus' within which member-states negotiate on concrete matters, as well as, the general direction of institutional development of the EU.

Strategic adaptation has to do with the response of the policy-makers to the need to develop a bargaining strategy for coping with the interaction between the national and European decision-making levels and the frequent informal transnational contacts among officials beyond the formal diplomatic channels. Here we are interested in the ways in which either the political leadership or the individual actors attempt to gain and exercise influence in the pursuit of their substantive and institutional objectives. We focus on the emerging formal and informal patterns of coalition behaviour among member-states and address the question of whether specific national circumstances result in a particular pattern of behaviour with regard to action at the European level.

National actors need to be aware that an understanding of the attitudes of one's partners and the dynamics of EU institutions is increasingly important if one wishes to be effective in the complex negotiations in a multilateral and multi-cultural environment. This new context makes new demands upon those who would be effective and have influence in the representation of national interests in the making of European policy. To what extent do key actors in the different countries have an adequate appreciation of the context within which they operate and the institutions and procedures through which decisions are taken? Is there evidence for some kind of conscious, systematic strategy for making the most of a country's decision-making 'resources' and having its weight felt in Brussels? What are the patterns of coalition-building during negotiations (at all levels)? With whom do these small countries align? Do they seek to join together or do they seek the protection or support of the larger member-states? Are there stable patterns of cooperation or do these vary from issue to issue? To what extent do the smaller states try, and with what degree of success, to shape the agenda and to take initiative rather than reacting to steps taken by other, larger states? To what extent have these strategies shifted or been modified as a result of SEA and TEU with the more frequent use of qualified majority voting? Have the direct transnational contacts with counterparts in other member-states been intensified as a result of the incorporation of new policy areas into the competence of Community institutions?

The concept of 'strategy' need not be limited to attempts to gain influence through the formation of coalitions and the development of effective bargaining techniques within the existing institutional arrangements. A country can also seek to influence decision-making with regards to both the structures and procedures that will determine the future shape of the EU and define the 'rules of the European policy game'. Likewise, attempts to affect the course of further integration can include preferences regarding the substantive objectives to be sought through joint efforts. The 'quality' of the life shaped by the decisions of the EU can also be an item of strategic concern.

It is the nature of edited volumes such as this, no matter how heavy the guiding hand of the editors, that the introduction often promises much more than the later chapters can deliver. Despite the solemn collective vows of the participating authors, the contributors to such volumes remain relatively untameable: each goes its own way, to some extent, even though all use a common terminology and follow a shared general plan of analytical attack. Nevertheless, the following chapters have been prepared with a common set of questions in mind. The first drafts were discussed at a meeting of the research group on Crete in December 1995. On the basis of a critical evaluation of the initial concept of the book, the authors redrafted their chapters. The result is a collection of short descriptions of the essential changes that have been introduced to adapt the national politico-administrative systems and policy style to the exigencies of membership of the EU. Taken together, the country chapters make visible to what extent and in what ways these small states have responded to a common set of external inputs into their domestic policy systems.

References

Amstrup, N. (1976) The perennial problem of small states: a survey of research efforts, *Cooperation and Conflict*, vol. 11, no. 3, pp. 163–82.

Bulmer, S. (1983) Domestic politics and European Community policy-making, *Journal of Common Market Studies*, vol. 21, no. 4, pp. 349–63.

Bulmer, S. and Paterson, W. (1987) *The Federal Republic of Germany and the European Community* (London: Allen & Unwin).

George, S. (ed.) (1992) *Britain and the European Community* (Oxford: Clarendon Press).

Haas, E. (1990) *When Knowledge is Power* (Berkeley: University of California Press).

Handel, M. (1981) *Weak States in the International System* (London: Frank Cass).

Ladrech, R. (1994) Europeanisation of domestic politics and institutions: the case of France, *Journal of Common Market Studies*, vol. 32, no. 1, pp. 69–88.

Richardson, J. (1996) Series editor preface. In Y. Mény, P. Muller and J.-L. Quermonne, *Adjusting to Europe: The Impact of the European Union on National Institutions and Policies* (London: Routledge).

Weale, A. (1992) *The New Politics of Pollution* (Manchester: University of Manchester Press).

Wessels, W. (1995) Verwaltung im EG-Mehrebenensystem: Auf dem Weg zur Megabuerokratie? In M. Jachtenfuchs and B. Kohler-Koch (eds), *Europaeische Integration* (Opladen: Leske & Budrich).

Chapter 2

Belgium: The Dilemma between Cohesion and Autonomy

BART KERREMANS AND JAN BEYERS

Introduction

Most scholarly attention to European integration has been focused on the degree to which member-states' preferences can be translated in EU decision-making. Some looked at the role of the member-states in treaty revisions, others concentrated upon the degree of member-state influence in the EU Council and the relations between this institution and the Commission and European Parliament. Putnam has been one of the first to refer to the complex interactions between EU and national decision-making (Putnam, 1988). His 'two-level game' only referred, however, to the double role played by national representatives in the Council, the Committee of Permanent Representatives (COREPER) and the numerous working groups. The influence of the process of European integration for the member-states goes deeper, however. It is not only reflected in the double role of national decision-makers but also in the structural changes on the national level that have been entailed by European integration. Even here, the influence cannot but be underestimated. Structural changes that at first sight seem to be the result of national processes have been influenced by the 'European embeddedness' of the EU member-states.

Belgium is probably the member-state in which this has been most visible. Between 1985 and 1995, the Belgian political and administrative apparatus has not only been reformed in order to adapt to the challenges of the ever-expanding scope of European integration, but also in response to the domestic problems that the Belgian state had to face. Between 1985, when the internal market initiative was launched, and 1995, the centralized Belgian state has been reformed into a full-fledged federal one. This fact has played an important role in Belgium's adaptation to EU membership, as this chapter will show.

First, we present a general overview of the Belgian political and administrative system with the focus on relevant aspects for the assessment of Belgium's adaptation. To put it more concretely, the proliferation of Belgian ministries in EU decision-making as a consequence of the enlarged EU agenda after 1985 has been reinforced by the creation of subnational ministries after the state reforms of 1980, 1988 and 1993. In the second part we describe how the Belgian administrative and governmental system works formally. The third part focuses on the strategic adaptation of

Belgium. This analysis will be based on data gathered by interviews with those who have to work with and within the Belgian coordination system.[1] How do they perceive their role in Belgium's decision-making on EU issues? Is there a difference between the structures and the processes? The fourth section aims to describe the Belgian pro-European attitude and the consequences of the Belgian position on its political and strategic adaptation. Is Belgium now better equipped to face the European challenges? How are the expansion of the national involvement in the EU, the European involvement in the national political systems and the far-reaching effects of this on structural and political adaptations to be evaluated?

Belgian adaptation in general

Contextual factors that have affected the Belgian adaptation process

As in every country that has to adapt to European integration, the Belgian process of adaptation has partly been shaped by a number of contextual factors. It concerns factors such as political culture, institutional traditions and the general political attitude towards European integration.

Although it is difficult to delineate the exact meaning of political culture, it is sometimes possible to discern some aspects that certainly are part of it. If there is one such feature in Belgium, it is the tradition of coalition politics. Not coincidentally, Belgium has been ranked by Lijphart as one of the most typical examples of a consociational democracy (Lijphart, 1981). Generally, the reason for this can be found in the different cross-cutting cleavages that characterize Belgian politics: the cleavage between Catholics and free-thinkers, between employers and employees, and between the Flemish and the Francophones. The existence of these three cleavages made coalition politics both necessary and possible (Huyse, 1986; De Wachter, 1992: 167–72).

Within governing coalitions a constant search for consensus exists. This is reflected in the way in which complicated consensus-building devices have been created to secure a consensus on the Belgian position on European integration and on important decisions of the EU institutions. Despite the increased number of protagonists in the preparation of the Belgian position in the EU, this search for consensus has remained. The result is an intricate web of institutions and organs that aim at finding compromises among the increased number of actors.

A second element in the Belgian adaptation to EU membership consists of an institutional tradition that emphasizes ministerial autonomy (De Wachter, 1992: 163–7). This seems to contradict the coalition and consensus-building character of Belgian policy-making, but, in fact, it does not. Only in cases where politically sensitive issues are at stake are consensus-building mechanisms mobilized. In all other cases the ministerial autonomy is widely respected.

A third element consists of the 'behind the scenes' mentality in Belgian politics. Despite existing formal institutions, decision-making tends to take place elsewhere (Denis, 1992: 91; De Wachter, 1992: 174). The role of the formal organs is, then, to act as rubber stamps. This makes Belgian politics both more flexible and less visible to the outside world. This informalism does not contradict the consensus-building attitude. On the contrary, in cases of highly politicized matters consensus tends to be built outside the formal circuits.

Last but not least, an element that has largely influenced Belgian adaptation is its traditional position in favour of European integration. That Belgium can be considered 'more European than the European Union itself' is reflected in its official position on the Intergovernmental Conference of 1996: 'As determined by the government program, the construction of the European Union on a federal basis is a priority of Belgium's foreign policy.' Since this pro-European position of Belgium has major consequences for the political adaptation of Belgium, we will deal with it in a separate paragraph.

A factor unique to Belgium: the state reforms

As already mentioned, the Belgian answer to European integration has also been influenced by particular developments in the Belgian political system. In the successive state reforms of 1970, 1980 and 1989 Europe was not a big issue. Very few people asked the question of how to preserve the effectiveness of the Belgian EU policy after these state reforms. The fulfilment of the wish of Flanders and Wallonia to get more autonomy dominated these reforms. It was only in the 1993 reform that Europe became a real issue, due to the lack of implementation of EU directives by Belgium between 1988 and 1993. Also the granting of foreign policy competencies to the Belgian subnational entities made an adaptation of the coordination system necessary. On the other hand, however, the Belgian state reform also triggered some requests for changes on the EU level itself. Article 146, dealing with the composition of the Council of Ministers, was changed at the demand of Belgium and Germany. This article allows member-states to be represented in the Council by ministers of subnational governments (Beyers and Kerremans, 1995).

In what follows, it will become clear that the Belgian answer to European integration has been influenced, if not determined, by the mixture of its particular political culture, its institutional traditions and its successive state reforms. This mixture makes the Belgian adaptation process quite a complex story. But whatever the complexities, Belgium has succeeded in building up both institutions and practices to cope with the challenges of an ever more important European Union.

The governmental and administrative adaptation of Belgium

If one wants to assess the extent of the Belgian governmental and administrative adaptation to EU membership, one has to look at two levels on which this adaptation has taken place: the federal (e.g. national) and the federated (e.g. subnational) level. The first refers to the adaptations among and within the federal ministries and within the federal government. The second refers to the way in which the subnational entities have become involved in Belgian EU policies.

Governmental adaptation at the federal level

As in all EU member-states, European integration, and especially the enlargement of its scope in 1987 and 1993, has increased the number of Belgian ministers that are involved in EU policies. This required the adaptation of ministerial departments that had never previously been involved in EU decision-making. These adaptations took place within each ministry and in the system that governed the relations among them.

Adaptations in the principal ministries

One has to take into account that many national ministries have been reformed in the 1970s and 1980s due to different reasons, only one of which has to do with the EU. The principal reason has been the Belgian state reform which necessitated the transfer of large groups of civil servants from most federal ministries to new sub-national ministerial departments. Some ministries (like education) have been completely transferred and no longer exist on the federal level. Another reason for these reforms was the need for more efficient government services at a lower cost. This was the consequence of the economic recession, prevailing neo-liberalism since the 1980s and the budgetary problems of the Belgian state.

Administrative adaptations to European integration have been conducted for two important reasons: first, to prepare the Belgian representatives in the working groups of the Council for their task; second, to guarantee the transposition of EC directives in Belgian law. But both adaptations have occurred on an *ad hoc* basis. No central reorganization has taken place to prepare Belgium better for the enlarged EU agenda after 1986 and 1993. In some ministries, adaptation was a consequence of coincidences like the nomination of a senior official with a personal interest in European integration. This happened, for example, at the VAT division of the Ministry of Finances.

At the Ministry of Economic Affairs, which has been reduced as a consequence of the state reforms of 1980 and 1988, a general simplification of the structures has taken place. The principal reason for its reorganization is not, therefore, the EU agenda, but the Belgian state reform, as is indicated in the new manual of the ministry (Ministerie van Economische Zaken, 1995: 5). The proliferation of directions and divisions that were responsible for EU matters (Ministerie van Economische Zaken, 1992), has been suspended by concentrating them in the Division Integrated European Policies of the Direction for Economic Relations (Ministerie van Economische Zaken, 1995: 14–15).

At the Ministry of Agriculture, the same thing happened. Major adaptations took place as a consequence of the initiation of the Common Agricultural Policy (CAP) in the 1960s. Until 1972 the effect of the CAP had been reflected in annual changes in the structure of the ministry. After 1972, two major reforms took place: one in 1980 and one in 1994. Both were largely the consequence of the state reforms of 1980 and 1993. In the 1994 reform, however, which simplified the ministry's structures to a large extent, the adaptation to the ministerial structures of the other EU member-states was said to be one of the reasons. As a result, EU agricultural and fisheries policies have been concentrated in DG 2 (Direction for the Agricultural Policy). But in terms of concentration of EU policies within one division of the ministry, the 1994 reform just changed names, nothing else.

The Belgian Ministry of Finances conducted its adaptations before 1985. Thereafter, no major changes have been conducted. Adaptations took place whenever the EC agenda necessitated this. The VAT division, for instance, had already been adapted in 1978 when the EC started to issue its VAT directives. In 1993 a new section was founded (within the division of EEC legislation and disputes) in order to deal with the administrative cooperation with the other member-states (the so-called Mathew Programme). In the customs division, no major adaptations took place; 1992 only led to a shift in numbers of officials between the different sections.

In the Ministry of Home Affairs and the Ministry of Justice, the influence of European integration has been more visible during the last few years. The influence of the Maastricht Treaty and the Schengen Agreement has engendered structural adaptations in both ministries. In the Ministry of Justice, a special service for the coordination of EU affairs has been set up to coordinate Belgium's policy towards the subjects of Article K.4 of the Maastricht Treaty. In the Ministry of Home Affairs, the introduction of new treaty provisions by the TEU is reflected in a number of adaptations. Within the Direction for the State Police, a new section on international police cooperation has been set up. This section is responsible for Schengen, Europol and police cooperation within the EU. Within the Direction for Foreigners, a new office for international relations has become responsible for the implementation of the Schengen Agreement. Finally, the new Direction for Prevention Policies contains a special section for juridical and European affairs. Concerning the Ministry of Home Affairs, it is important, however, to notice that major reforms have taken place in 1988 as a consequence of the state reforms. Additional adaptations were needed, however, to take into account the consequences for Belgium of the 'third pillar' of Maastricht.

The conclusion, as far as the administrative adaptation of the Belgian ministries is concerned, can be simple. One cannot speak of a high level of adaptation to EU membership since 1985. Adaptations that took place were mostly the consequence of the state reforms that took place between 1980 and 1993. Whenever Europe was a reason to adapt the structures, the adaptations occurred on an *ad hoc* basis and were limited to a few services within some ministries. There was certainly no general Belgian policy to adapt the ministries in general to the challenges and requirements of the 'new' Europe.

Coordination among the federal ministries

As far as coordination among ministries is concerned, one can barely speak of 'adaptation' after 1986 or 1992. The system was already in use for much longer. The only slight changes that have been made have to do with the increasing number of actors involved because of the expanding scope of European integration and the inclusion of subnational authorities since the state reforms.

An important change took place in 1974. In that year the Directorate-General for Political Affairs of the Ministry of Foreign Affairs strengthened its role in the

Belgian coordination system on EC affairs. A system was created to coordinate between the then two most important participants: the Ministry of Economic Affairs and the Directorate-General for External Economic Affairs of the Ministry of Foreign Affairs. In this new coordination system the Directorate-General for Political Affairs of the Foreign Ministry played a central role. According to Franck (1987: 70–1), this was mainly due to the increasing importance of European integration for Belgium's foreign policy and to the strong personality of the director-general for political affairs of that time, Etienne Davignon. In 1974, this system was known as the 'European Coordination'. Since 1985 it is called the P.11 Coordination, after the Direction for European Affairs (known as P.11, see below) of the Foreign Ministry.

One of the remarkable aspects of the Belgian federal coordination on European issues is the absence of one ministry responsible for all European issues. In the first instance, this has led to a formal system with two coordinating bodies. The above-mentioned Direction for European Affairs (P.11) is the first one and belongs to the Ministry of Foreign Affairs. The second is the Interministerial Economic Committee (CEI) and belongs to the Ministry of Economic Affairs. Whereas the CEI coordinates between the different federal ministries when economic and technical questions are involved and acts on the level of seniors officials (Denis, 1992), the P.11 meetings of high officials and personal collaborators of ministers (called the *cabinets*) aim at coordinating the Belgian position from a political and institutional perspective. Practice shows, however, that it is very difficult to delineate sharply between the functions of these two bodies (Lejeune, 1993: 14) and that the role of the CEI is less important than the role of P.11. This is especially the case for highly politicized questions. In that case P.11 becomes more involved. The same happens when different departments cannot agree on the department that is going to represent Belgium in one of the working groups of the Council. In that case, a P.11 meeting will designate the so-called pilot department (Beyers, 1994: 14). Finally, P.11 meetings take place on all issues that are put on the agenda of the working groups, the COREPER's and the EU Council's. Therefore, P.11 meetings take place on a weekly basis. The composition of the P.11 meeting can change from week to week, although representatives of the prime ministers and deputy prime ministers are always invited.

On all levels of this structure the Belgian Permanent Representation (PR) to the EU is represented. This is because of its central role in the communication between the Belgian administrations and the EU institutions. As mentioned in the handbook of the Direction for European Affairs (P.11) 'the Permanent Representation is for the Belgian Administrations the only statutory channel for all communication with the EC institutions'. This seems to be logical since it is the PR that represents Belgium in the COREPER's. The PR is, together with the line departments, responsible for the representation of Belgium in the Council working groups. Furthermore, the PR acts as the mailbox for the communication of the EU institutions with the Belgian administrations. Proposals of the European Commission are communicated by the PR to the ministries that have to deal with it. As we will see later, the important formal role of the Belgian PR makes it an attractive partner in the informal networks among Belgian administrations.

Administrative adaptations and the Belgian state reform

The Belgian state has been reformed from a centralized state into a fully fledged federal state by four constitutional reforms during the last 25 years (Hooghe, 1995). These not only attributed a large array of competencies to Belgium's subnational entities, but also created new governments and parliaments. These new institutions can act independently from the federal state. In other words, there is no hierarchy between the federal level and the subnational level. The absence of hierarchy between the different governmental levels is of fundamental importance for understanding the consequences of the state reform for the Belgian position in the EU. A subnational law, called a **decree**, cannot be changed by a national law. Nor can a subnational executive decision be altered by an executive decision of the federal government.

The Belgian state reform has resulted in the formation of six constituent subnational units: the Flemish, Francophone and German Communities, the Flemish and Walloon Regions, and the Brussels Capital Region. Each of these units has its own directly elected parliament, a government and ministerial departments. Regions and communities largely overlap. Whereas the first refers to territories, the second refers to inhabitants. The competencies of the regions are 'territorially bound'. They refer to problems that are linked to a territory and concern issues such as regional economic development, employment, industrial restructuring, environment, land use planning, urban renewal, road-building, traffic, agriculture and export promotion. The competencies of the communities are 'personally bound'. They relate to problems that are linked to persons, i.e. culture, language policies, education, health care, welfare and family policies. The Flemish Community consists of the inhabitants of Flanders (the Flemish Region), and the Dutch-speaking inhabitants of the Brussels Capital Region. The Francophone Community consists of the French-speaking population of both Brussels and Wallonia (the Walloon Region). The German Community consists of the German-speaking population (65,000 people) of Wallonia. In Flanders, the Flemish Community and the Flemish Regional institutions have merged into the Flemish government and the Flemish council (the Flemish parliament). The Francophone Community is still separated from the Walloon Region, although personal links (ministers belonging to both the Walloon and the Francophone governments) exist. The German Community and the Brussels Capital Region have remained separate entities.

The relevance of the Belgian state reform for European integration has become clear in the last seven years. Many competencies attributed to the subnational entities have also partially been transferred to the EU.[2] Because of the lack of hierarchy between the federal and the subnational authorities, the consistency of the **Belgian** policy towards the EU's policies on such issues became a problem. But the problem was not limited to policy formulation only. For the same reason the federal government could not force subnational authorities to implement EC directives. The result was that the **Belgian** state has been regularly condemned by the EC Court of Justice for failure to fulfil its obligations because the subnational authorities failed to implement EC directives. In other words, the reformed Belgian state has been confronted with a dilemma between autonomy and coherence. In the state reform of 1993, which made the regions responsible for international cooperation within the range of their competencies,[3] the question of the reconciliation of autonomy and coherence in Belgium's European policies became an urgent one.[4] This necessitated a **Belgian** and a **European** adaptation. The Belgian adaptation consisted of the creation of a system of concertation and coordination among the different authorities, similar to what has been called German executive federalism. On the European level, a revision of Article 146 of the EEC Treaty was needed to guarantee the respect for the prerogatives of the Belgian subnational authorities up to the level of the EU Council of Ministers. We start by outlining the adaptation on the EU level since the adaptation on the Belgian level has partly been influenced by the new EU arrangement.

The European adaptation

It is difficult to imagine that authorities negotiating on an issue (e.g. education) in the EU Council are those without the competencies, either completely or partly, on this issue (e.g. the Minister for European Affairs) in the legal order of their home country. This was the case with the Belgian representation in the EU Council before the Maastricht Treaty and its new Article 146 came into force. According to the Secretariat of the Council, the meaning of this article was clear (our translation): 'According to Article 2 of the Merger Treaty of 1965 (former Article 146 EEC) the Council consists of the members of the governments of the member-states, which means either ministers or secretaries of state from the national governments.'

It was logical, therefore, that the Belgian subnational authorities, anxious as they are to secure their new prerogatives, wanted to change that system. At the Intergovernmental Conference (IGC) of 1991 on the European Political Union, the Belgian delegation asked for a revision of Article 146 and got it. In return, the French delegation asked for a guarantee that all member-state representatives in the Council would bind their member-state **as a whole** and not just parts of it (Ingelaere, 1994: 69). Therefore Article 146 has been reformulated as follows: 'The Council shall consist of a representative of each Member State at ministerial level, authorized to commit the government of that Member State'. The first part of the new Article 146 reflects the Belgian concerns, the second part those of the French.

The Belgian adaptation

That representatives bind their member-state as a whole necessitated the establishment of coordination systems among the subnational and national authorities. Because of the right of the Belgian subnational authorities to develop their own external relations autonomously, there was a problem of cohesion. If Belgium wanted to commit itself as a whole, the subnational authorities, whenever an issue belonging to their competencies was to be discussed in the Council, had to determine the Belgian position among themselves. In the case of mixed competencies between the subnational and the national levels, the position had to be the outcome of concertation between the federal and the subnational governments. Therefore a system to determine the Belgian position was needed. In addition, if Belgium could be represented in the Council by members of its subnational governments, it had to be determined which subnational government would represent Belgium in which case. These two elements (coordination and representation) are regulated by the Co-operation Agreement (CA) between the federal government, the communities and the regions of 8 March 1994. This agreement forms the core of the Belgian governmental adaptation to EU membership after the Belgian state reforms of 1988 and 1993.

Coordination

Concerning the problem of coordination, the old system (with the CEI and P.11) has been largely kept intact. For each issue on the agenda of whatever EU Council, a coordination meeting has to be organized by P.11 (Direction for European Affairs). The meeting is chaired by someone from P.11 and attended by representatives from federal and subnational ministries, depending on the issues that will be discussed (Art. 2 CA). If it concerns issues within the scope of the subnational entities, these entities will be invited to the meeting. Important, however, is the fact that the representatives of the federal prime minister, deputy prime ministers and the minister-presidents of all the subnational governments have to be invited to every P.11 coordination meeting, whatever the issue on the agenda. The same is true for the representatives of the Belgian PR to the EU.

The Cooperation Agreement has provided the possibility of *ad hoc* meetings that aim at preparing the P.11 meetings for technical issues. All such meetings have to be notified to P.11. For political questions, no such meetings are possible (Art. 4 CA). The existence of *ad hoc* technical meetings means that the state reform has further eroded the role of the Ministry of Economic Affairs in EU decision-making. For technical issues belonging to the exclusive competencies of the federal government, technical preparations can take place in the CEI or in one of its subcommittees. These meetings are not possible for mixed competencies or for exclusive competencies of the subnational entities. In such cases, *ad hoc* meetings outside the CEI prepare the P.11 meetings. In this way, the subnational governments have the guarantee that the federal economic ministry cannot involve itself in issues that are exclusively their concern.

Important in the Cooperation Agreement is its commentary. Therein it is clearly stated that in the case of absence of a compromise on the Belgian position, the Belgian representative will have to abstain in the case of a vote in the Council. The commentary clearly mentions the possible consequences. Whenever unanimity is required in the Council, an abstention is equal to a positive vote. In the case of a qualified majority, however, an abstention is a negative vote, since Belgium cannot add its five votes to the votes of the other member-states in order to attain the required 62 votes. The commentary concludes (our translation): 'Because of the effects of a Belgian abstention in the Council, the Belgian coordination system is almost obliged to reach an outcome on a Belgian position. Only this will allow Belgium to participate in the negotiations in the Council.'

Coordination in Belgium means consensus-building. Because of the need for consensus, every participant has the guarantee that no decision can be taken against its will. It may seem that this system lacks efficiency, because it can take a long time before the Belgian position is determined. On the other hand, however, it is the price that an ethnically divided state has to pay for the maintenance of a minimum level of federal loyalty from its constituent parts. Federal loyalty is also one of the assumptions that lies at the basis of this system. Whatever the number of consensus-building devices, no compromises will be possible if the participants refuse to cooperate in a spirit of mutual understanding and with a willingness to make concessions. Therefore the principle of federal loyalty has even been included in the Belgian constitution (Art. 143 NBC, Lejeune, 1994: 235; Peeters, 1994: 241).

Representation

A problem that had not been resolved by the Cooperation Agreement is the one concerning Belgium's representation in the Council. The Interministerial Conference for Foreign Policy has found a solution to this problem. All the EU Councils have been divided into four groups (see Table 2.1).

Table 2.1 Representation of Belgian authorities in the Council of Ministers

Category	Type of Council of Ministers	Examples of Council of Ministers	Example of issues	Representation
I	Exclusive federal competencies	General Affairs ECOFIN Budget Telecommunication Development Cooperation	Directive on voting	Federal government
II	Shared competencies with a dominant federal share	Agriculture Internal Market Public Health Energy	Directive on waste and packaging waste	Head of delegation is the federal government assisted by someone from the subnational entities (dependent on rotation)
III	Shared competencies with a dominant subnational share	Industry Research	Proposals concerning the restructuring of the steel industry	Head of delegation is someone from the subnational entities (dependent on rotation) assisted by someone from the federal government
IV	Exclusive subnational competencies	Education Tourism Land Use Planning	The Socrates programme	Someone from the subnational entities (dependent on rotation)

For each of these groups, the Belgian representation is determined. For category I (e.g. the Council of Financial and Economics Ministers – ECOFIN), Belgium is represented by representatives of the federal government only. For category II (e.g. environment), the head of the delegation is someone from the federal government, assisted by a member of a subnational government. The function of the latter is to consult Belgian authorities during the negotiations in the Council. For category III (e.g. industry), the head of the Belgian delegation is a member of one of the subnational governments, assisted by a member of the federal government who has to consult the other Belgian authorities during negotiations in the Council. For category IV (e.g. education), Belgium is represented by a member of one of the subnational governments only.[5] This system is based on the kind of Councils that meets and not on the kind of issues that are on the agenda of a particular Council. That makes the Belgian representation in the Council stable and predictable. This is important for the relation with the Commission and with the other member-states. The subnational membership of the Belgian delegation rotates among the subnational governments every six months (the period of a Council presidency).

The strategic adaptation of Belgium

Despite the existence of structures to coordinate the Belgian position, one can ask whether such structures really play a role in the way that Belgium adapts itself to European integration. Our empirical analysis of the Belgian strategic adaptation to EU membership indicates that this is not the case. Strategic adaptation is defined here as the development of **practices** in decision-making and implementation in order to adapt oneself to the consequences of EU membership.

Belgian adaptation on decision-making

Networking on the federal level

According to the formal Belgian coordination system, all coordination is centralized into one ministry, the Ministry of Foreign Affairs. This has to happen through the meetings organized on a weekly basis by the Direction for European Affairs (P.11).

In Table 2.2 we show the strength of the mutual contacts of different groups of Belgian officials in the coordination of the Belgian position. Three groups of actors have been distinguished: the officials of Foreign Affairs (N=22),[6] the representatives of the other ministries (line departments) at the Belgian PR (N=8), and the other officials from the line departments that have been involved in EU decision-making (N=65). The pattern of contacts clearly indicates the central role of the foreign ministry. As an object of contacts, the foreign ministry plays a much more active role than the line departments do. This can be seen in the significant differences between the first and the third column of Table 2.2. Officials of the foreign ministry also initiate more contacts. To a certain extent, this is logical since the foreign ministry contains both the P.11 service, and the PR; two services that play an important formal role in the Belgian coordination system on EU issues.

Table 2.2 Strength of internal administrative contacts of respondents at the federal level in the sample of 1994

Partners (source of contact)	Respondents (initiators of contacts)		
	22 interviewees belonging to the Foreign Affairs Ministry	8 interviewees of line departments seconded to the PR	65 interviewees working in line departments
Prime minister's office	Weak	Weak	Weak
Cabinet of Foreign Affairs	Very Strong	Strong	Weak
Officials of Foreign Affairs	Very Strong	Strong	Strong
Cabinets of other ministries	Strong	Strong	Weak
Officials of other ministries	Very Strong	Strong	Strong

The second column is more revealing, however. This column enables us to look inside the Belgian PR by providing the contact patterns of the representatives of the line departments in the PR. In general, they initiate less contacts with most other ministries than do their colleagues from the foreign ministry. The scope of the contacts of these representatives is by definition more restricted than the one of the foreign affairs officials in the PR. Each of the line department representatives limits its contacts to issues of direct concern for its own ministry. Furthermore, such representatives are mostly members of working groups in one policy domain. This is also reflected in the division of labour between officials in the PR. The officials of foreign affairs at the PR have to deal with more varied policy domains than the officials of the line departments. This obliges them to develop and to maintain contacts with officials from many ministries at the same time.

The role of the line department officials (not working at the PR) as initiators is less important than the one of their colleagues from the foreign ministry. This does not mean that their role is unimportant. Far from that! The first column of Table 2.2 indicates that such officials have established communication networks, especially with the officials of line departments seconded to the PR and the officials of the foreign ministry. The contacts with the foreign ministry are not surprising because of its formal role in the Belgian coordination system. Besides these contacts, Table 2.2 also indicates that contacts among line departments are strong. This is especially the case for the ministries that have no representatives in the Belgian PR. For ministries that do have such representatives, the PR provides the context for direct contacts with other line departments. For the others, the need for such contacts is fulfilled by the establishment of informal coordination networks. The context of such networks may be different from those of the ministries that are represented, although the pattern and the intensity of these contacts is quite similar.[7] This confirms the conclusion that the Belgian coordination system consists of a double network: one network in which foreign affairs plays a central role, and one system of direct contacts among the different departments. The second part of our empirical research proved to be revealing on this point.

Table 2.3 Strength of involvement in formal and informal networking for three cases

Case	Waste	Socrates	Voting
Representation in the Council of Ministers	Head of delegation is federal government assisted by subnational entities (category II)	Representation by one of the subnational entities (dependent on rotation) (category IV)	Federal government (category I)
Politicized	Limited	Limited	High
Number of interviewees	10	17	15
Strong involvement in the formal network			
at the working group level	Permanent Representation Federal cabinet of Ministry for Environment	P.11 Permanent Representation Subnational actors	P.11
at COREPER level	P.11 Permanent Representation Federal cabinet of Ministry for Environment	P.11 Permanent Representation Subnational actors	P.11
at Council level	P.11 Permanent Representation	P.11 Permanent Representation Subnational actors Subnational actors	P.11
Strong involvement in informal network	P.11 Permanent Representation	P.11 Permanent Representation Subnational actors	P.11 Permanent Representation Cabinets of prime ministers and deputy prime ministers Cabinets of subnational ministries

Networking between the federal and the subnational level

As has been mentioned above, the low number of officials in the first part of our empirical research necessitated a second round of interviews in which the intergovernmental coordination in Belgium was analysed. By 'intergovernmental', we refer to the coordination and collaboration among the federal and sub-national governments of Belgium. And the importance of the involvement of sub-national authorities in the Belgian coordination system, as compared with those of the other member-states, was a significant finding in the first part of the interviews.

In this second round of interviews we also tried to elaborate on the different roles of the P.11 and the Belgian PR. In addition, our hypothesis presented in the previous section, that especially highly politicized matters are treated by cabinets and politicians, was based on interpretation, but not on real empirical findings. This was the reason that we chose the study of three cases in the second part of our research. For each of these case studies (the Socrates programme, the Waste Directive, and the Voting Directive), the respondents were asked to outline their contacts with other Belgian authorities, for each of the important decision moments in the EU Council (common position, informal agreement, formal decision), and this on the three decision-making levels in the Council: the working group meetings, the COREPER meetings and the meetings of the Council itself. The questions concerning their contacts referred to contacts both within the framework of the formal institutions (CEI, P.11 meetings, Interministerial Conference for Foreign Policy) and outside these. The results are summarized in Table 2.3. More empirical details are presented elsewhere (Beyers and Kerremans, 1995; Kerremans and Beyers, 1996).

Table 2.3 shows that most of the contacts take place according to the formal coordination system. The meetings organized by the Direction for European Affairs (P.11) function as the central forum for negotiations between the Belgian adminis-trations and ministers, both on the national and the subnational level, as required by the Cooperation Agreement. What cannot be deduced from Table 2.3, but what was visible in the answers of the different respondents, was the very restricted scope of direct communication outside the P.11 framework among the Belgian subnational authorities. The Flemish and Walloon governments seem to prefer communications within P.11 to direct communications between themselves.

Furthermore, Table 2.3 indicates that there is one actor in the Belgian coordina-tion system that has a much more prominent role than one would suspect from the Cooperation Agreement. It concerns the Belgian representation to the EU. In the formal system, the PR is one of the participants in the P.11 meetings, and functions as a mailbox between the EU and the Belgian institutions and authorities. It also chairs the Belgian delegations in the working groups and the COREPER (I and II). In reality, the role of the Belgian PR is much more important. It is not just one actor among the others, but functions as an important informal coordinator besides P.11. Many of Belgium's positions in the working groups and the COREPER are determined at a meeting organized by the Belgian PR. In our case studies, only in the Voting Directive did no such meeting take place.

This has something to do with the highly politicized nature of this question in Belgium. In other member-states the Voting Directive was not as important as it was in Belgium. The Flemish were afraid that unrestricted voting rights for European citizens would lead to increased electoral support for Francophones around Brussels, because more 'Eurocrats' speak and understand French than understand or speak Dutch.

The comparison of the results of the Voting Directive with the two other cases is very important. The Voting Directive was handled in a relatively short period of time at the EU level (about one year), while the Waste Directive took several years and the Socrates programme about one year. Related to the relatively short time, the network of the Voting Directive is considerably different from the other networks. The formal meetings were rather limited while the informal network was very dense. Furthermore, this dense informal network was highly political in character. Contacts took place at the level of cabinets. Therefore the Voting Directive is a good example of informal decision-making working towards getting a consensus on highly politicized issues in a relatively short period of time.

There is another, more formal, reason for the important role of the Belgian PR. From a formal point of view, the subnational governments had nothing to do with the Voting Directive. It is outside the scope of their competencies. The involvement of these governments was secured, however, not in PR meetings, but in the meetings of P.11, where the representatives of the minister-presidents of the subnational governments have permanent seats. But even in this case, the Belgian PR remained an attractive partner as the figures on the informal contacts show. This was due to the fact that the PR, as the Belgian 'mailbox', was a good source of information on this question, especially during the preparatory phase in the EU working groups. This emphasizes that the central role of the Belgian PR in the informal Belgian network is largely due to its important role in the Belgian delegations in the working groups of the Council and the COREPER. The chair of the Belgian delegation belongs to the PR, which makes direct contacts among the subnational authorities less useful. Coordination will take place in the PR meetings anyway.

Another important aspect concerns the development of additional informal coordination systems in cases of repeated decision-making in the same policy area. This has been shown by the Belgian coordination on the Waste Directive and has been confirmed by previous research (Beyers, 1994). In those policy areas where there is a high frequency of EU decision-making (as in agriculture and environment), the specialized ministries of both the federal and the subnational authorities have developed their own specialized coordination systems. In the case of environment, this informal (or semi-formal, because it is used on a regular basis) system consists of coordination meetings at the cabinet of the federal minister of environment. This meeting is attended by the members of the cabinets of the ministers of environment of the Flemish Region, the Walloon Region and the Brussels Region, and by the PR official who chairs the Belgian delegation in the concerned working group. Sometimes, subnational administrations are also involved. A similar system exists for agriculture, economic affairs (in that case, the CEI is used) and research and technological development. These 'semi-formal' networks allow for a very quick coordination, whenever necessary. In addition, these semi-formal networks avoid an overloading of the PR and the P.11 coordination. It is a typical example of how the 'efficiency gap' caused by the Belgian state reform has been filled in a spontaneous and informal way (Pijnenburg, 1993: 165). It also reflects the quest for consensus in Belgium, even after the subnational entities became more autonomous.

The political adaptation of Belgium

A limited permissive attitude of Belgian élites towards European integration

The pro-European position has been reflected in the positions of the successive Belgian governments and parliaments towards European integration. In addition, Belgian political leaders are associated with some successful moments in the process of European integration (P.H. Spaak, L. Tindemans), and the Belgian Council presidencies are generally expected to be both maximalist (in terms of European integration) and successful (Beyers and Kerremans, 1994). Furthermore, the best way for Belgian politicians to prove that they are statesmen is to present themselves as European leaders. Wilfried Martens, the former prime minister, and Jean-Luc Dehaene, the current prime minister who was about to become president of the European Commission in 1995, are examples of this. The same can be said about the former NATO Secretary-General Willy Claes who showed his capacities as statesman during the Belgian presidency of 1993. For Jean-Luc Dehaene, for instance, his (abortive) candidacy for the Commission presidency in 1994 (Corfu Summit) caused a change in his popularity in Belgium. Before Corfu, Dehaene was not very popular. Since Corfu, and despite many criticisms on his policies, he is widely respected in his home country.

For Belgium European integration has mainly political objectives. Franck describes this in the form of three equations (Franck, 1996: 151). The coherence equation implies the linkage between economic integration (i.e. the first pillar) and political integration (i.e. the second pillar). Second, integration in the field of foreign policy also means integration in the field of security policy and excludes the neutrality option. Third, for Belgium the political union has primarily federal aims. As a consequence the Community procedure should become the main decision-making procedure. Belgium was always worried about the attitude of some member-states to take decisions in an intergovernmental way on economic issues that were linked to the third pillar (e.g. economic sanctions). This tendency is viewed as hollowing out the supranational features of the first pillar. This federalist option of Belgium is inspired by the principle of 'unity in diversity' which also characterizes the heterogeneity of the country and the institutional adaptation to it. The Belgian adaptation to heterogeneity has been a multiplication of institutional structures at different levels. A similar option is preferred for Europe.

Belgium is not the only member-state with a pro-European position, but it is certainly the most radical in its pro-European rhetoric. The Netherlands, Luxembourg, Germany and Italy also have a pro-European attitude, but their positions are generally more moderate. This extreme pro-European attitude was also reflected in the interviews we carried out. Several items measured the European ideology of our respondents. On all dimensions the Belgian officials were more pro-European than their colleagues of other member-states. Thus the official pro-European position of the country is reflected very well in the general attitudes of the officials who represent the country in day-to-day negotiations.

Within and between political parties European questions are seldom an issue of debate. In general Belgian political parties are in favour of European integration. The pro-European attitude can be partly explained by the important role that Christian Democrats play in Belgian politics. Generally, Christian Democrats are known for their pro-European position. But the influence of the Christian Democrats is not a sufficient condition. Other political parties have a pro-European orientation as well. Especially for the Social Democrats, this issue has become more salient recently. Within the Social Democratic family, however, the French-speaking part of the Socialist Labour Union has reservations towards the Economic and Monetary Union (EMU) project. The green parties are most divided on European issues. They are generally in favour of positive integration when it comes to environmental and social policies but are opposed to the internal market programme and the EMU project. But the reservation within some political parties are rather limited and are generally not provoking major political problems. The only political party that is strongly against European integration is the extreme right-wing Vlaams Blok. A coalition between the Euro-sceptical forces has no great chances: the salience is not high enough and the reasons for scepticism are rather heterogeneous (Hooghe, 1995: 163).

Does this mean that there are no limitations on this rather permissive attitude? We must admit that Belgians are equally concerned about their identity as the Euro-sceptics in general are. They fear the increased influence of big states and they are equally aware of the possible effect of integration on cultural diversity (*ibid.*: 161–3). Especially the Flemish show a very high level of sensitivity to this issue. Restricting the number of working languages in the EU is therefore unacceptable. This is less the case for their Francophone counterparts and their colleagues of other member-states. European integration may be perceived as a good thing in Flanders but it also has its limits. It cannot intrude into the highly sensitive question of language rights. The Voting Directive is a concrete example of how the limited permissivity of the Flemish works in a concrete issue. Since most of the EU issues do not concern languages, the highly supportive attitudes of the Belgian respondents towards European integration can be seen as an indicator that political adaptation towards EU membership has been realized in the minds of the Belgian decision-makers.

The consequences of the permissive attitude for adaptation

One could expect that a pro-European member-state has a very pro-active European policy-making process and that Europe is a central topic for politicians. This is not the case for Belgium, as the problems with implementation and the absence of a general strategy to adapt the Belgian administrative system to EU membership indicate. There may be a general pro-integration attitude among Belgian political and administrative élites; but the internal problems of the Belgian state and the ensuing adaptations of its structures and institutions have relegated Europe and European integration to a secondary importance in day-to-day politics. This has been reflected in the state reforms, in the adaptations of the parliamentary structures, in the changes in interest representation at the national level (Bursens, 1996) and in the limited involvement of ministers in EU issues. Their involvement is restricted to highly politicized matters. In all other cases, ministers rubber-stamp the compromises that have been reached among civil servants without giving much political input.

The latent pro-European attitude of Belgium is also reflected in the role perception of the Belgian representatives in the EU Council and its auxiliaries. Instead of making difficulties on specific questions, these representatives see their role as supporting the Commission in finding integrative compromises among the member-states. Of course, there are issues in which Belgium plays an active role or decides to oppose a specific proposal or decision. But such occasions are rather rare, and even then the Belgians almost never take the lead but support the opposition of another, mostly bigger, member-state.

This is confirmed by the attitudes of officials responsible for day-to-day nego-tiation in the working groups of the Council of Ministers. On the one hand, Belgian negotiators have excellent opportunities for pro-active behaviour. Their offices are situated in Brussels and their policy position is generally close to the position of other important institutional actors like the European Commission and the European Parliament. On the other hand, our research shows that Belgian civil servants have a very low self-esteem in comparison with their colleagues from other member-states. Belgian negotiators generally found that they were not well prepared, that they lacked clear instructions, that they did not have political backing and that negotiators of other member-states performed much better in Council negotiations. In more extens-ive qualitative interviews Belgian officials complained of the fact that a general broad policy view was missing and they pointed out that a very pro-European position can limit creative negotiation behaviour. Interviewees said, for instance, that there is a general attitude of 'waiting for ideas from the European Commission' and that Bel-gians are sometimes too 'dogmatic in approving the proposal of the Commission'.

The low self-esteem of Belgian negotiators is one factor. Their networking attitude is another. Being close to Brussels could be an advantage for Belgian decision-makers: however, we find that Belgian officials are not well integrated in the networking activities in Brussels. The communication networks of Belgian officials are less dense than the communication networks of officials from other member-states. The relations of Belgian officials with politicians (in the European and Belgian parliaments), with officials of the European Commission and with interest groups are less extensive than the relations developed by their colleagues from other member-states.

Conclusions

Our analysis of how Belgium adapted to European integration leads to several conclusions.

First, the Belgian coordination system reflects a high level of policy centralization. The different authorities coordinate their EU policies through a central system: the P.11 meetings. This is due to the formal obligation to prepare the Council meetings through P.11. In the P.11 meetings the Belgian position on each of the EU issues is evaluated according to three criteria: the compatibility with the general pro-European position, the respect for the institutional balances in the EU (role of the Commission, subsidiarity) and the consequences for the EU budget and Belgium's contribution to it. Other considerations are taken into account in the more specialized coordination networks.

Second, the important role of P.11 in the Belgian coordination leads to a high level of functional centralization. Functional centralization refers to networks in which both generalists and specialists participate. Functional decentralization means that coordination takes place among specialists in a specific policy domain only. In P.11 meetings, specialists and generalists participate, and the generalists (the prime minister, the deputy prime ministers and the subnational minister-presidents) have a permanent seat. However, the development of specialized coordination networks in policy domains for which EU decision-making takes place has frequently eroded the degree of functional centralization of the Belgian coordination system. The formal coordination system may be for generalists; part of the informal coordination has a more specialized character.

Between the formal coordination system of P.11 and the semi-formal coordination on specialized issues, the Belgian PR functions as a kind of gate-keeper (see also Lejeune, 1993). It provides the guarantee that there will be coordination and that this coordination will lead to a conclusion. This is most obvious in cases where no semi-formal coordination system has been developed because of the lack of frequent decision-making on particular issue areas in the EU or in cases where the internal coordination did not suffice to allow for a clear Belgian position in the EU Council. In such cases, the gap that exists because of the absence of a semi-formal system is filled by the informal networks that are built by and through the Belgian PR. In this way, there is a guarantee that, despite the high number of authorities and institutions in Belgium, there will be a Belgian coordination on EU issues.

Third, the Belgian response to European integration has been an incremental one. This is reflected in the *ad hoc* adaptations of the different ministries to the new requirements of a changing EU and in the slow reaction of Belgium to its poor record on implementation. Belgium's internal problems have monopolized the Belgian political agenda and its administrative and political adaptations. Belgium is just too busy with itself and has granted Europe the benefit of the doubt.

The incremental attitude in governmental, administrative adaptation and implementation is also reflected in the political sphere. Generally Belgian officials defend the federal option in European decision-making. Although their work is clearly affected by ideological aspirations and ambitions, the political input in day-to-day proceedings is rather limited. Belgian officials also lack, despite their ambitions, a positive self-esteem and are less integrated in the European networks.

Belgium, as a loyal member of the EU, has conducted a number of administrative, political and strategic adaptations as a consequence of its EU membership. One could raise the question, however, of whether all these adaptations really adapted Belgium to its changing European environment. This question is relevant because European integration was only one of the factors that determined the Belgian adaptation process. In some cases, it was even a minor factor. Structural changes took place, not as a response to Belgium's EU membership, but to its domestic problems. The effects of these changes on the efficiency and efficacy of Belgium's policies towards the EU were only of secondary importance. Nevertheless, the changes in the Belgian coordination system on EU policies have shown that the coherence of these policies started to play an important role after the state reform of 1988 and after the scope of European integration had been expanded by the SEA in 1987 and the TEU in 1993. But even in these new adaptations, the concern for autonomy of the Belgian subnational entities played a larger role than the concern for coherence in the Belgian EU policies.

Our analysis shows, however, that it is risky to look at structural changes only to assess fully the nature of the adaptation process of Belgium (see also Kerremans, 1996). Despite the weaknesses of the formal coordination system, with its time-consuming logic of consensus-building, the different subnational and national authorities have succeeded in filling the gap between autonomy and coherence by a system of semi-formal and informal coordination. This suggests that adaptation has to be considered as partly a process of structural changes and partly a process of attitudinal changes. The example of Belgium shows that adaptation is basically a social process in which an institutional setting is shaped and reshaped, and in which previously centralized functions and roles are reallocated among different political actors from different government levels, both in a formal and an informal way. This implies that the Belgian efforts to overcome the discrepancy between autonomy and coherence has to be considered as a permanent process of dynamic adaptation.

Notes

1. The data have been collected as part of a research project on the national and European communication networks of civil servants, the promoter of which is Guido Dierickx. The data collection and analysis was made possible by a grant from the Belgian Fonds voor Kollektief Fundamenteel Onderzoek to the University of Antwerp (075/1557).
2. Note that for many issues, no strict division of power exists between the federal and the subnational levels, which makes concertation and coordination towards the EU even more necessary (see for instance Baeteman, 1994: 57).
3. The communities had already got that right in 1988.
4. Important is the fact that, despite the lack of hierarchy, the Belgian subnational authorities have to respect the general foreign policy of Belgium. They cannot conclude agreements with countries with whom Belgium has no diplomatic relations. The federal state determines with which countries Belgium will maintain such relations (see article 167 §1 NBC; Documents Belgian Senate, 91/92, no. 100–16/1: 2 & Documents Belgian House of Representatives, 92/93, no. 797/3: 5).
5. The categorization of the EU Councils has been based on the issues that are dealt within these Councils and the concomitant competencies in Belgium. If a specific Council deals most of the time with issues that belong to the subnational sphere of competencies, Belgium will be represented according to category IV, even if a specific issue on the agenda of that Council belongs to the federal competencies only.
6. In order to simplify the table no distinction is made between foreign affairs officials and diplomats working at the Belgian PR. Furthermore the differences between the two were not significant.

7. This is indicated when, for the figures of the third column of Table 2.2, the distinction is made between line departments with and those without PR representatives. In that case, the intensity of communication of the PR representatives with other ministries and with foreign affairs is similar to those of the officials belonging to departments that are not represented at the PR.

References

Baeteman, G. (1994) Aspecten van het Belgisch federalisme anno 1994–1995. In *Publiek recht, ruim bekeken: opstellen aangeboden aan Prof. J. Gijssels*, (Antwerp: MAKLU), pp. 29–74.

Beyers, J. (1994) De Structuur van Besluitvorming in de Raad van Ministers van de Europese Unie, *Res Publica*, vols 3–4, pp. 381–98.

Beyers, J. and Kerremans, B. (1994) Relativiteit en Succes van een Europees Voorzitterschap. Het Belgisch Voorzitterschap van Naderbij Bekeken, *Res Publica*, vol. 2, pp. 129–41.

Beyers, J. and Kerremans, B. (1995) De plaats van de federale overheid, gewesten en gemeenschappen in de Europese Unie: consequenties van de staatshervorming en de wijziging van artikel 146 EU, *Tijdschrift voor Bestuurskunde en Publiek Recht*, vol. 11, pp. 647–57.

Bursens, P. (1996) European integration and environmental interest representation in Belgium and the EU, paper presented at the workshop on 'The transformation of governance in the EU' of the ECPR Joint Sessions, Oslo.

De Wachter, W. (1992) *Besluitvorming in Politiek België* (Louvain: Acco).

Denis, C. (1992) De Interministeriële Economische Commissie: Beperkte herziening of grootscheepse hervorming?, *Kwartaaloverzicht van de Economie*, vol. 3, pp. 78–93.

Franck, C. (1987) La prise de décision belge en politique extérieure: cohésion, tensions, contrôle et influences, *Res Publica*, vol. 1, pp. 61–84.

Franck, C. (1996) Belgium: the importance of foreign policy to European political union, in W. Wallace and C. Hill (eds) *The Actors in Europe's Foreign Policies* (London: Routledge), pp. 151–65.

Hooghe, L. (1995) Belgian federalism and the European Community, in B. Jones and M. Keating (eds), *The European Union and the Regions* (Oxford: Clarendon Press), pp. 135–65.

Huyse, L. (1986) *De gewapende vrede. Politiek in België na 1945* (Louvain: Kritak).

Ingelaere, F. (1994) De Europeesrechterlijke draagvlakken van de nieuwe wetgeving inzake de internationale betrekkingen van de Belgische Gemeenschappen en Gewesten, *Sociaal-Ekonomische Wetgeving*, vol. 2, pp. 67–82.

Kerremans, B. (1996) Do institutions make a difference? Non-institutionalism, neo-institutionalism, and the logic of common decision-making in the European Union, *Governance: An International Journal of Policy and Administration*, vol. 2, pp. 217–40.

Kerremans, B. and Beyers, J. (1996) The Belgian subnational entities in the European Union: 'second' or 'third level' players?, *Journal of Regional and Federal Studies*, vol. 2, pp. 41–55.

Lejeune, Y. (1994) Le principe de la loyauté fédérale: une règle de comportement au contenu mal defini', *Administration publique*, vol. 18, pp. 233–8.

Lejeune, Y. (1995) The Case of Belgium, in S.A. Pappas (ed.) *National Administrative Procedures for the Preparation and Implementation of Community Decision.* (Maastricht: EIPA), pp. 59–112.

Lijphart, A. (1981) *Conflict and Coexistence in Belgium: The Dynamics of a Culturally Divided Society* (Berkeley: Institute of International Studies).

Ministerie van Economische Zaken (1992) *Organigram* (Brussels: Ministerie van Economische Zaken).

Ministerie van Economische Zaken (1995) *Praktische gids van het Ministerie van Economische Zaken* (Brussels: Ministerie van Economische Zaken).

Peeters, P. (1994) Fédéralisme et relations extérieures, *Administration publique*, vol. 2, pp. 239–42.

Pijnenburg, B. (1993) Belgium: federalized EC lobbying at home, in M.P.C.M. Van Schendelen (ed.), *National Public and Private EC Lobbying* (Dartmouth: Aldershot), pp. 155–82.

Putnam, R. (1988) Diplomacy and domestic politics: the logic of two-level games, *International Organizations*, vol. 3, pp. 427–60.

Chapter 3

The Netherlands: Growing Doubts of a Loyal Member

BEN SOETENDORP AND KENNETH HANF

Introduction

The Netherlands was not only one of the six founding members of the EEC, it also played a critical role in the creation of the EEC. Together with the Belgian foreign minister Paul Henry Spaak, its former Foreign Minister, Jan-Willem Beyen, carried out in 1955 much of the preparatory work for the negotiations among the six members of the European Coal and Steel Community (ECSC) that would ultimately lead in 1957 to an agreement among the Six to establish an internal common market free of custom duties. As a trading nation (about 55 per cent of the GNP consists of exports), Dutch policy-makers have always considered the removal of trade restrictions very beneficial for the country and an essential requirement for its prosperity. This basic attitude has not changed over the years. The integration process remains important for the economic development of the country as exports to the other EU member-states still account for a significant proportion of Dutch trade. In 1995, for instance, about 80 per cent of all Dutch exports went to the twelve member-states that at that time formed the EU (Ministry of Finance, 1995).

Consequently, Dutch governments have always been strong advocates of the further expansion of European integration. During the diverse Intergovernmental Conferences (IGCs) aimed at institutional reforms necessary for the further development of the EC/EU, the Netherlands has repeatedly put forward proposals to enlarge the involvement of the institutions of the Union in common policy-making and to improve the functioning of its decision-making bodies. However, in recent years some policy-makers in the Netherlands have begun to have doubts regarding the benefits of further integration, emphasizing the need to balance national interests against community interests. Dutch politicians and officials have started to question the unconditional transfer of national financial resources to the EU budget and have become much more concerned about the loss of national autonomy in certain policy fields. As we will discuss later, the main source of this emerging reluctance among Dutch policy-makers is the fundamental change in the financial relationship of the Netherlands with the EU. Since the early 1990s the country has become a net contributor to the EU (in the sense that the Netherlands' share in payments to the EU is higher than its share in receipts from the EU budget). This has made Dutch politicians and officials much more aware of the budgetary consequences of further integration as well as further enlargement.

These small, but in the long term probably quite important, changes in political attitudes towards European integration are not yet broadly shared. European policy-making is still a bureaucratic process carried out according to standard operation procedures established in the early days of European integration. The completion of the single market and the signing of the TEU have, however, enlarged the number of policy issues that fall under the scope of common policies and have quite significantly multiplied the number of officials involved in European decision-making.

Governmental adaptation

The way that the Dutch negotiation position in the various Council meetings of the EU is prepared and decided indicates great respect for two basic principles underlying governmental policy-making in the Netherlands: namely, the principle of departmental autonomy and the principle of collective decision-making in the Dutch Council of Ministers. In the early stages of European integration, when economic issues dominated the EEC agenda, it was therefore not the Ministry of Foreign Affairs but the Ministry of Economic Affairs that was given the leading role in the preparation of the Dutch position on EC matters. This resulted, however, in problems of competence between the two ministries which were resolved in 1972, when the chief responsibility for the overall preparation of the Dutch position in the Council of Ministers on both the national and European level was formally entrusted to the Ministry of Foreign Affairs.

Since 1972 the minister of foreign affairs has been able to maintain his position as the major agent of interministerial coordination on European affairs. This role has occasionally been challenged by the suggestion of some politicians in parliamentary debates to transfer the overall responsibility for policy-making on European affairs to the prime minister. However, an official review of the foreign policy of the Netherlands, carried out in 1995 to examine ways in which the organization of the country's foreign policy could be restructured to improve the overall international performance of the Netherlands (including the need to ensure greater cohesion of Dutch activities in the EU), consolidated the pivotal position of the Ministry of Foreign Affairs in this respect. As a result of this review, the Ministry of Foreign Affairs itself underwent a fundamental reorganization in 1996, but the ministry was very careful to maintain the national structure of European policy coordination wherein it fulfils an important role almost unchanged. However, in many specialized issues, as we will illustrate, the Ministry of Foreign Affairs carries only the formal responsibility for the formulation of a coherent national negotiation position. The actual preparation of the negotiation positions regarding European dossiers remains within the specialized sectoral ministry which bears the main responsibility for the relevant issue.

Departmental autonomy

The greater impact of European policies on a large number of domestic policy areas and the increasing involvement of national officials from the various ministries in the EU decision-making process has blurred the distinction between foreign policy and domestic politics. It has also made the coordination of the many EU-related activities of the diverse ministries, in an attempt to achieve a coherent Dutch policy on the various EU topics, more complex. At present, besides officials of the foreign ministry, a large number of civil servants from every ministry is involved in the process of European policy-making, at the European level as well as the national level. Every ministry has its own representatives at the PR in Brussels. These officials act not only as the guardians of the specific interests of their department in the EU's policy-making bodies; they are also the eyes and ears of their home ministries in Brussels. They provide the sectoral ministries at home with a direct line of communication to the PR, which makes these ministries less dependent on the information given by the foreign ministry. Together with officials from the sectoral ministries who come over from The Hague, they participate on behalf of the Netherlands in the specialized working groups of the relevant sectoral Council, where the initial preparation of the Council decision-making takes place, and assist their minister during the Council meetings.

In every ministry the EU-related activities are dealt with by several divisions which handle the specific European component of its work. To manage the internal coordination of its European activities every ministry has a European affairs unit, staffed by officials with a more broad knowledge of EU matters and decision-making procedures. The organizational structure and size of these European affairs units differ per ministry. Some ministries, like the Ministry of Economic Affairs or the Ministry for Agriculture, which have long experience in European matters and are deeply involved in the making of European common policies, have a large European affairs unit that supervises the internal policies on various European dossiers through weekly meetings in which all relevant policy-makers participate. Newcomers to the European stage, such as the Ministry for Health or the Ministry for Environment, have a smaller European affairs unit, whose main task is to serve the minister and the various divisions in the ministry in the handling of European dossiers. However, all the European affairs units fulfil a key role in the various interministerial coordination fora in the Hague. Senior officials of these units participate on behalf of their ministry in the weekly meetings at the Ministry of Foreign Affairs. In these meetings the instructions are discussed for the Dutch Permanent Representative, who participates in the weekly meetings of COREPER, and for the sectoral ministers, who represent the country in the relevant specialized sectoral Council meetings in Brussels.

The national interministerial coordination on European matters in the Hague follows in general lines the different stages of European decision-making in Brussels. It starts when the European Commission proposals for decision-making by the European Council of Ministers are transferred through the Permanent Representative to the foreign ministry. In The Hague the Commission proposals are initially reviewed by the so-called Interministerial Working Group to Assess New

Commission Proposals (or BNC, according to the Dutch acronym), which is composed of representatives from every ministry and is chaired by an official from the Ministry of Foreign Affairs. The working group estimates the financial and legal consequences of the Commission's proposal for the Netherlands; evaluates whether the proposal meets the requirements of the subsidarity principle; and determines which ministry is to have the principal responsibility in the negotiations on the specific proposal. The analysis, which is based on an initial assessment report of the Commission's proposal prepared by the ministry with the major responsibility for the policy area affected by the proposal, is also sent to Parliament to inform its members about the ongoing proposals from the Commission.

During the first stage of the Council decision-making in Brussels, which takes place within the various working groups set up by COREPER or one of the other preparatory committees, such as the Special Committee for Agriculture or the so-called 113 Committee, it is officials coming from the sectoral ministries rather than the foreign ministry who will carry the main burden of the pre-negotiations. Thus the Dutch negotiation position in the working groups prepared within the ministry is charged with the major responsibility for the handling of a certain dossier. It is also up to the sectoral ministry to decide whether the representative of the ministry at the PR or the relevant official from the home ministry will be entrusted with negotiations, as well as to what extent other ministries should be involved in the deliberations. The almost exclusive participation of the sectoral ministries in the various working groups gives them quite some leverage to try to settle the disagreement with their counterparts on a dossier without the intervention of other ministries before it reaches the next preparatory stage of COREPER. As much of the bargaining between the officials of the various member-states is already done in the working group and many of the compromises are already accomplished at this point, the sectoral ministry also has a unique opportunity, at the beginning of the multilateral negotiations, to determine the Dutch stand in the next phases of the Council decision-making. The foreign ministry is informed by the relevant sectoral ministry about the outcome of the discussions in the working groups, but it plays no active role in the deliberations. As a matter of fact, the foreign ministry will participate directly at this stage only in the working groups that fall under its own competence, such as those established by the Political Committee or the COREPER that deal with foreign policy and security issues or institutional questions, as well as environmental matters, where the foreign ministry shares a common responsibility with the Ministry of Environment.

The foreign ministry's role as interministerial coordinator

The Ministry of Foreign Affairs resumes its role as coordinator of the national position in the Council, when the instructions for the Permanent Representative and his or her deputy who meet weekly with their counterparts from the other member-states in the COREPER I and the COREPER II meetings in Brussels have to be approved by the so-called COREPER instruction meeting in The Hague. The instructions for the negotiation position for the COREPER meetings, where the national ambassadors to the EU and their deputies prepare the work of the various councils, are drawn up each week in a gathering at the foreign ministry. This meeting, which is attended by representatives from every ministry, is chaired by a high-ranking official from the foreign ministry.

Although the draft texts of the COREPER instructions are prepared by the Directorate for European Integration at the foreign ministry, the first draft of these instructions are actually formulated in the ministry that has the major responsibility for the dossier and whose officials have already tried to settle the matter in the relevant working group in Brussels. Formally, each item on the agenda of these COREPER instruction meetings are open for discussion, but the participants usually intervene only when the specific item involves their own ministry. It is also common not to intervene when the instructions concern a dossier on which a working group has already reached complete agreement. These COREPER instruction meetings are, nevertheless, the first opportunity for other ministries to see the outcome of the deliberations in the various working groups. This gives those ministries who are not satisfied with the result a chance to redraft the instructions to the Permanent Representative. The COREPER instruction meetings are therefore an important forum where interministerial conflicts come to the surface and where a first attempt to resolve these national conflicts is undertaken by the foreign ministry. In these meetings officials from the foreign ministry also receives a first chance to relate the negotiations on a specific dossier, where the working groups were not able to agree on a proposal of the Commission, to negotiations on other dossiers. It gives them the chance to place the outstanding problems in the broader context of the ongoing bargaining in COREPER meetings in Brussels. In this way they can suggest issue linkages and package deals – ways to settle the outstanding problem in an overall strategy.

The cabinet's role as ultimate decision-making unit

When the decision-making on a proposal of the Commission reaches the final stage at the Council meetings in Brussels, the Dutch position taken by the minister participating on behalf of the Netherlands has already been determined at the weekly meetings of the Dutch Council of Ministers in the Hague. In this way the Dutch cabinet, chaired by the prime minister, is actually the ultimate decision-making unit where the final coordination of the Dutch negotiation position in the coming Council meetings is determined. The ground work for the cabinet meeting is done by the Coordination Committee for European Integration and Association Issues (known by its Dutch acronym as Co-Co). The state secretary of European affairs who has the major political responsibility for European affairs at the Ministry of Foreign Affairs chairs the Co-Co meetings. Since the state secretary also participates in the cabinet meeting where the conclusions of the Co-Co are considered, he or she figures in fact as the link between the highest bureaucratic level and the highest political level. The administrative preparation of the Co-Co meetings is once again prepared by the Directorate for European Integration at the Ministry of Foreign Affairs in close cooperation with the leading ministry on the specific dossier. The proposed negotiation positions are formulated as draft conclusions which are sent to all the other ministries in advance of the Co-Co meeting. Although any ministry can respond to these draft conclusions, the high-ranking officials from the different ministries represented in the weekly Co-Co meetings usually focus the discussions on those issues that have not yet been settled by COREPER and which need further interministerial coordination. In cases where conflicts of interests arise among the various ministries, the foreign ministry will act as an honest broker. If the Co-Co is still unable to reach a consensus on an agreed negotiation position, the Dutch cabinet makes a final decision on the preferred position. However, some politically sensitive dossiers are deliberately not settled at the Co-Co level and passed to the cabinet for final decision-making. All the points on which a consensus has been reached in the Co-Co meeting as well as the points on which agreement has emerged in earlier stages of the decision-making process are grouped together as the 'Co-Co final conclusions', and sent to the cabinet for final approval. At this point it is important to note that since both the Co-Co and the cabinet act under the pressure of the deadlines of the coming ministerial councils in Brussels, another high-level coordination committee has been created in the Hague alongside the Co-Co. This committee is composed of the most senior officials from the key ministries and meets less frequently than the Co-Co. It offers its participants an opportunity for a more substantial discussion of the preferred Dutch policy with respect to some longer-term European topics. It is also the major forum where the initial debates on the Dutch strategy in the coming European councils takes place.

Departmental autonomy ends, in practice, at the cabinet level, where a collegial mode of decision-making and the principle of collective responsibility prevails. Departmental interests may still determine a stand taken by ministers at the cabinet meetings. But once the cabinet has agreed on a negotiation position, every Dutch minister who participates in any of the Council of Ministers meetings in Brussels is not allowed to act independently of the mandate given by the cabinet. At the cabinet meeting a distinction is made between 'A points' and 'B points' on the cabinet's agenda, in a similar way to the distinction made at the Council meetings in Brussels. 'A points' are those items on which complete agreement has already been reached in COREPER and which makes further discussion in the Council probably unnecessary, while 'B points' refer to the items on which the Permanent Representatives were unable to reach agreement and as such are subjected to further discussion in the Council. In advance of the cabinet meeting the prime minister, in the capacity of the chair of the Dutch Council of Ministers, may decide to refer some politically sensitive matters that need a thorough discussion at the cabinet level (such as items addressed at the European Council of heads of government or institutional questions considered at the IGCs) to the Council for European Affairs (REA, according to the Dutch acronym).

The REA is actually a subsidiary of the cabinet's Council for European and International Affairs which meets in two separate compositions with a strict separation of labour, namely as a Council for European Affairs and as a Council for International Affairs. While the REA focuses solely on matters related to the EU, the latter deals with almost every international topic that falls outside the scope of the EU, varying from peace operations to development cooperation. The prime minister chairs the REA meetings and the minister of foreign affairs is responsible for the interministerial coordination in advance of the meeting. However, the prime minister's office is responsible for the administrative preparation of the REA meetings. Almost every minister is a member of the REA. Even where that is not the case, all ministers are entitled to attend the REA meeting if they wish to do so. Ministers may also be accompanied to the meeting by one of their senior civil servants. The prime minister may invite the Dutch member of the European Commission and the Dutch Permanent Representative at the EU to participate in the REA meeting. However, in spite of the growing importance of REA, the Dutch Council of Ministers itself remains the ultimate national decision-making unit on EU policies.

As we mentioned earlier, the latest review of Dutch foreign policy has also left unchanged the relatively modest role of the Prime Minister's Office in the national decision-making process on European matters. Despite the increasing role of the European Council, the Dutch prime minister has not become the leading figure in European policy-making on the national level. The main formal responsibility has remained with the foreign minister, while the prime minister has kept the traditional role as *primus inter pares*. As such the prime minister acts, in the first place, as the chair of the Dutch Council of Ministers and its various subcouncils. Like fellow ministers, the prime minister is also allowed to manoeuvre in the meetings of the European Council only within the margins of the mandate given by the Dutch Council of Ministers. Nevertheless, the larger scope of European issues dealt with by the cabinet has increased the role of the prime minister and senior officials in the formation of the Dutch positions in the EU. This is a result of the growing necessity for mediation at the cabinet level between rival ministries. Arbitration when controversies over competence arise among members of the government has always been one of the specific tasks of the Dutch prime minister. Consequently, along with the minister of foreign affairs, the prime minister also carries, in an indirect way, special responsibility for a coherent Dutch performance in the diverse decision-making bodies of the EU.

A limited parliamentary involvement

The Dutch Parliament has traditionally kept a low profile with respect to involvement in European policy-making. It was not until 1986 that Parliament decided to set up, for a period of two years, a temporary standing committee for EC affairs. The main task of this committee was to exercise some parliamentary control over the decision-making in the EC Council of Ministers. On the basis of an evaluation report, it was decided in 1988 to continue the activities of this committee, which changed its name in 1994 to the General Committee for EU Affairs. The committee deals essentially with issues discussed at the General Council and the European Council, whereas the other sectoral councils are dealt with by the relevant sectoral committees in Parliament. Until 1996 it was common that the Committee for EU Affairs as well as the other specialized committees would receive the agenda of the relevant council meeting before the council meeting. However, the members of the committee were only able to exchange views with the relevant minister – or the minister-president in the case of the European Council – after the meeting has taken place. This means that Parliament could exercise its control on the performance of the Dutch ministers in the various council meetings, if they wished to do so, only after the meeting – never in advance. Moreover, since the deliberations of the various councils are in principle secret, the minister could easily withhold information from Parliament.

A change in this practice was introduced in 1996. Ten years after its involvement with the decision-making in the Council of Ministers had started, Parliament decided to introduce a new procedure, again on a temporary basis for six months, called 'Europe Consultation', which allows members of Parliament to exercise better control over the performance of the Dutch ministers in the Council meetings in Brussels. In June 1996, Parliament decided that on a fixed day of the week, members of Parliament would have a chance to exchange views with the relevant minister, not only on recent Council meetings but also on the agenda and the position to be taken by the relevant minister in the Council meetings of the next week. Thursday afternoon was chosen as the fixed day of the week. This is just after the Co-Co has drawn (on Tuesday) its conclusions about the preferred Dutch position for the Council meeting the next week, and just before cabinet has endorsed the Co-Co conclusion at the cabinet meeting (on Friday). Were this new practice to become institutionalized, the Dutch Parliament would be much more involved in the formal cycle of European policy-making. However, this involvement is still not binding in the sense that the members of Parliament cannot determine the Dutch negotiation position, which is still fixed by the cabinet. The only exception concerns matters that are related to the provisions concerning cooperation in the fields of justice and home affairs. During the parliamentary debate on the ratification of the TEU, the government accepted an obligation not to commit itself to any decision of the Council for Justice and Home Affairs before the Dutch Parliament had been consulted and approved the proposed decision. This was done because the member-states had decided to avoid any control by the European Parliament over policies that are related to cooperation in the field of justice and home affairs.

National implementation

As EU legislation has become more important for what the Netherlands can and must do within its domestic borders, questions of prompt and effective implementation of Community legislation have become increasingly frequent items on the agendas of both the cabinet and Parliament. Although the Netherlands has long considered itself to be a model of good implementation of EU legislation, evidence indicates that the Netherlands has been increasingly less able to transpose EU directives within the time limit set. In the Netherlands, about 30 per cent of the directives were not implemented by the deadline set for implementation.

Since there is no special implementation procedure for EU directives, the procedures used to transpose Community law into Dutch law follow the constitutional procedures laid down for the legal instrument to be used to incorporate Community measures into national law. Although the Dutch constitution sets limits to what kind of instrument can be used under particular circumstances, whatever the instrument, it has become increasingly recognized that the manner in which national execution is prepared will have important consequences for both the speed and effectiveness of the implementation of a directive. This preparatory activity is usually in the hands of a single ministry. Effective implementation requires that these preparations begin as soon as possible. Best of all would be when they occur in conjunction with the decision-making on the directive itself. In this way the Dutch government can still try to influence the proposed directive, while at the same time having an opportunity to anticipate possible implementation problems and to determine how responsibility for implementing the measure is to be allocated once the measure has been passed.

Although there are a number of causes for the delays in implementation, attention has been particularly focused on shortening the lengthy legislative procedures by which European law is incorporated into the Dutch legal order. In this connection efforts have been made to involve implementing officials – especially the legal experts of the various departments – in the earlier phase of community decision-making, instead of waiting until the directive has already been formally passed and submitted to the member-states for implementation. This would enable potential implementation problems to be signaled already during the preparation of the directive. Up until then, negotiations in Brussels had been almost exclusively in the hands of the policy experts. There have also been serious coordination problems in those cases where an EU directive cuts across the boundaries of separate policy fields and the jurisdictional lines of the individual ministries. Such directives require changes in regulations under the competence of a number of ministries, which can lead to substantive disagreements, jurisdictional disputes and problems of coordination.

A well-prepared national input into Community decision-making requires, among other things, the timely involvement of the national Parliament in the Community phase. This is better than waiting until the national implementation phase or until a directive is already in effect. Earlier involvement of Parliament in Community decision-making would contribute to speedier transposition, since Parliament would be able to devote less time and attention to details of the subsequent incorporation measures. To this end, there has been a number of changes in the Netherlands. Parliament now receives more information from the government regarding pending EU matters, e.g. annotated agendas and reports of meetings of the Council of Ministers, fiches or information sheets from the Ministry of Foreign Affairs regarding the content of new Commission proposals and the deadlines and measures for national transposition, together with overviews from the various ministries concerning Community developments in their particular areas.

In general, what has been happening is that the point of involvement of the various actors participating in the legislative process at the national level in the Netherlands is shifting from the implementation phase, i.e. involvement in the passing of the statute by which EU law is transposed into national law, to the Community legislative process. To this end, for example, the government has decreed that no external advisory opinions or consultations with affected interests will be requested with regard to the transposition measures (except in those cases where such inputs are required by law – and efforts are also being made to cut back on such formally required advisory opinions – or are necessary in order to prepare the transposition measures thoroughly). On the other hand, such inputs will be encouraged in considering new Commission proposals. It will be up to the individual ministries to decide whether it is necessary to consult advisory boards and other interested parties at this stage. This includes providing access for provinces and muncipalities, through their associations, to national decision-making on European matters.

With regard to speeding up national implementation the cabinet has followed, in large measure, the recommendations of the Committee for the Testing of Legislative Proposals. A number of measures has been introduced, affecting all aspects of the implementation process. Most of these are contained in the Guidelines for Rule-Making. Within one month after the joint position of the Council of Ministers has been formulated, the lead ministry in The Hague must present a concrete implementation plan to the Work Group on the Evaluation of New Commission Proposals. If there is a delay in meeting this deadline, or there are substantive points of dispute, the cabinet must be informed. Once the EU measure has been formally passed, the draft of the measures designed to transpose the directive intro Dutch law must be presented, in principle, one month after the period set out in the EU measure for the transposition has begun.

The cabinet is supposed to check each month whether the ministries are meeting these deadlines and whether any problems have arisen that require its attention. The cabinet also looks at any substantive difficulties or jurisdictional disputes that may have arisen and tries to resolve them. Prior to this, the legislative policy staff of the Ministry of Justice try to mediate in the interest of resolving this kind of bottleneck as much as possible. An attempt is also made to prevent national policy measures from being attached to measures intended to transpose EU law into Dutch law. In the past, such implementing statutes were often used as vehicles for adding on new or revised national policy. The more general intention is, as well, to make sure that the transposition legislation is 'implementable and enforceable'. This means that, in addition to procedural improvements to ensure that deadlines will be met, efforts are being made to make sure that the substantive provisions of the implementing measure are also adequate. Here, too, measures have been taken to assist the sectoral ministries in achieving this goal.

As the coordinator of EU policy within the Dutch government, the Ministry of Foreign Affairs is also suppposed to monitor the progress achieved in carrying out this policy. But the Ministry of Economic Affairs coordinates on directives that have to do with the realization of the internal market. Recently, however, both the Ministry of Justice and the Prime Minister's Office have become increasingly more involved with these issues. The Ministry of Justice sees itself called to safeguard the quality of legislation used to implement EU directives. In light of this competition for a piece of the coordination action, the situation has been described as follows: 'The co-ordination structure in the Netherlands becomes complicated and unclear, which can lead to further problems. The status of the co-ordinating Ministries of Foreign Affairs and Justice is low in the eyes of the policy-oriented ministries, because these two ministries do not have the professional knowledge to judge the contents of impementation measures' (Bekkers *et al.*, 1992: 25).

When a new directive has been received from Brussels, the Ministry of Foreign Affairs sends it to the sectoral ministry into whose jurisdiction, according to the present division of labour, the matter falls. This ministry bears the primary responsibility for seeing that the EU legislation is properly executed. In cases where there are differences of opinion between two or more ministries regarding who is supposed to implement a particular directive, it is not the foreign ministry but the ministries themselves who have to work this out. If they cannot do so, then the cabinet will decide.

Since June 1989, the state secretary for European affairs of the Ministry of Foreign Affairs presents a quarterly overview of the situation in the Netherlands with regard to the implementation of EC legislation. This overview is prepared by the interministerial work group 'Implementation of EU Directives', under the direction of the Ministry of Foreign Affairs. The report is discussed in the Co-Co before being approved by the cabinet. It is then presented to Parliament. Although the function of this report is, in the first instance, to provide both the government and Parliament with the information necessary to monitor and control the implementation of EU policy, it also serves the purpose of providing a 'score card' for judging the efforts of the individual ministries. In this way the laggards can be 'shamed' by making their relative position public and, it is hoped, in this way spurred on to greater efforts in promptly implementing EU legislation.

Political adaptation

As mentioned in the introduction, Dutch policy-makers (both politicians and officials) have traditionally been strong supporters of a European integration that would ultimately lead to the united states of Europe. Neither the signing of the SEA nor the ratifying of the TEU has triggered any fundamental debate about the direction and speed of the integration process. The mainstream political parties in the Netherlands were always true believers in a federal structure and the need to strengthen the supranational institutions of the Community. A powerful European Commission, European Parliament and European Court were, in the view of the Dutch political élite, the best safeguard for small states against the formation of an informal directorate of the larger states within the principal decision-making body, the Council of Ministers. Only some politicians of small marginal parties on the right as well as the left of the political spectrum have expressed opposition to European integration. But the process of European integration has never been a real issue of public debate in any election campaign. The initial opposition of the Netherlands to the proposed 'three-pillar' structure of the EU, during the IGC over the TEU, reflected very much traditional Dutch ideas regarding European integration. This also explains the abortive attempt by the Netherlands in September 1991, in its capacity as president in office, to move the EU as a whole in a more federal direction. This objective reflected very much the traditional Dutch perceptions about European integration.

While the national consensus on the need to continue the process of European integration still exists, one can nevertheless sense a departure from the almost dogmatic belief in the advantages of European integration. As a result of this change of mentality among Dutch politicians and officials regarding the merits of European integration, it has become common among Dutch policy-makers to express their doubts as to whether the Dutch government should approve initiatives of the Commission to start new European action programmes, given their misgivings about the lack of budgetary discipline of the European Commission and the European Parliament. It is not unusual to employ in this connection the principle of subsidiarity as an argument against the transfer of certain responsibilities in a specific policy area from the national to the European level. In the Dutch memoranda prepared for the IGC to review the TEU, the Dutch government has explicitly stated that European government and legislation are not an end in themselves. Stressing that decisions should be taken as closely as possible to the citizens, the Dutch government argues that in its view the EU must take action only where the member-states are no longer able to offer satisfactory answers to social, economic and political questions. It has emphasized that when the Commission submits a proposal it is obliged to explain why regulations at European level are necessary (Ministry of Foreign Affairs, 1995).

The Dutch government is proposing, therefore, that the TEU be revised in a way that would make the vague formulation of the principle of subsidiarity, as it is laid down in Article A and Article 3b of the TEU, more explicit. When the Commission presents a proposal to the Council, it is, according to the Dutch view, not sufficient that the Commission confirms that it has assessed a proposal in the light of the subsidiarity principle. The Commission has to do more and should answer three concrete questions. First, the question of subsidiarity: Why is regulation at the EU level necessary? Second, the question of proportionality: Would a less stringent regulatory instrument and a less detailed form of rules suffice? Third, the question of costs versus benefits and enforceability: What are the costs for the EU, the national government and the business community of the proposed regulation and how easily can implementation be monitored? The argumentation of the Commission should be made public and should lead to a public admissibility debate in the Council if at least one member-state asks for such a debate. The admissibility debate should be based not only on the arguments of the Commission and the reactions of the national governments, but also on the responses received from the public, interest groups, national parliaments and decentralized authorities (*ibid.*). Such a political consultation is contrary to the current practice where the proposals of the Commission are first discussed by officials of the national governments and the Commission in the secrecy of the Council working groups. At present the political debate can take place only at the very last stage of final decision-making in the Council, and again in secrecy. The Dutch government, which has always been a strong supporter of strengthening the powers of the Commission *vis-à-vis* the member-states, stresses, however, that the subsidiarity test should not be used as a covert means of limiting the Commission's power. The government has therefore been careful to present its proposal for a subsidiarity debate as a means to reinforce the democratic working of the Union. But in the view of the post-Maastricht debate among the member-states and the Commission on how to operationalize the concept of subsidiarity, where some countries indeed see the subsidiarity principle as a useful instrument for putting a limit on the activities of the Commission and shifting the division of powers between the EU institutions and the member-states in favour of the latter, the Dutch proposition is quite remarkable. Although after the signing of the Maastricht Treaty the Commission expressed its willingness to apply the test of subsidiarity to all its future proposals and to review past legislation, the Dutch proposition actually puts the Commission on the defensive since it is the Commission that has to explain why it wants Community action.

The more critical attitude of the Dutch government towards an extension of the activities of the Commission may result from the simple fact that the Netherlands has become the second largest net contributor (in relative terms) to the EU, after Germany. The main reason for this deterioration is that its share in payments to the EU is increasing, while its share in receipts from the CAP and the Structural Fund policy, the two main sources of receipts from the EU, are decreasing. In the agricultural sector alone the Netherlands has dropped from a net receiver of over 2.5 billion guilders in 1988 to a net contribution of almost 1 billion guilders in 1995. The recent reform of the CAP will further worsen the net position, as the Netherlands is expected to benefit the least of all the member-states from this reform. The Dutch net position in relation to the Structural Fund is very similar. While the net contribution to the Structural Fund continues to rise, the Netherlands receives the smallest amount per capita of all member-states (Ministry of Finance, 1995). According to estimations made by the Dutch Ministry of Finance, the country is expected to become in 1999 the largest net contributor in relative terms to the EU. While in 1988, for example, the Netherlands still received from the EU three guilders for every guilder it paid to the EU, in 1995 it received back from the EU only one guilder of every two guilders it has paid.

Whereas the Netherlands accepts that the EU cannot avoid a situation where some members are net receivers and others are net contributors, the government is nevertheless concerned about its relatively high burden compared to the other more prosperous member-states. The Dutch government realizes that the benefits of its EU membership for the economy as a whole outweigh the costs of being a large net contributor. But Dutch politicians also realize that, since the financial contribution to the EU involves a diversion of funds from national priorities, there is a limit to the extent to which a position as a net contributor can be accepted by the public. Although even in 1999 the Dutch contribution to the EU will not account for more than 4 per cent of the Dutch government expenditure, Dutch politicians find it increasingly difficult to justify significant cuts in the national budget and, at the same time, to support an increase in the contribution to the EU budget. The Dutch government does not yet follow the policy of Britain under its former Prime Minister Margaret Thatcher, who demanded its money back. Nevertheless, the prospect of bearing the relatively largest share of the cost of financing the EU by the turn of the century has caused a more critical attitude on the part of the Netherlands towards the financial consequences of some common policies. The government is, for instance, in favour of the accession of countries from central and eastern Europe. However, it has also indicated that it will resist any further rise in the total expenditure of the CAP and the Structural Funds as a result of an enlargement to the east. This means that it will be necessary first to review the financial implications of such an enlargement for the current CAP and the Structural Funds policy. The government resists, in fact, any rise in the future budget of the EU and seeks support from other countries, Germany and Britain in particular, for a policy of restraint with respect to future expenditure. In order to achieve a reduction in the costs of the CAP when the Union is enlarged, the government has suggested, in addition to a further rationalization of the CAP, a re-nationalization of the agricultural policy. The government has also questioned the current practice in the distribution of the social funds which allows not only the poor countries of the Union, but the rich member-states as well, to use the structural funds to finance their own regional policy. The government favours some kind of ceiling on payments to member-states which would eliminate the current large differences between payments and receipts. Since the Dutch government wants to keep the EU budget as low as possible, it argues also in favour of a ceiling on the annual EU budget, which would fix the maximum sum of annual expenditure. It is obvious that, besides the Dutch officials and politicians, the Dutch electorate also, as it becomes more aware of the financial burden of further integration, will adopt a more critical attitude towards the blessings of further integration in general and the Commission in particular. When one talks to the officials who deal on behalf of their ministry with the daily practice of European integration, one can sense in some governmental circles a growing reluctance to support new initiatives of the Commission. There is, in other words, a growing gap between the political élite, which still believe in European integration as such, and an officialdom, which raises some questions regarding the need to deepen that process further. However, some politicians are already beginning to express their doubts as to whether the Netherlands should accept blindly every further extension of the powers of the European institutions to new policy areas. This might be a beginning of some second thoughts about the merits of further integration and the start of some kind of political debate about the limits of European integration.

In the intergovernmental negotiations over the revision of the TEU, the Dutch government has already taken a more pragmatic position towards the institutional structure of the Union. This time the government has not challenged the 'three pillar' structure of the Union as such. Instead, it has focused on safeguarding the irreversibility of the achievements of European integration thus far, as well as the improvement of the functioning of the Union within its current structure. But the Netherlands still advocates a stronger role for the Commission in the preparation and implementation of the Common Foreign and Security Policy (CFSP), and the extension of qualified majority voting to this policy area. It should be pointed out that the extension of the activities of the Commission in the CFSP area does not carry any financial costs. This is also the case with regard to Dutch support for increased cooperation in the field of justice and home affairs in the third pillar, greater parliamentary involvement and more involvement of the European Court of Justice. All these proposals have a high symbolic value, while the price is almost nil. It seems that this also explains why the Dutch government focuses now on demands for more democratic legitimacy and transparency in the working of the EU institutions rather than extension of the EU powers to new policy areas, and why Dutch policy-makers insist on the improvement of the functioning of the institutions of the Union within its current structure before further enlargement can be realized. It is perhaps not surprising that, at the same time, the Dutch government is considering the idea of a smaller Union. While the Netherlands has always been against a differentiation in EU membership, the present government has dropped the traditional Dutch opposition to multiple-speed integration. It emphasizes in its IGC memoranda that it continues to advocate that the Union as a whole should travel in a single direction. However, if that is not possible, a smaller group of member-states should be allowed to integrate more closely. The only condition is that the single institutional framework of the EU must remain intact (Ministry of Foreign Affairs, 1995).

Strategic adaptation

Until the failure of the Dutch government, during its presidency in 1991, to receive support from the other member-states for its own ideas about the way that the EU should be arranged, Dutch policy-makers were quite confident of their relative influence within the EC decision-making process. But the failure of the Dutch government to get the Dutch draft on political union accepted, as well as the abortive attempt, shortly thereafter, to get the Dutch Prime Minister Ruud Lubbers nominated as the president of the European Commission raised some doubt about the influence of the Netherlands within the Community. Moreover, the recent enlargement to the north and the prospect of an enlargement to the east has made it even more crucial to develop a more strategic approach towards the exercise of influence on the decision-making process in the EU. As mentioned in the introduction to this chapter, this concern received special attention in the governmental review of the foreign policy of the Netherlands. In order to safeguard Dutch interests, the government has decided to pay much more attention to the building of the necessary coalitions in advance of the Council meetings in Brussels. In this respect the improvement of the relations with Germany and France has gained high priority in an effort to facilitate the formation of coalitions with these two key actors. However, with the exception of the traditional cooperation with its Benelux partners, little effort has been made in building more permanent and stable coalitions with other small states. Coalition-building with like-minded states like the Scandinavian members is still on an *ad hoc* basis when the Council discusses regulations in the environmental field or regulations that give citizens a substantial right of access to information on EU decision-making.

Some sectoral ministries are also paying special attention to the improvement of the performance of their officials in the decision-making process at the European level. For example, several sectoral ministries organize special visits of Dutch officials to their counterparts in other European capitals, in order to establish bilateral contacts which would make coalition-building, when necessary, much easier. To improve the way in which their officials deal with European issues, some sectoral ministries also organize seminars and visits to the European institutions to increase the knowledge of their officials about Europe. In advance of the Dutch presidency of 1996, the government even organized special training courses in multilateral negotiations for those officials who will chair EU meetings during the presidency.

In conclusion we may say that, because of the Dutch respect for the principle of departmental autonomy, a more integrated approach to the Dutch performance on all the levels of European decision-making seems unfeasible. As the recent reorganization of the Ministry of Foreign Affairs illustrates, the national system of European coordination, which involves other ministries as well, was left intact. This does not mean that, over the years, cooperation between officials from the foreign ministry and other sectoral ministries has not improved. Still, the Dutch government is unable to embark on a new strategy that would have the permanent rotation of officials from the foreign ministry and officials in the sectoral ministries involved in European affairs as its main core. But the participants in the weekly COREPER instructions meetings and the weekly Co-Co meetings, together with the national officials placed with the PR in Brussels and the Dutch officials seconded to the European Commission and the secretariat of the Council in Brussels, do informally constitute a hard core of European policy officers. These officials try to bridge, in their daily activities, the barriers between the national ministries in a collective effort to secure the Dutch interests in the EU.

References

Bekkers, V.J.J.M., Bonnes, J.M., de Moor-van Vugt, A.J.C. and Voermans, W.J.M. (1992) The implementation of Community legislation in the Netherlands: processes and problems, Tilburg: Tilburg University.

Ministry of Finance (1995) *Memorandum to the Lower House on the Net Position of the Netherlands vis-à-vis the EU Budget*, internal document (The Hague).

Ministry of Foreign Affairs (1995) *The Netherlands and the Future of the European Union* (The Hague: SDU).

Chapter 4

Denmark: The Testing of a Hesitant Membership

SØREN Z. VON DOSENRODE

Introduction

Apart from the short period between the acceptance of the Single European Act (SEA) in 1985 and the refusal of the Treaty on European Union (TEU) in 1992, Denmark has been a pragmatic and reluctant member of the EC (EU). One could expect such a cautious approach to be reflected in the adaptation of the political system to the EU. On the other hand, in order to be able to profit as much as possible from the membership of the EU, certain adjustments were necessary. In this chapter, I analyse how Denmark, with its preference for intergovernmental cooperation, has attempted to adapt to the demands of the increasingly supranational EU.

The highest Danish administrative authority is the government.[1] All bills are presented at the weekly cabinet meeting before they are passed on to the parliament (Folketinget). Likewise, all important administrative decisions are presented in the cabinet before they are put into force. However, the individual ministers are responsible both politically and administratively for their departments (minister governance).[2] Since 1901, when cabinet responsibility was introduced, the ministers and the government answer to the Parliament. The *raison d'être* of the department was its function as the secretariat of the minister. Without the minister the department has no administrative authority. Compared to the number of ministries in other Scandinavian states, Denmark holds the record with twenty in 1996 (two less than in 1994). One can trace this large number back to political rather than functional reasons.

Along with its large expansion after the Second World War, the Danish civil service changed character as well. Today it can be described as reasonably open and informal. Although 'the fundamental basis for the activities of the administration is the rule of law' (Nielsen in Gammeltoft-Hansen *et al.*, 1982: 50), the central administration, and public administration in general, are pragmatic, not rigidly law-bound. There is, for example, no general law governing the organization and the procedure of the administration. There are no general rules on deadlines by which a case must be closed (*sagsbehandlingen*) and a decision taken; there are no general rules on sending proposals for comments (Rasmussen, 1985: 216). As a result, 'unwritten rules are of major importance in the field of administrative law' (Nielsen in Gammeltoft-Hansen *et al.*, 1982: 50). Likewise, there remains an imminent danger of arbitrariness and abuse of power.

A last characteristic of the central administration is its very close cooperation with the influential interest organizations. As Katzenstein suggests, Denmark, too, is a good example of corporatism. We shall return to this later in this analysis.

Institutional adaptation

The Danish EU coordination system

Denmark joined the EC on 1 January 1973, i.e. at a time when the EC had already had approximately twenty years to build up an administrative tradition of its own. Thus the basic organizational principles of the EC were already well established. That they had to relate to something already existing was an obvious advantage for Denmark.

The administrative preparation for the Danish EC membership first began seriously in 1971. The market section of the Ministry of Foreign Affairs had intended to give itself a central position, stressing the foreign–political dimension of membership (Notat af 21. Januar 1972). The motives of the market section were fairly obvious. During the long negotiations leading to membership, this section had been the most important actor, with all the prestige and power that this implied. Once the negotiations were concluded, the section risked losing prominence. The market section's proposal was opposed vigorously by most of the other ministries. They wanted as decentralized a decision and coordination system as possible (Auken *et al.*, 1974: 245f.). Grønnegård Christensen described this as a clear case of fighting for one's institutional interests. Since the sector ministries saw no reason to give up their strong independence, the result was a compromise. It was laid out in a memorandum from the Department of Foreign Economic Policy (the second half of the Ministry of Foreign Affairs) from 12 December 1972. The structure and the process have remained the same up until now (1996), apart from small changes.

The formal part of the Danish EU coordination and decision-making procedure is built up around coordination and consultation committees on various levels, with different actors. On the lowest level there are the EC Special Committees[3] (EF-Special Udvalgene), of which there were 19 in 1972 and 30 in 1996. Their task is to coordinate the points of view of the involved ministries on a single issue or policy area, e.g. agriculture or the internal market. The work of this level was expected to be of a specific and technical nature, but it also includes strong political elements. The next level is the EC Committee (EF-Udvalget), a coordination committee composed of senior officials. According to Thygesen, this committee has three tasks (in Haagerup and Thune, 1986: 58): to solve the rare conflicts at the level of the Special Committees according to the general principles of Danish EU policy; to filter political from administrative issues and to pass the former on to the government; and to monitor the development of the EU in general. It should, moreover, be stressed that with 30 Special Committees, coordination is one of the EC Committee's most important tasks. The committee is supposed to ensure that the recommendations of the Special Committees are not contradictory in order to prevent Denmark from having to defend contradictory positions in Brussels. The highest administrative level is the cabinet, especially its Foreign Political Committee (Regeringens Udenrigspolitiske Udvalg). The main task of this committee is to decide on the Danish position on issues that are being negotiated in the EU (in all three pillars). Due to the tradition of not interfering in the affairs of other ministers, only cases of general interest and political importance are brought up for discussion here.

Before the government can participate in the meetings of the Council in Brussels, it has to get the approval of the Folketing, or rather it has to ensure that there is not a majority against its stand. This is done in the Parliament's European Committee (Europa Udvalget).

In general, the Danish EU coordination process can be characterized as strongly centralized compared to the traditional administrative tradition. However, it is, at the same time, flexible, and many questions are solved informally (von Dosenrode 1993a: 460). The formal structure does not reveal the whole truth about Danish EU decision-making. One can speak of two important networks in Danish EU policy formulation: the administrative–corporative network, and the parliamentarian network.[4]

The administrative–corporative network consists of 32 subnetworks: the 30 Special Committees' networks, the coordination network and the ministerial network. Its main task is to prepare the administrative part of the Danish EU decision-making process as well as to help with the implementation of the EU directives. The Special Committees subnetworks are the most important in Danish everyday EU policy formulation. They can be involved at an early state of the EU decision-making process. Here we can speak of strong subnetworks, with authority towards the outside. The strongest are those with known contacts, formal or informal in nature, with the interest organizations (IOs). In the subnetworks where some of the actors come from outside the civil service, the actors from the interest organizations have achieved a certain equality with the civil servants. To coordinate the recommendations coming from the Special Committees network, a coordination network has been set up around the EC Committee. Its tasks are important, but it rarely changes the recommendations of the Special Committees network substantially. The third part of the network is the ministerial network, which has several important functions. Among others, it bridges the gap to the parliamentary network, and it prepares the negotiations in Brussels. In this network, the minister has a role as political legitimizer for new bills; the minister and the Foreign Political Committee of the cabinet serve as troubleshooters; the minister or the cabinet may lay down guidelines for Denmark's overall EU policy; and the minister may serve as an important contact for his or her counterparts in other countries. Altogether we have a network with fairly clear roles and functions. It is a strong network that decides most of Danish EU policy.

The second important network is the parliamentary network, centred around the European Committee of the Parliament. Its functions are to inform the Parliament about developments in the EU in general, and on concrete Danish positions in particular; to give the Parliament an opportunity to influence Danish EU policy, thus legitimizing it; and to provide the last possibility of coordination. Unintentionally, the meetings of the committee also serve as a rehearsal for the minister for his or her 'performance' in Brussels. The committee's task is to control and influence Danish EU policy in the name of the electorate. The committee is the meeting point of the parliamentary and the administrative cooperative network. (A discussion of the EU Committee's work and power follows below.)

The Special Committees networks

Since the Special Committees (sub)networks are very important, we will take a closer look at them.

The first official level of the coordination and decision-making process is that of the Special Committees. From the very beginning, the functions of the Special Committees were to coordinate the points of view of the involved ministries and to make recommendations for a Danish position. A Special Committee sends its recommendation to the ministries that are responsible for the policy area (*ressortområde*). They, in turn, then pass it on to the EC Committee. Already in 1972, in a decision from the government's EC Committee, it was stated that the ministries were responsible for taking the opinion of the IOs into consideration, although it was also suggested that the chair of the Special Committee invite the IOs to participate in the relevant meetings. Thus the network's tasks involve establishing contact between the civil service and the IOs, exchanging information, coordinating actions (both civil service and the IOs have contacts with the European Commission) and cooperating in policy formulation, implementation and the subsequent legitimation. In short: the main functions of the Special Committees networks are to formulate Denmark's stand on a given issue, and to help implement it later.

As soon as a proposal takes shape during the agenda-setting phase, and the civil service knows about it, it can be discussed at a Special Committee.[5] At the latest, a proposal will be placed on the agenda of the relevant Special Committee when it is officially handed over to the European Council of Ministers by the European Commission. If a proposal is changed, new meetings will be convened.

When an initiative from the European Commission has been through the European Committee of the Danish Parliament, and has been negotiated and decided in the Council of Ministers in Brussels, a directive will normally be the result. This has to be implemented back in Denmark. Traditionally the IOs are involved in the preparation of the implementation of Danish laws; it is the same with EU laws. Approximately 85 per cent of the EU directives are administratively transformed into Danish rules through a law of authorization (*bemyndigelseslov*), not through the Parliament (Steen Gade, interview November 1995). This procedure creates a problem in that the Parliament is often excluded from the important part of the implementation procedure. Due to their heavy workload the ministers frequently also do not have time to participate in the phase where an EU directive is being formulated into concrete Danish legal terms (*bekendtgørelser*). Thus a good deal of the implementation activity is left to the civil servants and the IOs.

Structurally, each Special Committee can be regarded as an interdependent network with a high degree of autonomy. It has a core network, consisting of the main actors centred around the relevant Special Committee, and a broader network, where other important actors are active, e.g. ministers, the EC Committee and the Ministry of Foreign Affairs, which all have a (rarely used) chance to change the decisions made by the core network. Around these actors, the borders of the network are closed. In spite of the generally horizontal character of the networks, it is easy to identify a central unit, formed by the chair and his or her ministry. Normally, it is the minister or the ministry that formulates the proposed Danish position, and guides it through the decision process. The pattern of interaction is well structured and ordered.

In this context it should be remembered that the networks are tied together by formal as well as informal links on several levels. A recent survey indicates that an important part of the civil service (38 per cent) has contacts on EU matters with IOs either on a daily or monthly basis (Pedersen and Pedersen, 1995: 19). It is therefore justified to talk about a generally high density of relations. A recent analysis of corporatism in Denmark shows the growing importance of informal, 'routinized' contacts in different forms between the civil service and the IOs. These contacts have increased since the SEA came into force (*ibid*.: 17–20).[6]

The Europeanization on the departmental level

Apart from introducing the coordination and decision-making system outlined above, EC membership only led to quantitative changes in the overall organization of the Danish civil service. Jørgen Grønnegård Christensen estimated that in 1973 between 200 and 300 civil servants were occupied with EC affairs (in Amstrup and Faurby, 1978: 89). Excluding the Ministry of Foreign Affairs, the civil service used 2,000 'work years' for international tasks;[7] of these, only 277 'work years' or 13.5 per cent were related to the membership of the EC (Betænkning nr. 1209 vol. 2/ 360f.). In spite of the developments caused by the Maastricht Treaty, the number today probably does not exceed 15 per cent of the time used on international work.

But 'Europe' spread quickly to most of the ministries; already in 1973 there were 40 sections in 15 out of 19 ministries working on EC affairs (von Dosenrode 1993a: 457). This development has continued: in 1995 there were 77 sections in 17 out of 20 ministries working on EU affairs. In this sense a Europeanization has taken place (Hof and Stat, 1995). This trend has been confirmed by a survey conducted by Pedersen and Pedersen according to which nearly 38 per cent of the ministries or their agencies have daily or weekly contacts with directorates-general of the EU Commission. On the other hand, 50 per cent of the ministries or their agencies were of the opinion that they did not have any direct contact at all to the European institutions (1995: 18f.). Comparing Pedersen and Pedersen's figures, which look at the civil service *en bloc*, with von Dosenrode's figures describing the Europeanization of the individual ministries (1993a: 457; Hof and Stat, 1995), it is obvious that there is a core of ministries which have very intensive contacts with Brussels (e.g. Foreign Affairs, Finance, Commerce, Agriculture and Fisheries, Public Tax, Energy and the Environment). The rest of the ministries have less intensive relations. This is not a surprising conclusion. But, on the other hand, it is not as trivial as it may seem, since it indicates a potential clash of cultures within the civil service. In this sense, we can see a differential Europeanization of the civil service.

The increasing Europeanization has forced the ministries to consider the question of coordination within the department and its agencies. From the very start, each ministry had to have an 'EC responsible', someone to whom the Ministry of Foreign Affairs could send mail. This person, normally a head of section, was in charge of the ministerial basic coordination beside other duties. This modus still prevails.[8] Naturally, the coordination system is most elaborated in the ministries with many EU-related duties.

In spite of this Europeanization, it is not possible, either on the interdepartmental or on the departmental level, to detect any major structural administrative adaptation due to the extended use of majority voting in the Council of Ministers. The situation is the same regarding the new procedures involving the European Parliament more in the Union's decision-making procedure. These changes at the EU level have not led to changes in Denmark. The subnetworks centred around the Special Committees have, however, gained power since the SEA and the TEU. At the same time, the EU procedures have been tightened up in some of the ministries (see below).

Procedures

As we have seen, the overall procedure for coordinating and deciding on the Danish input into the EU decision-making process was laid down in the memorandum from the Department of Foreign Economic Affairs from 1 December 1972. In addition to allocating competencies among the different actors, it contained a rigid time schedule for the coordination and decision-making process. It also included rules for the communication with the PR in Brussels (everything written has to pass through the Ministry of Foreign Affairs and from there to the ambassador, who passes it on to the attachés), and obliged all ministries to appoint a person in charge of distributing EC material to the relevant persons and sections. Compared to the Danish administrative tradition, this is a very rigid procedure. The reason for this formalism was the notion that a small state would only stand a chance if it spoke with one voice and if its statements were well prepared and logical, i.e. if it had a good case.

Due to the principle of departmental autonomy as well as the different degrees of involvement in EU matters, the ministries have different standard operating procedures on EU affairs. The Ministry of Commerce is a good example of a ministry that is seriously involved in EU affairs. After the SEA, an EU secretariat was created in order to handle EU legal questions and to coordinate EU affairs internally. The need of coordination increased after the TEU. The ministry now covers five different EU councils. In the beginning of 1995 the ministry's EU secretariat drafted and implemented a set of detailed rules concerning the ministry's EU planning.[9] Other heavily involved ministries have introduced similar systems. The guidelines are a sign that EU-related tasks are expanding within the ministries, and that EU affairs are no longer isolated and treated by only a few civil servants per ministry. But this has not changed the fundamental principle that EU cases generally are to be handled as 'normal' Danish cases by the sections in charge of the corresponding Danish cases.

Implementation

The basic Danish attitude concerning the implementation of EU law is that when the law-making process has been completed, the law must be implemented and obeyed. Even if a directive does not correspond to Danish wishes, it still has to be implemented. The argument from all ministers except one is that it is in the overall interest of Denmark that EU laws are implemented in the other member-states too. To set a bad example by only implementing such law in a minimalist way would be damaging to Danish interests in the long run.[10]

It suits Denmark's interests to live up to agreements. A good indicator for this is the number of cases in which Denmark was a party before the European Court of Justice in Luxembourg. At least since 1991, Denmark has been the *Musterknabe* (paragon) concerning implementing EU directives. All others were rebuked more frequently by the EU Commission (Udenrigsministeriet, Notat, Oversigt over traktatkrænkelsessager mod Danmark, 1992–95). The main reason for the Commission to ask the Danish government for an explanation concerning a lack of implementation has been the lack of notification that a directive had been transposed into Danish law. For example, in 1994 this was the case in 51 out of 57 cases. Altogether it is not possible to observe any lack of will to implement directives, neither at the political nor at the administrative level. There is no tension between the political will to implement the directives and the administrative ability to do so.

The role of the prime minister

Before ending this section, we will take a brief look at the prime minister's role in Danish EU policy-making. The prime minister has always been a member of the cabinet's EC Committee (now the Foreign–Political Committee), but it is the foreign minister who chairs this committee. In the first years of Danish EC membership, the role of the prime minister was to arbitrate between the minister of foreign affairs and the minister of foreign economic affairs. This modest role was quite consistent with the tradition in Danish politics of letting the sectoral ministers manage their own business. This did not even change when regular European summits were introduced. The centre-right governments of Mr Poul Schlüter maintained a fairly rigid division of labour between the prime minister, who was in charge of keeping the government together and in office, and the minister of foreign affairs (a devoted pro-European), who was concerned with launching as positive a European policy as possible. This picture changed when Poul Nyrup Rasmussen and his government came into office in 1993. Prime Minister Rasmussen has a keen interest in foreign affairs in general, and in European affairs in particular. Shortly after taking office, he reorganized the Prime Minister's Office into a larger organization, with a better capacity to control what the other ministries are doing – not to the great joy of the other ministries. Now, in 1996, the Office is divided into three 'areas', each with an official head. One of these areas deals with foreign affairs. It consists of seven civil servants and is headed by a senior ambassador. The new permanent secretary of the Office is a former permanent secretary of the Ministry of Foreign Affairs.

This reorganization has given the Prime Minister's Office a better organizational starting point for playing a more active role in formulating EU policy. This new situation has not escaped the eyes of the Ministry of Foreign Affairs.[11] Interviews with civil servants outside the Prime Minister's Office show that the idea of letting that Office take a larger responsibility in the coordination of EU affairs was not new. Some centrally placed civil servants were of the opinion that the Ministry of Foreign Affairs, in the long run, could turn out to be a bottleneck for the decision-making and coordination system and that the Prime Minister's Office could be a suitable alternative. But with only seven civil servants taking care of foreign and EU affairs, the Prime Minister's Office still lacks the necessary human resources to be a fundamental threat to the Ministry of Foreign Affairs. On the other hand, it is clear that the prime minister and the Prime Minister's Office play a considerably more active role today than in the 1970s and 1980s.

It is symptomatic for the new role of the Prime Minister's Office that the political negotiations about the IGC in 1996 are taking place in the Prime Minister's Office and not in the Ministry of Foreign Affairs. It is Mr Rasmussen who chairs the meetings and there are civil servants from both the Ministry of Foreign Affairs and the Prime Minister's Office present.

In conclusion, the role of the prime minister concerning European affairs has been strengthened considerably since the change of power in 1993. But the reasons probably are to be found on the domestic level; they are not due to the TEU.

Institutional adaptation: summing up

Adaptation has taken place in the Danish civil service. The increasing Europeanization has called for increased coordination, both at the interdepartmental and the departmental level. In the ministries most affected by the membership this has led to a tightening up of the procedures during recent years. On the other hand, no fundamental structural changes have taken place. The adaptation has taken place in an incremental way – except for the time around the beginning of Danish EC membership.

As a consequence of the SEA and the TEU, the actors of the administrative–corporative network have been able to achieve tighter cooperation. This has strengthened it *vis-à-vis* the parliamentary network (see below).

In the constant institutional in-fighting, the Ministry of Foreign Affairs has been under severe pressure from the Prime Minister's Office as well as from the Ministry of Finance. This pressure, together with the routine that the sector ministries have obtained in handling EU affairs, has seriously challenged the Ministry of Foreign Affairs' prominence in European matters.

The European Committee of the Danish Parliament

As a transition from the administrative to the political level, we will now turn to the parliamentary network, centred around the parliamentary European Committee (formerly the Market Committee), which is often hailed as something 'especially Danish'.

The Folketing (Parliament) has tried from the start to exert influence on Danish EU decision-making and coordination process. This aim was pursued with great vigour. The parliamentary network's task is to control and influence the Danish EU policy in the name of the electorate, thus adding democratic legitimation to the Danish EU policy. As we have seen, the European Committee is the meeting point of the parliamentary and the administrative–corporative networks.

The seventeen members of the Committee meet every Friday. On its agenda are the issues of the Council of Ministers meeting for the following week. The minister or ministers who are going to negotiate in Brussels go through all points on the agenda; the minister can choose whether he or she just wants to brief the committee (*orientere*) on an item on the Council of Ministers agenda if the government does not expect a decision to be made on the Council's meeting; or the minister may choose to present a concrete negotiation proposal (*forhandlingsoplæg*), if he or she expects the Council to decide on the item. But the members of the committee may ask questions and make suggestions on all points on the agenda. The minister has to be certain that there is no majority against his or her proposal. When this has been secured, the minister has got his or her 'mandate'. The 'mandate' has three aspects: agreement on the subject matter; agreement on which allies to search for; and 'the elastic', i.e. the freedom of action for the negotiator (Steen Gade, interview 1995).

The potential power of the European Committee rests on three components. First of all, most Danish governments are minority governments. Thus they risk a vote of 'no confidence' in the Parliament if they do not follow the European Committee. Second, the members of the European Committee are generally senior members of Parliament, often former ministers, having had their seat in the committee for several years. Therefore they have had previous experience in EU affairs. Finally, these deliberations take place under a certain time pressure. The Committee meets on Friday, and the minister(s) go(es) to Brussels the following Monday. Therefore there is no time for the normal political to and fro. If Denmark's voice is going to be heard, the Committee has to find a common stand on the case before the ministers leave for Brussels.

The problem of the Committee is that it is not able to use its power effectively. As we shall discuss further below, the parliamentary network, and indeed most of the political system, is almost paralysed concerning EU affairs when dealing with highly political issues such as the future development of the EU. And when low political issues are on the agenda, the administrative–corporative network's influence prevails. This situation has persisted since 1992, when the TEU was turned down by the electorate and only accepted with a tiny margin at a second referendum. If the IGC negotiations do not give rise to further integration in the form of the handing over of more sovereignty, it can be expected that the parliamentary network will regain some of its power.

A prerequisite for serious and efficient work in the European Committee is that it has access to relevant material. The committee receives the initiatives of the EU Commission together with the agenda of the Council of Ministers. An important help in digesting the vast amounts of information from the Commission are the memoranda made by the relevant ministries. For certain directives and decisions made by the EU Commission this kind of memoranda is made automatically.[12] But the European Committee can request such a memorandum from the government on any case it wishes. These memoranda state the legal basis of the directive; its content; how the directive relates to existing Danish law; which interest organizations have been heard on it; whether Danish law has to be changed; what financial consequences it has for the state; and, finally, the economic consequences for the nation as a whole. The memoranda are not supposed to make any political recommendations or assessments. As a matter of fact, the committee does not know the position of the government before it is revealed by the minister.

It is symptomatic that major developments in European integration have fostered much public and parliamentary attention in Denmark. Both the SEA and TEU affected the committee's powers and procedures directly. Both treaties were used by the European Committee to enlarge its influence.[13]

In spite of the parliamentary network's currently weakened position, it still plays an important role in informing Parliament, legitimizing the ministers' negotiation basis and functioning as a potential emergency brake. To limit the dependence on the civil service somewhat, the committee has the best-staffed secretariat of Parliament. Altogether it plays an important, and in the European context, rather unique role.

Political adaptation

Denmark and the EU

Denmark's membership in the EU (EC) was never unquestioned, either in the public or among the political élite.[14] This has made EU affairs 'an issue' outside the decision-making system, too, especially since the SEA was negotiated. Since the mid-1980s, the population has been roughly divided into two equally large blocks of opponents and proponents to further Danish involvement in European integration. This division runs through the largest Danish party, the Social Democratic Party, and through some minor parties as well. To some extent it follows an ideological line, where socialist parties are very critical of the EU, and bourgeois parties are positive in their attitude. This is important because coalition governments have been the rule since the 1930s, and because, in addition, governments very often have been minority governments too.

But after the Edinburgh Agreement, a move can now be seen towards a generally more positive attitude regarding the EU in Parliament (even the Socialistisk Folkeparti, an old strong opponent of the EC/EU, voted in favour of the TEU).[15] The electorate, however, is still divided into two equally large blocks. The EC (EU) was presented to the Danish electorate in 1972 and 1985 as a purely economic matter. If the Danes would just vote in favour of the SEA, it would, in the words of the then Prime Minister Schlüter, mean that any thought of a European Union would be 'stone dead'. With the two IGCs leading to the TEU, the EC suddenly turned political – suddenly for the Danes, that is. Notions like a Common Foreign and Security Policy and the prospects of a Common Defence Policy and a common currency did not fit into the traditional Danish conception of the EC as an intergovernmental organization. Moreover, the TEU did not bring any visible economic advantage to the Danes. Thus the TEU did not appeal immediately to the Danes.[16] One major reason for the Danes to vote in favour of the TEU at the second referendum was the fear of the economic disadvantages they would suffer if Denmark were to be left outside the EU. Thus the narrow 'yes' to the TEU did not have anything to do with supporting the European idea.

The Danish anti-EU movements outside Parliament, as well as a small party on the extreme left-wing (Enhedslisten) and two small parties on the right wing (Dansk Folkeparti and Fremskridtspartiet) in Parliament, are able to remind the political élite that around half of the population remains very sceptical of the EU.

These factors are important in explaining why Danish EU policy has its strictly functional and pragmatic appearance, with a total lack of vision. Too many 'fancy ideas' would break up the Social Democratic Party (in power since 1993), and it would not leave many of the other parties untouched either. It could easily cause serious trouble for the whole political élite. Thus political restrictions are imposed on the parties in Parliament by the electorate.

EU and political adaptation

How are the above-mentioned restrictions reflected in ministers' actions? Do decision-makers have Europe on their minds or don't they? That depends on which ministry one is talking about. The minister of economic affairs, who prepares the Danish position for ECOFIN, and the minister of trade and industry, who is in charge of the coordination of the internal market, spend more time on the EU than do, for example, the minister of religious affairs or the minister of defence. The same is true for the direct contacts to Commissioners or to fellow ministers in other European governments. The possibility is there and it is being used. Interviews indicate that an average Danish minister contacts one or more of his or her colleagues abroad once a month; and this tendency is increasing. But the bulk of these contacts is channelled via the civil servants. This is viewed positively by their political superiors. It seems correct to say that, on the whole, the ministers are embedded in the European environment, and that they have regular contacts with colleagues abroad and in the European institutions.

Although one minister very diplomatically answered that it was a question of taking both the European and the Danish consequences into consideration when looking at an EU initiative, the clear tenor was that Danish ministers, relying on a Parliament chosen by Danes, would have to give the national interest first priority, no matter how 'European' they were themselves. This is reflected in the information given by the government to the European Committee of the Parliament: it always includes considerations about how a new directive will influence the Danish economy, law or other aspects of government policy or social activity, but nothing on the consequences for the European integration process. These questions will be considered carefully by the parliamentarians, who would like to get re-elected. While the so-called élite would like to promote European integration, the public is much more sceptical.

Since the SEA, more and more decisions of the Council of Ministers are taken by qualified majority vote. It is the general impression of all ministers questioned that there is a willingness to help a member-state with a genuine problem, but that the time has passed where negotiations would go on for days due to a minor problem. This has made the negotiations more effective and rational.[17] The only way to adapt to this has been to inform the European Committee of the Folketing, and to try to be as well prepared as possible in order to have a good and clear argument. Coming home after a meeting of the Council of Ministers in Brussels, the minister will report to the European Committee on the result of the negotiation. Having to account for one's actions in Brussels in this way can work as an incentive to do one's best.

The *White Book on the Internal Market* and the Treaty of the European Union have resulted in a strengthening of the role of the Commission. It seems to be the opinion of the ministers and parliamentarians interviewed that the Commission should have time to 'digest' its new powers, and that further development should lie within the realm of the Council of Ministers. The members of the Commission are seen as some kind of higher civil servants, and that role should not be changed.

The European Parliament (EP) is increasingly seen as a place where one can seek allies on an *ad hoc* basis, in case the Council does not react in a positive way towards Denmark. Thus the Folketing decided in May 1994 that the government had to inform the Danish Members of the European Parliament (MEPs) on the Danish policy. But on Danmarks Radio (20 January 1996) the foreign minister stated that the government only had a duty to inform the MEPs 'if possible', and that cases on environment, health and consumers' rights were complicated and time-consuming. What the government appeared to be saying was that, in fact, it was not interested in involving the MEPs.

Can one use the EU to promote internal, national policies? The ministers interviewed replied in the affirmative, at least in theory. Depending on the modus of voting in the Council of Ministers, a Danish initiative that had been turned down by the Danish Parliament could be passed by the Council of Ministers. However, this situation seems hypothetical. More likely is a situation where the Danish government – *contre coeur* – has to act according to a mandate from the European Committee. Here the government may be outvoted in the Council of Ministers, but it will not be unhappy about it. But the Danish minister always has to report back to the European Committee on the results of the negotiations in the Council of Ministers.

Summing up, one can say that the ministers dealing with EU affairs are generally pro-Europe. As we have noted, they are embedded in a European context, and have regular contacts with colleagues abroad and in the European institutions. At the same time, political reality often prevents them from internalizing EU policy to any larger extent, if they want to get re-elected. When looking at a proposal from the Commission, Danish interests are decisive for their recommendation. Further European integration is, therefore, seldom on the political agenda. It is only the Agrarian Liberal Party and the Centre Democrats who try to gain votes by being strongly pro-Europe.

We can, therefore, conclude that political adaptation is taking place, but only up to a point. Ministers, as members of the administrative–corporative network, may adapt but serious restrictions are put on them as members of the parliamentarian network.

Strategic adaptation

The 1996 Intergovernmental Conference

The motives for Danish membership of the EC, before actually joining, were economic in general and agrarian in particular. Membership was seen as a way out of total economic dependence on the EC and Britain, where export licences, especially for agricultural goods, had to be negotiated on an annual basis (von Dosenrode 1993b: 294–313). Thus Danish EU membership *per se* was and is a form of strategic adaptation. Denmark's contributions to the SEA and the TEU have to be seen in this light.

In the negotiations leading to both the SEA and the TEU, as well as in the present discussions in the IGC, Denmark's preferences were clearly intergovernmental and functional. In their *Basis for Negotiations*, the Danish government earmarks the enlargement of the EU as the main topic to be discussed, followed by 'fundamental rights of the citizens'. This is a course of action that does not provoke sharp reactions from the electorate.

Institutionally, the Danish government stresses the importance of all member-states being represented in the Commission, i.e. the role of the Commission as a clearing house. Moreover, Denmark advocates the involvement of the national parliaments in the decision-making process, and warns against disturbing the institutional balance. Under the heading 'Economic cooperation', the government stresses that 'improvements are to be achieved in two ways: firstly by improving practical day-to-day co-operation . . . , and secondly by amendments to the Treaty in order to provide for a better framework for cooperation'. As far as the CFSP as well as the cooperation on justice and home affairs are concerned, the government prefers to leave it intergovernmental, although it can be tightened up here and there. One can therefore conclude that Denmark's strategy is not to gain influence by innovation and visions.

Denmark's experiences

A small state can choose among a large number of strategies to enhance its influence. EU membership is in itself the major strategy for most small states (von Dosenrode, 1993b: 411). The question of small-state alliances within the EU is not new. In everyday life in Brussels it is the interests that lead to alliances, and because the interests of states have a tendency to change slowly, certain patterns emerge. The north–south division is one such persistent pattern (von Dosenrode, 1993b: 407).[18] For Denmark, the states with similar interests are Germany, the Netherlands and Great Britain; Sweden and Finland are aspiring to 'join' that group (interviews in Copenhagen in November 1995).[19]

Both Danish civil servants and ministers agreed that there was, of course, a difference in the influence of small states and great powers in negotiations. Denmark joined to gain influence over its immediate surroundings, and it has got that. Those interviewed agreed that the small-state strategy in the Council of Ministers was to be very well prepared and to have a good argument. This is considered the *sine qua non*, if a small state wants to be heard. There has been no change in that approach, at least since 1989 (von Dosenrode, 1993b: 337). Preparation for negotiations includes a mapping of the positions of the other EU members, as well as talks with potential allies on all levels (*ad hoc* allies are looked for early, and indicated on the government's memo to the European Committee of the Danish Parliament). But if a case turns 'political', one's allies may leave on very short notice.

The ultimate EU meeting is, of course, that of the European Council. Before the summit, the prime minister will have read reports from all relevant Danish ambassadors. The prime minister receives not only memoranda on all relevant topics but also 'travel literature', i.e. an update on topics that might turn up, on the character of the other participants, on their domestic problems, etc. The longer a prime minister is in office, the more experienced he or she becomes concerning the negotiations in the European Council. Thus Prime Minister Schlüter, who had been in office for nearly eleven years, is very qualified.

The ministers and civil servants interviewed in the summer of 1989 and in November 1995 agreed that the small state of Denmark 'got more than it gave', and that it was a great advantage to be a member. On the other hand, the SEA and the Maastricht Treaty have diminished the influence of small states. The use of qualified majority voting in the Council of Ministers has changed the atmosphere. While there was a great reluctance to vote on an issue before the SEA and the first years thereafter, this is not the case nowadays. The members of the Council still try to have regard for a member with a genuine problem, but the decision to resolve an issue by voting on it is taken more quickly than before. This is a procedure that is not to the advantage of the small states. On the other hand, small size is an advantage concerning payoffs and transition rules; granting favours to small states does not affect the complex calculations underlying the policy as whole, as would be the case if exceptions were granted to one or two great powers.

Danish diplomats and ministers are aware that one of the consequences of an enlargement will be less influence for the small states that are now members. But the political advantages of letting in the eastern European states are considered greater than the disadvantages concerning voting power.

Although all states got a right of veto with the Luxemburg Compromise, and despite the agreement on a 'blocking minority', small states seldom had a genuine right of veto. Thus, from the Danish perspective, the SEA and the TEU have not changed much in that respect. A strategic adaptation, involving a change of preferences and underlying motives for Danish membership, has not taken place.

Conclusion

The resistance towards further European integration, shared by large parts of the Danish population, poses serious restrictions for Danish EU policy and its strategic and institutional context.

It would be an exaggeration to say that all Danish EU policy is made in the administrative–corporative network, leaving out Parliament totally. But the division of the electorate into two blocks with regard to EU affairs, as well as the strong emotions that these questions call forth, have almost paralysed the European Committee of the Parliament. This leaves a lot of room for manoeuvre to the administrators and IOs. The more directives that have to be considered, the more influence the administrative–corporative network gets. Thus it is possible to argue that the SEA and the TEU have widened the gap between the two networks.

That the Danish parliamentary network is blocked is not an ideal situation. It is the administrative–corporative network that handles the day-to-day affairs. But when the future of the EU is being negotiated, it is obviously a great handicap that a member-state's government is not able to act freely.[20] Insights from studies on policy-orientated learning and the change of core beliefs indicates that the present situation may last a very long time (Sabatier and Jenkins-Smith, 1993). This would mean a long period during which Denmark might have to watch the further construction of the EU from the side-line.

Notes

1. For an introduction to the Danish public administration in English, see Peter Bogason in Rowat (1988), or Gorm Toftegaard in Gammeltoft-Hansen *et al.* (1982). In Danish, several authors have published on Danish public administration, e.g. Christensen (1984).
2. Closely connected with the principle of minister governance is the principle of direct approachability (*Ministerumiddelbarhedsprincippet*): the citizens have, as a matter of principle, the right to bring cases to the responsible minister.
3. Both the EC Special Committee and the EC Committee are called 'EC', not 'EU', as their field covers mainly the old EC Treaty. Thus there is no Special Committee for the CFSP.
4. For a detailed analysis of this approach as well as of the networks and their actors, function and power relations, see von Dosenrode in Branner and Kelstrup (1997).
5. It is the EU Commission that decides whom to consult. Thus it can vary a lot from case to case as to when the civil servants get to know about a draft proposal and when it is considered appropriate to inform the rest of the network.
6. Interviews made in 1995 and 1996 indicate that this tendency continues.
7. One 'work year' equals the work of one civil servant in one year.
8. Each minister has autonomy concerning the organization of their ministry. Thus there is a certain variation, although it should not be exaggerated. Some ministries have chosen to let their 'international section' handle the case, and a few have created an 'EU section' (Klöti and von Dosenrode 1994: 53).
9. It would go too far to describe the whole set of rules here. The rules are divided into a 'plan of action', which outlines the place that the ministry has in the EU decision-making process. The second part consists of specific 'rules of conduct concerning the preparation of EU affairs and EU Council of Ministers meetings'. These lay down strict procedural rules, guidelines and checklists for the formulation of memos for the minister, the Special Committees, the Parliament, etc. The handbook containing the guidelines and rules is intended to ensure that any section in the ministry will know how to handle EU cases.

10. One former minister expressed the opinion that if a directive was very unpleasant, one should only implement it as far as is necessary to have a good case if the Commission should ask questions. This opinion is not widely shared.
11. The source for this information is informal interviews with Danish diplomats. This development has been favoured by: the political constellation, with the prime minister belonging to the largest party in Parliament, and the Minister of Foreign Affairs to a minor coalition party; and the foreign minister having the reputation of being evasive and trying to avoid conflicts. The diplomats feel that he is giving up vital tasks of the ministry, without trying to get anything in return. In the *demi-monde* of the political élite, one hears Social Democrats boasting that the prime minister has twisted the arm of the foreign minister, reducing the Ministry of Foreign Affairs to an annex of the Prime Minister's Office. This may, of course, be exaggerated.
12. Those that influence the level of protection of the citizens, basically on health, environment, labour and consumer matters.
13. For an analysis and description of the development of this committee, see Klöti and von Dosenrode, 1994, pp. 65–9.
14. In the four referenda on the EC/EU there has been a steady decline in the number of votes in favour of the EU. In 1972, 63 per cent voted for a Danish EC membership, 37 per cent against. In 1985, 56 per cent voted in favour of the SEA, 44 per cent against. In 1992, 49.3 per cent voted in favour of the TEU and 50.7 per cent against. After the Edinburgh agreement, 57 per cent of Danes voted for the TEU and 43 per cent against (von Dosenrode, 1993b).
15. By granting Denmark four minor exceptions concerning the Maastricht Treaty, the other member-states showed a large degree of tolerance and flexibility. In that way the EU's reputation for being centralistic and dictatorial proved not to be true. This has given the EU a lot of goodwill in Denmark.
16. For an analysis of Danish EU policy, see von Dosenrode (1993b) or Laursen and Vanhoonacker (1992).
17. In any negotiation there can come a time where the parties involved see that they cannot give in any further. In that situation it is easier to vote, and it is easier to come home and say, 'well, we have been outvoted'.
18. Only one minister (Mrs Marianne Jelved) remembered one occasion where a small state had explicitly referred to small-state loyality: it was Greece on a personnel question. Otherwise she remembered none of these questions. Of small states using this strategy, Luxemburg is an example (von Dosenrode, 1993b: 232).
19. To talk of a 'Nordic bloc' would be exaggerated. But there are common interests and a deep cultural familiarity that create a common way to look at several problems.
20. The government in its dual role as member of both the administrative–corporative and the parliamentary network.

References

Amstrup, Niels and Faurby, Ib (eds) (1978) *Studier i dansk udenrigspolitik* (Aarhus: Forlaget Politica).

Auken, S., Buksti, J.A. and Lehmann Sørensen, C. (1974) Danmark – Tilpasningsmynstre i dansk politisk og administrative processer som følge af EG-medlemskabet, *Nordisk Administrativt Tidsskrift*, vol. 55.

Branner, Hans and Kelstrup, Morten (eds) (1997) *The Danish Policy Towards Europe after 1945* (forthcoming).

Christensen, Jørgen Grønnegård (1984) *Central administrationen – organisation og politisk placering*, 2nd edn (Copenhagen: DJØFs Forlag).

Gammeltoft-Hansen, H., Gomard, B. and Philip, A. (eds) (1982) *Danish Law*, (Copenhagen: G.E.C. Gad).

Haagerup, Niels Jørgen and Thune, Christian (eds) (1986) *Folketinget og udenrigspolitikken* (Copenhagen: Jurist- og Økonomforbundets Forlag).

Hof og Stat (Kongelig Dansk Hof-og Statskalender, Statshåndbog for Kongeriget Danmark), J.H. Schultz, various years.

Katzenstein, P.J. (1985) *Small States in World Markets* (Ithaea, New York: Cornell University Press).

Klöti, Ulrich and von Dosenrode, Søren Z. (1994) Anpassung von Kleinstaatexekutiven an die europäische Integration, *Vorläufige Bericht an den Schweizerischen Nationalfonds*, Universität Zürich (NF-Projekt 12-32365.91).

Laursen, Finn and Vanhoonacker, Sophie (eds) (1992) *The Intergovernmental Conference on Political Union*, Professional Research Paper (Maastricht: European Institute of Public Administration).

Pedersen, Ove K. and Pedersen, Dorthe (1995) *The Europeanization of National Corporatism: When the State and Organizations in Denmark went to Europe Together*, COS-rapport nr. 4/1995 (Copenhagen: Copenhagen Business School).

Rasmussen, Hjalte (1985) *Internationale organisationer*, (Copenhagen: Gads Forlag).

Rowat, Donald C. (ed.) (1988) *Public Administration in Developed Democracies* (New York and Basel: Marcel Dekker).

Sabatier, A. Paul and Jenkins-Smith, Hank C. (eds) (1993) *Policy Change and Learning*, (Boulder and San Francisco: Westview Press).

von Dosenrode, Søren Z. (1993a) Den optimale minimalløsning – Danmarks administrative tilpasning til EF', *Nordisk Administrativt Tidsskrift*, vol. 4.

von Dosenrode, Søren Z. (1993b) *Westeuropäische Kleinstaaten in der EG und EPZ* (Chur and Zurich: Verlag Rüegger).

Chapter 5

Ireland: The Rewards of Pragmatism

BRIGID LAFFAN AND ETAIN TANNAM

Introduction

Ireland joined the European Community in 1973 as part of the first enlargement. Since then its political, administrative and judicial systems have had to adapt to the demands of EC policy-making and the development of the Community. The Irish political system is no longer 'contained in a container', to borrow the phrase used by the French economist Perroux. Interaction with Brussels and bilateral contact with partners in other member-states has served to internationalize public policy-making in Ireland. Decision-making in many policy sectors dealing with such diverse issues as the environment, agricultural policy, health and safety in the workplace, technical standards and regional policy, take place within intergovernmental and transgovernmental policy networks that reach from Brussels into subnational government in the member-states. The nature and intensity of interaction, the balance between public and private actors and between national regulation and Union regulation differs from one policy sector to another.

Politicians, civil servants and representatives of interest groups straddle the EU domestic boundary in their day-to-day work. National actors have had to adapt to a system of public policy-making that involves complex games in multiple arenas. Putman's concept of two level games, although addressing vertical interaction between Brussels and the member-states, fails to capture the multi-layered and multiple arenas that characterize EU policy-making. Public officials are no longer just agents of the Irish state; they are participants in an evolving polity which provides opportunities for political action but also imposes constraints on their freedom of action. A keen understanding of the dynamics of negotiations and the attitudes of one's partners and EU institutions is as important as technical competence in the policy area. Judging the ebb and flow of complex negotiations in a multilateral and multicultural environment requires considerable skills. Assessing just what might or might not be in the so-called 'national interest' is an uncertain process in the multi-level structures of the Union. The need for compromise, log-rolling and package deals permeates the EU's policy process. Furthermore, EU membership is not just about involvement in Brussels-level decision-making because the EU can and does act as an agent of change in the member-states. The nature and extent of the EU's influence depends very much on endogenous factors in the member-states and their capacity to adapt.

The purpose of this chapter is to assess the process of adaptation to membership of a complex and rapidly evolving, partly formed polity. It examines administrative, political and institutional adaptation to the EU and concludes by considering the strategic challenges faced by Irish policy-makers. The first part of the chapter describes the background to Ireland's entry to the EU. In the second section the central level of policy-making – civil service departments, ministers and Parliament – is examined. In the third part of the chapter, the subcentral level of policy-making is looked at and the increased role of the subregions and of interest groups in decision-making is highlighted.

Ireland: the challenge of adaptation

EC membership was part of Ireland's drive towards industrialization and modernization which began at the end of the 1950s. A desire to lessen Ireland's economic dependency on Great Britain formed part of the motivation. The Irish economy is very open, with some 56 per cent of Gross Domestic Product (GDP) accounted for by exports. Moreover, the Irish economy is more dependent on agriculture, both as a source of employment and value added, than the average for the EC as a whole. The performance of Irish industry in the EC market is mixed; foreign multinationals located in Ireland have succeeded in penetrating the market whereas the performance of the indigenous firms has been weak. Population growth in Ireland has contributed to high unemployment and migration out of Ireland in the 1980s. Ireland was considered one of the lesser developed parts of the Community of Twelve and is a major beneficiary of EC financial transfers. All of these considerations have led Irish policy-makers and the Irish public to regard the Community as an economic entity. Ireland's neutrality during World War Two and the subsequent non-membership of the North Atlantic Treaty Organization (NATO) serve to reduce the saliency of the political dimension of integration. That said, the benefits of a multilateral framework for advancing Irish interests were recognized from the outset.

The early years

Membership in the Community imposed a severe burden on the Irish administration at the outset. It was ill-prepared for all that was demanded by involvement in the Community's intense negotiating process. The civil service had misjudged the personnel requirements that would be necessary. There was also a continuing dispute between the Department of Foreign Affairs and the Department of Finance as to which department should take the lead in the management of EC business. Ireland's foreign minister attended the opening of the accession negotiations flanked by the secretaries (official head of a department) of the four main government departments. The Department of Foreign Affairs was not involved in the 1961 decision to apply for membership, a decision that was taken by a core group of finance officials and the prime minister. During the 1960s, the Department of Foreign Affairs was a peripheral ministry responsible for the United Nations (UN). However, after accession, a government decision gave this department the main responsibility for managing the day-to-day issues of EC policy as this was the pattern in other member-states. Ireland's first presidency of the Council in 1975 served as the final apprenticeship for the civil service in adapting to EC membership. Management of the Council agenda and meetings for six months made Irish politicians and officials *au fait* with the nuts and bolts of the Community process. Thereafter, EC business became part of the normal flow of business in the administrative cycle. However, various aspects of the SEA and the TEU necessitated ongoing adaptation by Irish policy-makers and institutions.

Because the focus of this chapter is on developments since the relaunch of formal integration with the SEA in 1986, it is important to provide a synopsis of the key changes in governance structures of the EU and in the dynamics of integration which have moulded political and administrative adaptation. The intensification of constitution-building in the EU since the mid-1980s politicized the European project in Ireland. All changes to the Irish constitution are the subject of a national referendum which has meant that successive Irish governments have had to take the public opinion dimension of integration seriously during each round of treaty change. The EU's governance structures are in a state of considerable fluidity with repeated changes to the role and functions of EU institutions and the institutional balance.

The increased use of qualified majority voting altered the rules of the game in Council by speeding up the decision-making process and giving national officials less time to stall on proposals and enter scrutiny reservations. Preparation of negotiating positions works to a tighter framework than heretofore. The growing presence of the European Parliament in the legislative process means that more attention must be paid to the Parliament and the work of its major committees. Moreover, the growing Europeanization of public policy in Europe means that most areas of public policy have acquired a European dimension. The intensification of integration has brought many more actors into transnational networks at the EU level. The growth in lobbying in the EU and the mobilization of regional interests since 1985 changes the dynamic in many domestic policy networks.

Successive rounds of treaty change have increased the number of decision processes and rules in the EU, thereby adding to the complexity of the negotiating environment within which national officials operate. Coordinating mechanisms must encompass the pillar structure and variations within the Community pillar.

The internal market programme, the expansion in the flow of Structural Fund monies to Ireland, the prospect of EMU and developments in the political dimension of integration have led to institutional adaptation. In the remainder of the chapter the key changes in the Irish decision-making process are examined.

The central level

The cabinet

The overall coherence of public policy is the responsibility of the cabinet, which stands at the pinnacle of the Irish system of government. The constitution limits the cabinet to fifteen members which reduces the need for an elaborate system of cabinet subcommittees. That said, there is a tendency to establish *ad hoc* cabinet committees to deal with major issues on the EU agenda. For example, committees have been formed to manage the Irish Council presidencies, the Commission's May mandate, the reform of the CAP and the National Development Plan for cohesion monies. Usually the cabinet deals with EC business as it deals with public policy originating within the state. The government is sent a memorandum by the relevant minister on all major issues that will reach the Council. Issues that fall within the realm of 'high politics', that are likely to involve a cost to the exchequer or that will require primary national legislation, all reach the cabinet table. The cabinet is involved in deciding on negotiating strategies on major issues and would only deal with implementation in the event of a serious blockage or political problem.

The Taoiseach (prime minister) keeps a watching brief over major developments in the EU. The nature and intensity of ministerial involvement depends on their sectoral responsibilities. The ministers of foreign affairs, agriculture, finance and enterprise, and employment are intensively involved in EU matters. There are a number of ministers of state (junior ministers) attached to their departments who deputize for them at Council meetings on occasion. The remaining technical or domestic ministries are largely concerned with their own policy domain. Ministerial briefs for Council meetings are prepared by the relevant government department. Ministers who tend to have considerable leeway on sectoral and low-key issues would check back with the prime minister on sensitive issues. The extension of the EU's policy scope and the extent of the transfers coming to Ireland from Brussels means that almost all ministers have some EU involvement. That said, adaptation to the Community has not altered how the cabinet does its business. EC matters are dealt with in the same manner as purely domestic issues.

The Parliament

The Parliament (Oireachtas) is a bicameral legislature consisting of an upper and lower house. The lower house, the Dail, produces the government which is the product of a general election. The executive dominates the Parliament and can go about its business in an unfettered manner provided it has the support of a majority of the TDs (Members of Parliament).

In 1973 the Oireachtas established a Joint Committee on Secondary Legislation of the European Communities to oversee the implementation of EC law in Ireland. Subsequently its terms of reference were widened to include all Community legislation from the initial Commission document to the final stage when secondary legislation was being enacted in Ireland. The purpose of the committee was to ensure that ministers did not go beyond the powers delegated to them under the 1972 European Communities Act. Its capacity to act as a watchdog over the extensive range of EC policy was constrained because of its limited secretariat (two staff), the inexperience of Irish parliamentarians in working committees and the low priority accorded to European issues because of the high degree of consensus surrounding Ireland's membership of the EU.

One of the main problems of the Committee was that it did not have a specialized foreign affairs committee to provide the policy context for its deliberations. The Fianna Fail–Labour Party coalition which took office in December 1992 made an explicit commitment to establish a foreign affairs committee after years of debate on the matter. Composed of 25 Dail deputies and 5 senators, the Committee held its first meeting in May 1993. A former foreign minister, Brian Lenihan, was elected as chairman. The new committee subsumed the work of the Joint Committee on Secondary Legislation which become a subcommittee in addition to three other subcommittees on Northern Ireland, development cooperation and the UN. While it is too early to judge the effectiveness of the new committee, it does bring an added parliamentary focus to foreign policy matters and hence to the EU.

The Department of Foreign Affairs is working closely with the committee and has seconded an official to its secretariat. The Department of Foreign Affairs is also committed to supplying the committee with briefing papers, and officials attend its hearings. The presence of a former foreign minister in the chair gives added weight to its deliberations. The committee has the potential to provide a channel of informed debate on the many challenges facing Ireland and Europe in the post-cold war era. It may well act as a sounding board for changes in Irish security policy in the lead up to the 1996 intergovernmental policy. Following the change of government in January 1995, a separate European Affairs Committee was re-established. The Foreign Affairs Committee and the European Affairs Committee have enhanced parliamentary scrutiny on EU matters and the standard of debate on the European project in the Parliament. However, both committees continue to suffer from a chronic shortage of resources, a weak research capacity and the fact that only a limited number of parliamentarians are motivated to specialize in foreign affairs because of the unrelenting pressures of constituency matters. The existence of both committees does, however, add a degree of openness to Ireland's European policy.

The civil service

The arrangements for managing the interface with Brussels after accession endowed the Department of Foreign Affairs with primary responsibility for the day-to-day management of the policy process. This department is the main interlocutor with the EU system. Each domestic department manages those areas of policy falling within its competence. They service the relevant Commission expert groups and Council working groups and prepare briefings for their ministers for specialist councils. The Department of Foreign Affairs services the General Affairs Council, the Development Cooperation Council, meetings within Pillar Two and European Councils in conjunction with the Department of the Taoiseach. In addition, the Department of Foreign Affairs prepares briefings on the 'A' points in all Councils.

EC membership transformed the Department of Foreign Affairs. Membership of the Community blurred the distinction between foreign and domestic affairs which means that the Department of Foreign Affairs is now more intensively involved in domestic issues than at any stage in its history. Given that the EU provides the main context for Irish foreign policy with the exception of Anglo – Irish relations, the department is primarily involved in mediating between Ireland and the EU. There has been a number of administrative reorganizations and a significant expansion in the staffing levels within the department since 1973. At present there are three divisions within the Department of Foreign Affairs intimately involved in EC matters:

- the European Communities Division;
- the Development Cooperation Division;
- the Political Division. (State Directory 1995/6)

The European Communities Division, with a staff of nineteen, is responsible for monitoring the broad spectrum of EC matters including enlargement, constitution-building and internal Community policy. This division evolved from the Economics Division. Reports of working-party meetings are lodged in the European Communities Division. It tries to ensure that the domestic ministries service meetings in Brussels adequately and that policy developments in one policy sector do not impinge on general policy priorities. By and large the European Communities Division does not get involved in the detail of domestic issues unless the General Council is dealing with them. This section takes the lead on new policy areas, reform of major instruments or common policies, institutional change and enlargement.

The European Communities Division monitors the implementation of EC law in the system, a facet of EC membership that has received far more attention since the SEA. The Commission's monitoring of implementation and its publication of league tables acts as an external pressure on the domestic bureaucracy. The implementation of internal market legislation has proved difficult for the Irish bureaucracy with time lags and administrative blockages. Ireland's traditionally good record of implementation faltered under the weight of the intensity of legislation flowing from Brussels. Blockages in implementation can arise when the Attorney-General's Office is overburdened with legislation. An extensive legislative programme at national level makes it more difficult to get the Parliamentary draftsmen to draw up the legal instruments.

The Department of Foreign Affairs view is that Ireland must fulfil its obligations under EC law. There is a regular discussion of the pattern of implementation at the interdepartmental European Communities Committee. A letter of notice from the Commission which comes via the PR is usually enough to elicit compliance. Departments try to avoid going to the European Court of Justice because this requires the authority of the government and a cabinet decision.

The Political Division is responsible for matters that fall within the second pillar – the Common Foreign and Security Policy (CFSP). It has a staff of 26 and was created in response to the evolution of European Political Cooperation. It is organized on the basis of regional desks and issue areas. The head of this division is the political director. The Political Division services all meetings under the aegis of the second pillar, analyses the information received in the communication network of foreign policy cooperation (COREU) and sends messages to that network. Because of Ireland's non-membership in NATO, the security dimension of CFSP receives considerable attention. The Development Cooperation Division, with a staff of fourteen, is responsible for Ireland's bilateral aid programme and the Community's multilateral programmes – Lomé, aid to the non-associated states, association agreements.

The Irish PR in Brussels exercises a pivotal role in the policy process because of the small size of the Irish bureaucracy and the limited number of officials working on EU matters. The Permanent Representative is a career diplomat and is one of Ireland's most senior ambassadors. His deputy, Ireland's representative in COREPER 1, is also a career diplomat. The Department of Foreign Affairs supplies slightly less than half of the remaining officials in the representation. The need to provide detailed coverage of substantive policy sectors ensures that the remaining civil servants are drawn from the domestic departments. There are usually 29 staff in the PR, although this is strengthened during an Irish presidency.

The balance of influence between the PR and Dublin is difficult to establish. The preparation of dossiers and administrative coordination remains the prerogative of the national bureaucracy. The status and insider knowledge of the Permanent Representative ensures that his views carry considerable weight in determining strategy on issues of high politics. The PR acts as an early warning system and provides an insight on the thinking in the other member-states.

The Department of Finance could be said to have discovered the European Community. It was responsible for Ireland's first negotiations with the EEC in 1961, providing the initial expertise on the Community, and remains the most important government department. It is influential in determining Ireland's policy approach on: monetary matters, Structural Funds and cohesion policy, and the Community budget. The department also provides the expertise for contributions to the Community's general economic policy such as the *Delors Report on Growth, Competitiveness and Employment*. Although the department is primarily responsible for the national budget and public expenditure, Ireland's membership of the Exchange Rate Mechanism (ERM), the treaty on EMU and the doubling of the Structural Funds has enhanced the work of this department. The Department of Finance is largely responsible for drafting and implementing the National Development Plan which forms the basis of the Community Support Framework. The department services the regional review committees and evaluates the operational programmes.

The significance of the CAP, both in Ireland and in terms of Community policies, ensured that the Department of Agriculture would undergo major structural change at a result of Community membership. The operation and implementation of EC schemes and regulations forms the major work of this department. Staffing levels in the department had to be strengthened considerably to deal with the implementation of the CAP. The rhythm of work on the CAP is regulated by the weekly meetings of the Special Agricultural Committee and the many agriculture councils. Meeting agendas are circulated to the relevant sections and briefing material is drawn up. All observations, substantive material and position papers must be ready by Thursday for meetings taking place on the following Monday. Friday is allocated to defining instructions and ensuring that the brief is coherent. All senior officials are involved in the process.

The reform of the CAP and the General Agreement on Tariffs and Trade (GATT) round have posed a considerable challenge to this department in the 1990s. A related challenge was the need to address irregularities in the beef trade which were the subject of a national tribunal. The tribunal identified shortcomings in the management of the intervention system and the implementation of the CAP in the beef sector. As a consequence, the minister for agriculture established a special audit board in the department, consisting of private sector accountants and public officials, to enhance the auditing and the control of EU finances.

The Department of Enterprise and Employment combines the old Department of Industry and Commerce and the Department of Labour. This department is responsible for a range of Community policies relating to the internal market, competition policy, industrial policy, social policy and the Structural Funds. It is heavily involved in the EU's regulatory policies. Hence it is responsible for some of the most complex and technical areas of policy. The specialist sections are responsible for negotiating and implementing the directives falling within their areas of responsibility.

The department has a Structural Fund coordination unit and two units devoted to the evaluation of structural funds in training and industrial policy. This is a new feature of the management of the structural funds and reflects the interest that the Commission is taking in the evaluation of the Community Support Framework. There is considerable internal specialization on EU matters in the department; the Commerce Division deals with directives on insurance and company law.

The Department of Trade and Tourism has responsibility for the important Article 113 Committee on the Community's common commercial policy. There has always been an uneasy relationship between the Department of Foreign Affairs and this administrative unit dealing with trade matters. The tourism section of the department implements the operational programme on tourism which forms part of the Community Support Framework.

The remaining departments are involved to a greater or lesser extent in formulating policy responses to proposals falling within their realm, in negotiating within the Council system and in implementing agreed decisions. All have an EC or an international division which coordinates EC business but the substantive work is the responsibility of the functional divisions. The small EC divisions do not have the expertise to undertake the detailed work of policy formation. Functionalist specialists are now *au fait* with the Community system and tend to operate with ease at the European level.

The role of paragovernmental agencies in policy formulation should not be neglected because of the technical nature of Community business. Policies involving ionizing radiation, safety in the workplace, and plant and animal diseases, require scientific expertise. A myriad of agencies such as the Agricultural Institute, the Nuclear Energy Board and the Health and Safety Agency are involved in policy formation, thus extending the network of actors into the wider public service. Their role is particularly important because of the predominance of 'generalists' in the Irish civil service. Representatives drawn from these agencies attend Council working parties and provide technical back-up for civil servants at the later stages of the negotiations. Ireland's receipts from the structural funds flow through a vast array of state-sponsored companies in training, industrial development, research and development, tourism promotion, local authorities, local development agencies and the fisheries board (see below).

Coordination

The reach of the Community's policy process and the intensity of the negotiating process have led the member-states to establish standard operating procedures for managing the myriad of proposals that must be negotiated and implemented within the national system. The preparation of briefs necessitates intradepartmental and interdepartmental coordination. Coordination is not limited to what might be termed 'administrative coordination'. Governments must pay attention to the overall development of the EU, the institutional balance and the promotion of their priorities. From time to time, the fragmented nature of the policy process breaks down and issues are dealt with on the basis of a package deal. The Delors packages on financing the EU represent one such package deal.

There are a number of different levels of coordination within the Irish system. The cabinet is the juncture where major policy issues are resolved and the Taoiseach plays a leading role in determining governmental policy. At the administrative level, the main institutional device for formulating national strategy and deciding on priorities is the European Community Committee which actually predates Ireland's membership. The central departments or 'overhead' ministries dealing with Brussels on a continuous basis are represented on the committee. These are Foreign Affairs, Finance, Agriculture and Food, Enterprise and Employment, Trade and Tourism and the Prime Minister's Department. The committee has undergone a number of changes since 1973. It was chaired by the Department of Foreign Affairs until 1987 when its composition was altered.

The incoming Taoiseach, Charles Haughey, who tended to regard the Department of Foreign Affairs as too pro-European and who had opposed the SEA while in opposition, appointed a minister of state in his own department with responsibility for EC matters. The new minister, Maire Geoghegan-Quinn, took over the chair of the European Communities Committee. This added a political dimension to the committee and gave it the authority of the Taoiseach's department. Its work was overshadowed somewhat by the formation in 1988 of a joint Committee of Ministers and Secretaries which met on a weekly basis to plan the internal market publicity campaign and the preparation of Ireland's national plan for the Delors 1 round of structural fund monies. The committee clearly signalled the political priorities of the Taoiseach and the importance he accorded to structural fund monies.

When the national plan was submitted to Brussels, this committee was transformed into a ministerial committee to manage the preparations of the Irish presidency. Once the presidency was over, the European Community Committee and the Ministerial Committee fell into abeyance and were not active during the intergovernmental conferences. When Albert Reynolds become Taoiseach in February 1992, he reactivated the European Community Committee and gave a minister of state, Tom Kitt, responsibility for EC coordination. In January 1995, Gay Mitchell took over responsibility for the committee when a new government assumed office. Arising from the TEU ratification crisis in 1992, a task force entitled Communicating Europe and consisting of persons active in European affairs and in communications was established to analyse the level of public understanding of European affairs in Ireland.

The European Communities Committee meets on a monthly basis at assistant secretary level and provides a focus for coordination of the Irish approach and policy on all major strategic aspects of Community business. It is serviced by the Department of the Taoiseach and is attended by the Irish Permanent Representative. This committee deals with the big issues, particularly those involving a range of government departments. It will regularly review the programme of the member-state holding the presidency and periodically discusses implementation blockages within the Irish system. The committee establishes working groups on major issues. Although serviced by the Taoiseach's department, many of the detailed papers are compiled by the Department of Foreign Affairs or the relevant domestic ministry. The removal of the secretariat of this committee from the Department of Foreign Affairs to the Taoiseach's department may have reflected a down-grading of the role of the Department of Foreign Affairs in relation to EC matters. In reality, the addition of a political/ministerial presence and the authority of the Taoiseach's department has added to the status of the committee and the seriousness with which it is treated by the domestic departments. Day-to-day coordination resides with the Department of Foreign Affairs. Unlike other member-states, standing interdepartmental committees on sectoral matters are not common in Ireland. In 1976 there were eleven policy groups dealing with areas such as fiscal harmonization and science and technology that might cross departmental boundaries. The Committees met infrequently and gradually fell into abeyance. It is now more common to establish *ad hoc* committees when the need arises.

Administrative management of the Community's policy process in Ireland is far less institutionalized than is the norm in other member-states. There are fewer interdepartmental committees and those that exist meet far less frequently than those in other member-states. Contact and consultation in other member-states is more rigid and bureaucratic. The lead department in any particular area has considerable autonomy in working out the Irish response. Sectoral policy issues and low-key issues are the preserve of the responsible departments. The emphasis is on telephone contact and written observations rather than formal interdepartmental committees. Irish civil servants appear hostile to elaborate procedures and bureaucratic *lourdeur*. An understanding of this may be found in Ireland's administrative culture, the small size of the bureaucracy and the range of issues that are given high priority in Ireland. Personalism is a dominant cultural value in Ireland arising from late urbanization and the small size of the population. Personal contacts are extensive and easy to establish in a small administration. Irish civil servants know their counterparts in other departments, state agencies and representatives of the main interest organizations. The small nucleus of senior civil servants dealing with Brussels on a continuous basis meet frequently, either formally or informally, which reduces the need for formalized committees.

Pragmatism, a legacy of British rule, is apparent in Ireland's administrative culture. Administrative adaptation to Community membership has been characterized by pragmatism. An emphasis on the immediate to the neglect of the medium to long term is a feature of this administrative culture. Policy-making in Dublin tends to be reactive rather than active in nature. Position papers and negotiating tactics are worked out at each stage of the policy process. This policy style is reinforced by the Community's decision-making process which is dominated by negotiations and is highly segmented. Irish policy-makers try to avoid isolation during negotiations by aligning with like-minded states on an issue-by-issue basis or by hiding behind a larger state, if appropriate. Considerable attention is paid to the likely negotiating tactics of other member-states. It is claimed with considerable justification that:

> Although it is an oversimplification, there is some truth in the suggestion that Ireland's classic negotiating tactic is to sit on the sidelines during the Community's major debates, allowing the major players to sort out the broad lines of the deal, and then at the last moment to surrender on a range of nationally unimportant items in return for agreement by the others to a package of financially generous rewards to assist Ireland adapt to the changing circumstances. (Scott, 1994: 14)

Irish representatives will only go it alone and adopt a conflictual approach if they feel that the issue is of such importance that they have no choice. In fact, on all occasions when Irish representatives accorded overwhelming political priority to an issue (ERM, fisheries, super-levy), they succeeded in getting special treatment and side payments. In each instance considerable political and diplomatic resources were invested in the negotiations.

In a number of instances, the upper echelons of the civil service formed into a task force for the duration of critical negotiations. Size has implications not just for the policy process but for the range of issues that must be accommodated for Community negotiations. Interests are aggregated with greater ease in a small country as the potential for competing claims and conflict is reduced. Irish policy-makers have found it relatively easy to establish major priorities for the purposes of EC negotiations. However, it is also clear that the increased emphasis placed by the Commission on the subcentral level of decision-making has necessitated considerable administrative and political adaptation, complicating the centralized decision-making system.

The subcentral level

The Commission's emphasis on the principle of subsidiarity, the role of partnership, the reform of regional policy and the establishment of the Committee of the Regions, all point to a possible change in the role of subnational government and of interest groups in Ireland. The establishment of monitoring committees apparently strengthened the concept of partnership in the Irish planning system. These committees were given the power, assuming Commission agreement, to adjust financial plans in accordance with the original aims of a specific project: 'There was an extensive consultation involving the main bodies concerned with the development, the local authorities, state agencies and government departments operating through working and advisory groups in each subregion' (Mulreany and Roycroft, 1993: 199).

Indeed, there are clear differences between the Irish planning process for the 1990–94 National Development Plan (NDP) and the formulation of the 1994–99 NDP. For example, as regards the 1990 NDP, one of the criticisms levelled at central government by subregional representatives was that allocative decisions had already been made before they were consulted (Tannam, 1993: 281). It was argued that consultation was a cosmetic exercise (Coyle and Sinnott, 1993: 82). In contrast, in 1993, there appeared to be greater consultation. The seven subregional review committees were invited to present their opinions on the forthcoming development plan to the government, highlighting the development strategies that should be pursued in each subregion, how these plans should be pursued and the priority of each strategy in the overall subregional plan (NDP, 1993: 146). The government then attempted to include these priorities in the plan 'to the extent that these are consistent with the overall national objective of maximising sustainable employment and growth' (*ibid.*: 147).

However, on the other hand, the practical effect of consultation on national government's policies is questionable. There are still key weaknesses in the role of subnational government in the Republic of Ireland, despite the above changes since 1988. Change may still be cosmetic. For example, it is clear that subnational government still enjoys only consultative powers. It has no binding authority and no control over its own financing. Ultimate responsibility for expenditure continues to rest with the Department of Finance. Thus there remain obstacles to increasing subregional power in Ireland, despite EC membership.

As regards interest groups, the establishment of the Central Review Committee in 1989 to monitor the Programmes for National Progress (1987) and for Economic and Social Progress (1990) reflect the significance of key interest groups, as Figure 5.1 shows. As the numbers in the brackets indicate, some groups have more than one representative on the Committee. This committee was 'heavily involved in monitoring the implementation of the Structural Funds'.

This feature of the Irish decision-making process means that interest groups in the Republic have potential scope to influence decision outcomes. The importance of the agricultural and business sectors to the Irish economy implies that these sectors, in particular, form a potentially powerful force in Irish decision-making. They have also developed active lobbying centres in Brussels and have deepened their activity since the signing of the SEA.

In particular, the farmers' lobby group, the Irish Farmers Association (IFA) and the Irish Creamery Milk Suppliers Association (ICMSA) enjoy a close relationship with central government: ministers for agriculture tend to occupy a special place and have strong ties with their client groups, the farming lobby. For both groups, lobbying occurs at Brussels level and at national level, although national lobbying is of greater importance. Similarly, the main business and employees unions prioritize national rather than supranational lobbying. The Irish Congress of Trade Unions (ICTU) and Irish Business Employers Confederation (IBEC) have regular meetings with government departments, approximately once a month. The EC is perceived to have strengthened the unions bargaining position *vis-à-vis* national government. In particular, the inclusion of the social partners in the monitoring committee system has increased the role of the unions. According to both the ICTU and IBEC,

Fig. 5.1 Composition of the Central Review Committee

Secretary, Taoiseach's department
Assistant Secretary, Department of Agriculture
Assistant Secretary, Department of Enterprise and Employment
Assistant Secretary, Department of Finance
Office of the Tanaiste (deputy prime minister)
Irish Business Employers Confederation (3)
Construction Industry Federation (3)
Irish Farmers Association (3)
Irish Creamery Milk Suppliers Association (3)
Irish Cooperative Organization Society (3)
Macra na Feirme (Farming Organization)
Irish Congress of Trade Unions (8)

(*Source:* Jeffrey and O'Sullivan, 1994: 21)

there has been a marked improvement in consultation procedures since 1989 and the 1994–99 NDP reflected this improvement.

The ICTU is quick to point out that central government is the key decision-maker with binding power. However, the new system does allow for compromise and agreement to be reached. Moreover, it has caused the ICTU to develop alliances on certain issues with other economic groups, such as farming organizations, where few links existed before, thus strengthening interest groups' bargaining position. Thus, while the focus of interest group activity is the national level, membership of the EC has affected the main interest groups' bargaining position *vis-à-vis* national government.

Conclusion: Ireland's strategic adaptation to the EU

The Irish political and administrative system has adapted relatively easily to the demands of EU membership. Standard operating procedures are in place and work most of the time. The lack of dense bureaucratic foliage allows senior civil servants and politicians to be selective in the areas that are accorded priority. Hence political and administrative resources are utilized most heavily in those areas that are considered important. An awareness of resource constraints and limited personnel resources permeates the Irish civil service.

Irish civil servants have internalized EC business as part of the routine of their work and see it as a legitimate arena of public policy-making. Irish civil servants are by now well socialized into the norms and values of the Community policy. There is no in-built resistance to EC involvement in a wide range of policy sectors, provided that EC decisions take account of the Irish situation. The small size of the bureaucracy facilitates a flexible response to Commission initiatives. The existence of a generally favourable public opinion makes Irish policy-makers less constrained in their dealings with Brussels apart from issues touching on security and public morality.

Four main weaknesses have hindered Irish adaptation to the EU until recently. However, there is evidence that some of these weaknesses are diminishing. First, the Irish political system has not always produced the kinds of public policies that were consistent with membership of a large and competitive market. Pragmatism and an emphasis on the short term resulted in a severe fiscal crisis in the 1980s. A major challenge for Ireland is to produce public policies that allow the Irish economy to deal with the competitive pressures of the EC. Since the mid-1980s, there is some evidence that the government and the social partners are prepared to adopt cooperative strategies to manage the economic dimension of EC membership. Domestic economic management is critical to Ireland's ability to involve itself in EC policies, notably EMU.

Second, related to short-termism is the criticism that there has been a limited capacity within the Irish system for sustained thinking about the overall development of European integration and the role of small states in the emerging European polity. Ireland is not the source of new or novel ideas about the European project. Size and limited staffing resources reduced the scope for reflective position papers and the development of a strategic view of the EU. The fact that the European Communities Committee did not meet at all between 1983 and 1984 at a time of major development in the Community points to a certain institutional looseness in the past. The Irish system is heavily dependent on a number of severely overworked officials in the foreign ministry, the PR and the 'overhead' ministries. The expansion of the reach of EU policies and the growing complexity of EU regulation may leave Ireland exposed in areas where the system lacks technical depth and expertise.

Third, a highly centralized system of government militates against the involvement of subnational actors in the EC process. Moreover, there has been an excessive focus on receipts from the Community budget and a tendency to produce programmes that met the criteria without sufficient consideration given to the worth of the said programmes.

Finally, the Irish parliamentary model and the brokerage role of deputies limits the scrutiny of EC business. The establishment of a Foreign Affairs Committee has enhanced the Parliament's involvement in the Community process but this is hampered by a paucity of resources and research capacity.

However, despite these weaknesses there is evidence that a more strategic approach to EC membership is now being adopted. As was noted above, the introduction of the Community Support Framework has enhanced the weight given to evaluation and there is now a stronger planning focus. The decision by the National Economic and Social Council in 1988 to produce a major study on Ireland's membership of the Community, at the behest of the Taoiseach of the day, marked an important shift from the *ad hoc* approach of the past.

A further attempt to develop a considered approach emerged with the establishment in 1991 of the Institute of European Affairs in Dublin. The IEA is an independent forum with the aim of identifying strategic responses to the continuing process of European integration. The Institute is largely financed by private companies with some government backing. The main contribution of the Institute has been to harness and channel Ireland's limited expertise in this field by bringing together politicians, officials, academics and journalists to work on collaborative projects. Research output covers all of the major agenda issues for Ireland in the EC. Moreover, in 1994 the minister for foreign affairs proposed that a White Paper on foreign policy be prepared as part of Ireland's deliberations for the 1996 IGC. In order to involve Irish public opinion, the department held seven seminars throughout the country to hear the views of interest organizations and the wider public. Therefore, despite imperfections in Ireland's strategic approach to the EC, considerable adaptation has occurred. Overall, the intensity of change in the EU since the mid-1980s has prompted changes in Ireland's administrative and political system.

References

Coyle, C. and Sinnott, R. (1993) Regional elites, regional 'powerlessness' and European regional policy in Ireland. In R. Leonardi (ed.) *The Regions and the European Community* (London: Frank Cass).

Jeffrey, C. and O'Sullivan, B. (1994) The role of socio-economic interest groups *vis-à-vis* local and regional authorities, University of the West of England Papers in Politics, no. 4, Bristol.

Mulreany, M. and Roycroft, J. (1993) The EC structural and cohesion funds, *Administration*, vol. 41, no. 2 (Summer), pp. 191–229.

NDP (National Development Plan) 1994–99 (1993) (Dublin: Stationery Office).

Scott, D. (1994) *Ireland's Contribution to the European Union* (Dublin: IEA).

Tannam, E. (1993) Influence or power? The EC and the Irish administrative process, *Governance*, vol. 6, no. 2, pp. 275–84.

Chapter 6

Greece: Competing with Regional Priorities

MICHAEL CHRISTAKIS

Introduction

The European Community (EC) structure has witnessed a number of substantial changes during the course of its evolution since its establishment in 1957. Despite the problems, the regressions and the delays, it is generally accepted that European integration has moved forward and that the EC has moved towards closer unification.

To a greater or lesser degree, member-states have changed the way in which they traditionally approached the formulation of their domestic and foreign policies. For certain countries, their traditional role as independent policy-makers is not in conflict with their role within the European Union. Other countries, however, find it difficult to shape their policies at the level of the Union and within the Union. Each country's history, experience and tradition, its geographical position, its power and weaknesses, the time of accession to the EC, external threats and differing notions about them are all factors that lead to different considerations regarding the notion of national interest. The importance of this notion is crucial to the relation between national interest and what might be called a common interest for all member-states. Striving for European integration does not necessarily mean that geography, history or even mentality can be easily altered or changed.

This chapter examines the changes that Greece has had to undertake in adapting its governmental and administrative system to conditions arising from the evolving integration of Europe. The chapter focuses on the alterations that were the result of a more intensive cooperation between national authorities and the EC.

Since 1981, when Greece became the tenth member of the EC, and especially after 1986, when the SEA was signed, administrative and procedural mechanisms have been modified considerably. This was done in order to adapt to the demands and challenges put forward to the Greek state by an ever-increasing integration in all sectors, as agreed at the EC level.

Contextual factors affecting the adaptation process

Greece stands as a 'unique case' among the member-states of the EU in almost every respect. A peripheral country of the EU, Greece is geographically situated in the extreme southeastern corner of the EU. Besides being the member furthest from the centre of the EU, Greece is also the only country with no common borders with the other EU members. Furthermore, Greece is located in a turbulent region, the Balkans, surrounded by difficult neighbours. The crisis in the former Yugoslavia has evolved into a major destabilizing factor for the whole of Europe. But Greece's position in a fragile environment is not only because of the Balkans. It is also due to the critical situation in the Middle East. Another factor that should not be overlooked is that Greece is again the only member-state of the EU that feels an intense external threat to its national sovereignty and territorial integrity. The continuing territorial disputes with Turkey lie at the source of this perceived threat.

Important for Greece's understanding of its geopolitical position is the fact that it is surrounded by countries with different experiences in rule and culture. This creates difficulties in communication with these countries. Greece often feels that this reality creates problems not easily understood by the country's partners in the EU, as they live in a different, more stable and homogeneous environment (Kranidiotis, 1994).

This fragile security environment and the threats posed by it compel the Greek government to spend 7 per cent of the country's GDP – the highest percentage among EU members – on military expenditure. In the EU context, Greece is the country with the lowest level of development in terms of its per capita GNP, facing important structural problems at the same time. The economy of the country has, since its accession to the EC, steadily diverged from the European economy. For example, the per capita GNP of Greece, which in 1980 stood at 58 per cent of the EC's average, dropped to 52 per cent in 1992.

Furthermore, Greece is a country with a distinctive pattern of historical and political development rather different from that of the rest of Europe. In cultural terms, it is the only EU member-state that participates in two cultural formations, the Western liberal tradition and the Eastern religion-centred orthodox tradition. Nevertheless Greece, by virtue of its classical cultural heritage, more than any other member-state is entitled to the name 'European'; indeed the name Europe traces its origins to Greek mythology (Wenturis, 1994).

Attitude towards membership of the European Community

The evolution of Greece's attitude towards the EC and European integration in general is also characterized by a certain degree of uniqueness. In 1961, Greece was the first country to become an associated member of the newly established EEC. Its association status with the EEC was 'frozen' following the imposition of a dictatorial regime in 1967. After the restoration of democracy in 1974, Greece also re-established its relations with the EC. Within this context, the Greek government opted for full membership of the EC in 1975. After a long process of hard bargaining and negotiations, Greece was the tenth member to join the EC in January 1981. Still, accession to the EC was not a consensus choice for the major opposition party, the Panhellenic Socialist Movement (PASOK), which came to power ten months after the country's accession to the EC.

During the first decade of membership, the issue of accession turned from 'rather divisive' to 'strongly consensual'. Following three Greek presidencies of the EC, the principal political forces in the national politics, with the exception of the Communist Party (KKE), as well as the public at large, had turned in favour of the EC. To this extent, there was strong support for the efforts for greater political and economic integration, including the goal of full Economic and Monetary Union (EMU). An example of that is the overwhelming majority with which the TEU (the Maastricht Treaty) was ratified by the Greek Parliament. At the same time, despite the difficulties facing the economy, the public in Greece has demonstrated exceptionally high support for the criteria of economic convergence laid down in the Treaty to be met for full participation in the second phase of the EMU in 1999.

This strong pro-integration attitude that Greece has adopted is directly related to the actual and perceived gains that the country has obtained due to its membership of the EC. This was to a large extent expected by the conservative government which insisted that Greece should become a member of the EC as soon as possible. The fact is that Greece has made considerable gains mainly in the following two sectors:

- *Economically*, Greece has gained considerably from the flow of financial resources from the Community budget, now amounting to almost 5 per cent of the annual GNP of the country.
- *Politically*, Greece has strengthened its regional position, increased its bargaining power in its international relations and, last but not least, enhanced its political status and ability to deal with its traditional adversaries. (Plaskovitis, 1994)

However, Greece still encounters severe problems in adjusting its economy to the EU environment and, specifically, to the criteria for the second phase of the Economic and Monetary Union. Furthermore, there are certain aspects of the country's foreign policy positions that create tensions with its partners in the EU. All the aforementioned create a profile for Greece as a member-state of the EU as a 'special case'. These issues help to explain the fact that occasionally the country often appears to be 'out of step' with mainstream European thinking. Still, Greek governments have supported the deepening of the Union in the direction of some kind of federalist structure.

Greek foreign policy concerns

Since 1989, Greece has faced an increasing number of external problems. These include the crisis in Greece's relations with Albania and the former Yugoslavian Republic of Macedonia. The Greek government has had to deal with these problems at the same time that the country's relations with Turkey were increasingly strained and the Cyprus problem had to be confronted. The issues raised by these problems have created difficulties for Greece along a number of different fronts (see Couloumbus, 1994: 189–99). Greece did not manage in the period 1989–93 to exploit the emerging possibilities to play a crucial role and represent aptly the policy of the

EU in the Balkans. The successive Greek governments of the period failed to grasp the new realities in the post-Cold War era and the need to plan a new open strategy. A series of mistaken assessments led the country to an impasse which prevented it from formulating a sound Balkan policy, which instead created a number of disagreements with Greece's European partners.

The new Greek government, which took office in October 1993, is trying to change course and pursue a different policy. To this extent, both during and since the presidency of the EU in 1994, Greece has moved forward with the problem of Cyprus and Greek–Turkish relations, considering them as issues of first priority. At the same time, the government has sought feasible solutions to the problems and crises encountered in the country's northern frontiers with Tirana and Skopje. It should be noted that Greece is an important factor of peace and stability in the area of the Balkans, being a member of the EU, NATO and the West European Union (WEU). Its economic development is higher than its neighbours' and its gross annual income is almost equal to that of all the Balkan countries together.

Governmental adaptation

Following its accession to the EC, Greece had to undergo a process of adaptation at the central government level. This was imperative in order to endorse all the necessary changes decided at the EC level and to further European integration. This process was rather slow, as both the government and the administrative apparatus were not really prepared for the forthcoming accession.

The Greek government decided in 1975 to apply for full membership without waiting for the full implementation of the Association Agreement. Despite the fact that the transitional provisions of the agreement extended until 1984, and that only limited progress had been made in several important areas like agriculture, the government pressed ahead with its application for full membership. Overlooking a number of serious economic and social realities, the Greek government succeeded in accelerating the accession process, mainly for political reasons. The government of the day considered membership the best way of consolidating democratic institutions, following the collapse of the military regime in 1974. At the same time, membership of the EC was perceived as a way to protect the national security interests of Greece.

The Commission, however, was deeply concerned over Greece's ability to meet its obligations as a fully fledged member. The opinion of the Commission, which was presented to the Council in 1976, questioned the ability of the Greek state to handle effectively the obligations arising from accession, due to the problems in the economy. In fact, the necessary institutional and structural changes, even with the support of the Community, were a slow, complex and demanding task.

Adaptation to European integration in the principal ministries

As was the case with all the member-states of the EC, the enlargement of the scope of the Community activities during the 1980s gradually increased the number of

ministries involved in EC decision-making in Greece. This tendency was strengthened following the conclusion of the SEA in 1985 and the agreement on achieving
the single market in the EC.

The adaptation of the principal ministries was pursued mainly for the following
reasons:

1 There was a need to adjust the state apparatus to European norms and
   agreements in general. In other words, to transpose the *acquis
   communautaire* into the Greek legal framework. This also entailed the
   appropriate preparation of the Greek representatives for their task in the
   working groups of the Council and the proper organizing of the PR of the
   country in Brussels.
2 The Greek government was under pressure due to the inflationary and
   budgetary problems that Greece faced since 1979 and especially after
   1983.
3 Since the mid-1980s, the economic recession, which had hit western
   Europe and had become global in its impact, had already started having
   a negative effect in Greece, too. To this extent, the government and especially
   the key economic actors were gradually influenced by the neo-liberal
   ideas that were becoming dominant world-wide. A new need thus prevailed
   for the government, after the mid-1980s, to proceed to a better management
   of the state and to a more sound and consistent economic policy.

There were three ministries that established at an early stage – as early as 1976,
although Greece's accession to the EC took place in 1981 – by a ministerial decree
a special Department for Relations with the European Communities. This was in
accordance with the Law 445 of 1976 regulating the representation of Greece in the
EC. These three ministries were: the Ministry of Agriculture, the Ministry of Coordination (later renamed the Ministry of National Economy) and the Ministry of
the Presidency of the Government.

Due to its key role, the **Ministry of National Economy** was immediately organized to handle all the appropriate negotiations for the country's accession to the EC.
The adaptation of this ministry – which plays a key role in the government's policy
in the EC – to the increasing demands of European integration has been an ongoing
process since 1976. The impact of European integration has been more visible here
than in other ministries. This is due to the fact that this ministry is responsible for
managing Greece's economic relations with the EC. The principal units which handle
and monitor all issues related to the EC along with their implementation are the
independent Direction of Relations with the European Communities and a specially
established Office of EC Legal Affairs. The tasks of planning and implementing
EC programmes, initiatives and activities at the regional level have been allocated
to the General Secretariat of Investment and Development. Among the four directions included in this secretariat, two are directly related to the EC. These are the
Direction of Implementation and Funding from the European Regional Development Fund (ERDF), and the Direction of Special Programmes of the EC. This
allocation of responsibilities was made by a series of presidential decrees from
1976 to 1995.

The **Ministry of Agriculture** followed a similar pattern for two reasons: first, the need to carry out the difficult negotiations in the agricultural sector, and second, the need to prepare the appropriate mechanisms for the country to benefit from the CAP following its accession. To this end, a special Department for Relations with the European Communities was established, also based on the law regulating Greece's representation in the EC.

In the **Ministry of Home Affairs**, the influence of European integration has been more visible than in other ministries. This has to do with the fact that this ministry is responsible for organizing the elections for the national representatives to the European Parliament. The principal unit dealing with issues related to the EC along with their implementation is the Direction of Public Relations and International Organizations, especially its Department of European Communities and International Organizations. There are other minor and secondary tasks which have been allocated to other directions or their departments, the most important being the assistance provided for the local government associations in order to cooperate with the EU bodies. This division of labour within the ministry was introduced by two presidential decrees in 1988. It is expected that additional adaptations will take place soon to the ministry organization due to the 'third pillar', which is related to home affairs, endorsed by the Maastricht Treaty.

In the **Ministry of Justice**, the influence of European integration is less visible than in other ministries. The principal direction to handle all issues related to the EC, along with their implementation, is the Direction of Law Preparation of Special Legal Affairs and International Relations and especially its Department of International Relations. The distribution of responsibilities regarding the planning and implementation of EC programmes and other activities was made by presidential decree in 1988. Here, too, it is expected that additional adaptations of the ministry's organization will take place soon, as a consequence of the elaboration of 'third pillar' tasks in the area of justice.

In the organization of the **Ministry of Public Order**, the influence of European integration is easier to distinguish in comparison with other ministries since it includes specific directions set up as a result of European integration. The principal direction dealing with all issues related to the EC, along with their implementation, is the Direction of International Police Cooperation and especially its Department of European Communities. This organization of the ministry was decided by a presidential decree in 1993. Additional changes will be necessary in connection with the public-order issues falling under the 'third pillar'. The expected changes are related to police cooperation within the EU along the lines spelled out in the Schengen Agreement.

The **Ministry of Industry, Energy and Technology** seems to be the administration best prepared to face the demands of European integration. The influence of European integration has been obvious because this ministry is responsible for following up on the proper implementation of the Integrated Mediterranean Programmes (IMP) in Greece.[1] This task is the responsibility of the Department of the Integrated Mediterranean Programmes, a unit in the Direction of Industrial Development. However, the principal direction handling all issues related to the EC is the Department of European Communities located in the Direction of International

Industrial Relations. This ministry has had a more pro-European profile than others, in part because the head of the ministry has, for a long period, been Costas Simitis, a well-known pro-European in PASOK and, since January 1996, the prime minister of Greece.

The **Ministry of Labour** is considered to be well prepared to face the demands of European integration and, especially, the initiatives undertaken in the employment sector. In 1989 the influence of European integration resulted in important changes within the ministry. The principal body established to deal with issues related to the EC is the General Secretariat for Handling Community and Other Funds. In addition, there were two directions and three departments established: the Department of Coordination of European Union Affairs; the Direction for Planning and Implementation of Programmes of the European Social Fund (ESF) with a special Department of Planning and Coordination of the Initiatives of the European Social Fund; and the Direction for Community Initiatives and Other Funding with a special Department of Community Initiatives. The latter two directions have the tasks of managing EC programmes, initiatives and activities in the employment sector.

In the **Ministry of Commerce**, the direction in charge of matters concerning the EC is the Central Direction of the ministry and especially the Department of European Communities. The current allocation of tasks for this ministry was decided in 1988.

A similar pattern is found at the **Ministry of the Environment, Town Planning and Public Works**, where there is a special department concerned with all issues related to the EC in the Central Direction of the ministry. This is the Department of International Activities and EC Affairs.

There has been an ongoing discussion over the adaptations that have to be made in the organization of the **Ministry of National Defence** so that it is prepared for the common security policy, which is part of the 'second pillar' of the EU. If the effort to make the WEU the defence organization of the EU were to be successful, the Ministry of Defence would have to be reorganized since the issue of defence is crucial for Greece.

From the review of the new structures that have been established in all principal ministries as a result of an increasing integration within the European context it is clear that the crucial year for governmental adaptation of Greece is 1988. From the beginning of 1988 to the early months of 1989, all the principal ministries, one after the other, proceeded either to establish new directions and departments or to reshape already existing units. These changes were directly related to European affairs and took place in order to accommodate the ever-increasing importance of the EC for what was going on in Greece.

The SEA, the regulations agreed to be carried out as part of the single market (by 1992) and the ever broadening scope of cooperation in sectors such as environment, tourism, consumer protection and emigration were crucial factors in causing the Greek government to proceed with a major reshaping of the governmental and administrative apparatus of the state. These changes in the state organizations were necessary in order to make it possible for Greece to deal effectively with the plethora of new challenges within the European context.

The Ministry of Foreign Affairs and coordination with the sectoral ministries

Every ministry in Greece is responsible for the issues of its sector and for the harmonization of the EC legislation to the relevant laws of the country. In case there is a conflict of interest with another sectoral ministry during the preparation of Greece's positions on certain EC affairs, then the Ministry of Foreign Affairs takes over.

The Ministry of Foreign Affairs, which has the major coordinating role, puts the issue under discussion to the Governmental Committee (the small Ministerial Council as it is otherwise called) in order to resolve the conflict of interests between the two (or more) ministries and to achieve a greater agreement before these positions are negotiated with the other EC partners. If the conflict cannot be resolved at the lower level of representatives of the ministries, it goes to the ministerial level. If agreement still cannot be reached, it then goes to the prime minister for a final resolution. The objective is always to determine the priority to be given to the interests of sectoral ministries viewed from the perspective of the general interest of the country (Stoforopoulos and Makridimitris, 1996). An example of this process is the case of the programme of measures to ensure that the Greek economy will meet the criteria agreed in Maastricht, which was the result of a lengthy negotiation between principal ministries. The Governmental Committee met repeatedly at the level of ministers or general secretaries in order to achieve better coordination.

In the Ministry of Foreign Affairs a special bureau was established in 1986, the Special Legal Service for the European Communities (ENYEK), to handle all EC affairs. The main role of ENYEK is to coordinate and closely follow issues such as the harmonization of the EC directives to the Greek legislature. During the years it has been in operation ENYEK has proved very useful for the purposes for which it was designed.

At the end of the 1980s, a large part of the responsibilities handled by ENYEK was transferred to the Legal Council of the State (Nomiko Symvoulio tou Kratous). However, they were returned to ENYEK in 1993. This temporary transfer of responsibilities was mainly due to political expediency in the period between the change of the two main political parties in power.

It is generally accepted in political, governmental and higher administrative circles that ENYEK is doing a very good job. This appears to be due to the fact that ENYEK employs a large number of analysts and experts with deep knowledge and long experience in their fields. This experience was accumulated during the three Greek presidencies of the Council of Ministers. In functioning as the presidency of the different Councils, the officials had to face and resolve all the problems connected with 'running a presidency'. This played a crucial part in enhancing the role and maximizing the effectiveness of ENYEK. Still, all agree that ENYEK needs further financial support.

However, there is a problem, which appears occasionally, of not making appropriate use of the officials of ENYEK, either in Brussels or in Greece. In other words, there is the paradox of an official serving for three to four years in Brussels and then being transferred back to Greece to a position not at all relevant to his or her knowledge and experience. This is done either out of considerations of political expediency or for purely personal reasons. As a result of this practice, the effectiveness of the country's representation within the Community, especially with regard to economic issues, has suffered.

During the early 1980s, the Junior Minister of Foreign Affairs, Yannis Kapsis, in order to promote better coordination of Greece's policy in the EC, proceeded to establish in the context of the information service of the ministry a small group of external experts, consisting of university professors in the field of international relations. With the junior minister's participation, this group held weekly meetings to analyse current international affairs and to make proposals for the best promotion of Greek interests. Even though this arrangement produced results, the appointment of a new minister led to the gradual decline and ultimately to the abolition of this institution.

Another attempt to maximize the use of external advisers was made in the early 1990s by the then Minister of Foreign Affairs Antonis Samaras. He established the policy planning service, which functioned for three years. The job of the service was to analyse current international affairs and to make proposals for promoting Greek interests. This unit appeared to have good prospects for further development, but again a change of leadership in the ministry led to the gradual decline of this effort as well.

There is a strong need for further increasing the financial resources allocated to the general direction handling the affairs and relations of Greece with the EC. There is a strong tendency for further specialization in the sectoral fields of the EC, so that the new officials will need to possess appropriate expertise and be well prepared for the negotiations within the Community context. There is also under discussion the idea that officials dealing with the EC be given diplomatic status (Kofos, 1995). Nevertheless, there are strong doubts as to whether this discussion will prove fruitful, since there are strong objections to it from the *corps diplomatique* of the Ministry of Foreign Affairs.

The role of the Ministry of Foreign Affairs has been evolving since Greece's accession to the EC in 1981. This had begun as early as 1976. The importance of the Ministry of Foreign Affairs is considerable with regard both to the relations between Greece and the EU and to the relations between Greece and the other member-states. In this connection, it is generally accepted that the Ministry of Foreign Affairs currently has a threefold mission:

1   **the role of coordinator** between sectoral ministries in order to achieve the best representation of Greece in the EC;
2   **the role as main communication channel** with the sectoral ministries and the Community bodies; and
3   **the function of the main post office** between the sectoral ministries and the Community bodies.

The role of the Ministry of Foreign Affairs has grown dramatically since 1987, after the SEA came into force and especially after the signing of the TEU in Maastricht. Besides this continuous broadening of its role, there has also been an increasing tendency for the ministry to orient its activities toward the EU. This is due not only to the evolution of the EC to the EU, but also to the enlargement of the scope of policies and activities of the Community in the daily life of the member-states.

Administrative adaptation

The Ministry of Foreign Affairs plays the key role in coordinating the sectoral interests of the government and the major economic and social associations, such as the Organization of Local Government Associations, the General Confederation of Greek Workers, the Association of Greek Industrialists, and so on. To this extent, there are liaison officers not only to ensure regular contact but also to exchange information between these associations and the ministry.

The leadership of the Ministry of Foreign Affairs, along with the officials of ENYEK, follow all EC-related affairs closely. This follow-up takes place at all levels, from the working groups to COREPER and to ministerial level. Within this context, the ministry provides instructions on the Greek positions on issues for the Greek representatives. These positions may, of course, change in the course of the discussion and the negotiations with the other member-states as the balance between benefits and losses are redefined as new alternatives or combinations are developed. The Greek Permanent Representative plays an important information- and 'intelligence'-gathering role in its contacts with the representatives of other member-states. The priority to Greek interests may change eventually during the negotiations. The same may easily happen during the negotiations in the Councils of Ministers as well.

Every week, before COREPER, there is a meeting at the Ministry of Foreign Affairs of all the officials involved in order to prepare the agenda, led by the director-general of the EC Direction. Officials from the sectoral ministries, who work on the issues under discussion, are invited. At this meeting, the final telegram and the instructions are agreed, which spell out for the PR of Greece in Brussels how Greece's interests are to be represented in COREPER. Depending on the results of this meeting, some issues under discussion are sent on to the ministerial council, some of them to the working group, and some return to the ministry for discussion.

Before the meeting of the sectoral Council of Ministers in Brussels, there is a meeting in the Ministry of Foreign Affairs in Athens with all the officials (from the other ministries as well) involved with the issue under discussion at the ministerial meeting. This meeting is held in order to determine the appropriate strategy for dealing with the issue under discussion in Brussels (or elsewhere). All conclusions are included in a file which the Greek representative uses during the negotiations at the ministerial meeting in Brussels.

The day before the actual meeting of the sectoral ministers, there is another meeting held at the country's PR in Brussels with the group of officials coming from Greece. During the meeting, a mutual briefing, updating and documentation on the issue under discussion in the ministerial meeting take place between the two groups. The objective of the meeting is to formulate the final positions and strategy that Greece will adopt and pursue at the ministerial meeting.

There is also a telegram sent before every COREPER and every meeting of the sectoral councils to the ambassadors of Greece in every member-state. They are responsible for informing the Ministry of Foreign Affairs of those countries about the Greek positions, asking their positions in return and informing Athens immediately. This procedure is intended to provide the ministry with information on the initial reactions and plans of the other member-states. Based on this feedback, the leadership of the ministry can decide on the strategy and the alliances that Greece will try to form with other members of the EU. This is the process by which Greece forms its multi-level alliances for the coordination of its strategy within the EU.

The alliances that Greece enters into with other member-states of the EC on issues where a common interest exists, as well as the general lines of the strategy to be followed, are largely decided at an early stage. This was the case on the occasion of the signing of the customs union agreement between the EU and Turkey.[2] Greece had formed its position and strategy long before the signing of the customs union. All the interconnections with the other countries had already been decided, including questions as to the timing of when to press ahead with the issue, when to use the veto, how and when to coordinate with the decision of the European Parliament on the issue, and what actions should be taken in the context of the Commission.

This process entails a significant number of trips and contacts during which a large number of issues are discussed. For example, when the Greek representatives made contact with their partners in the EU in order to discuss the signing of the customs union agreement between the EU and Turkey, they also discussed issues related to the IGC of 1996, the enlargement of the EU in eastern Europe and the Mediterranean policy of the EU as well. This is an ongoing process.

Political adaptation

A reference should be made to a certain paradox existing in the relations between the EC and Greece. This is the duality that exists in the leadership of the Ministry of Foreign Affairs in Greece, expressed in the positions of the minister and the junior minister (or sometimes referred to as the alternate minister), responsible for EC affairs.

It is a standard procedure for every member-state to be represented in Brussels at the Council of General Affairs by the minister of foreign affairs. There are occasions when the junior minister will also be there to take part in the discussions of the current issues, but only on specific occasions will the junior minister represent his or her country. For Greece, though, it is customary that the junior minister (or the alternate minister) of foreign affairs represents the country in the Council of General Affairs. It is only on rare occasions that the minister represents the government at the above Council. This paradoxical situation has led to two problems:

- *internally*, a problem of coordination between the minister and the junior minister, when a decision has to be made on an important issue but the minister is not present; and
- *externally*, a diplomatic nuisance to Greece's partners in the EC, when the Greek minister is not there, a decision on an important issue has to

be made but Greece is represented at a lower level – this can create a coordination problem and, from a general point of view, a problem of diplomatic protocol.

The continuation of this paradoxical situation is considered to be detrimental to the interests of Greece. That it has persisted is, in great measure, due to the strong personality of Theodore Pangalos, who occupied the position of the junior or alternate minister of foreign affairs for most of the 1980s. Indeed, this may explain this duality phenomenon to a certain extent.

Another important development that should be mentioned is the establishment of the Commission of European Affairs in the Hellenic Parliament. This committee consists of MPs and MEPs and holds meetings on a regular basis. The occasion that produced a considerable package of proposals was the issue of the 1996 IGC. The strong interest shown by the Greek Parliament since 1993 is directly related to the personal interest of the president of the Greek Parliament, Apostolos Kaklamanis.

The political adaptation of Greece to European integration as an ongoing process is advancing slowly but steadily. The implementation of EC policies, though, has not progressed at an equal pace. There are still administrative problems affecting the capacity for absorbing the funds available to Greece from the EC, and in properly following up the implementation of the EC programmes and the proper channelling of the related funds. This is an area that creates major problems for the Greek government, since it does not wish to lose the substantial funds which are indispensable for the local economy, or to be accused of mismanagement, both by the opposition and the Commission.

Since its accession in 1981, Greece had the experience of three successful presidencies of the Council of Ministers of the EC.[3] These presidencies served as an apprenticeship for the civil service of the country for adapting gradually to EC membership. It was extremely helpful to learn how to cope with the management of the day-to-day issues of EC as it is the pattern in the other member-states as well. A successful presidency for a small state like Greece increases its potential in EC circles. On the one hand, the presidency gives to a small state a number of tactical advantages, e.g. the setting of the agenda, while on the other hand it serves as a good period for intensive training both for the country's civil service and political officials. On the whole, a small state usually comes away from a successful presidency of the EC with a strengthened profile.

Strategic adaptation

Greek governments, in general, have followed an increasingly strengthened pro-European policy since 1984. This is reflected in Greece's positions in a large part of its affairs with the EC. The only exception to this policy are the issues related to Greece's foreign policy. Greek governments decided, eventually, on a shift of their policy toward the EC. The main focus of the country shifted from a policy to increase the funding gained from the EC Structural Fund to one aimed at enhancing the country's participation in major EC projects. Hence the case of Greece participating actively in the drafting of the SEA with the concept of cohesion and economic convergence between member-states. Greece also played a major role in the drafting of the EC's Social Charter with the initiative of the Greek Commissioner at the time, Vasso Papandreou. The concept of social area in the EC was the main objective of the second Greek presidency of the Community (July–December 1988). Another important contribution of Greece was the idea of Yannos Kranidiotis, junior minister of foreign affairs in 1994, to establish a reflection group, which played a crucial role in the better preparation of the IGC of 1996.

All the above indicate that Greek governments have gradually come to recognize that the EC is not only a structural fund but mainly a forum where political ideas, programmes and initiatives can be brought for discussion. This is an attitude that has steadily created a pro-European profile for Greece. Greek governments soon realized that being in favour of the EC did not mean that the country was losing out as a result. It meant also that the country, as a member-state, was able to use the EC for promoting its national interests as well. This is a concept that has become policy and is followed by both Conservative and Socialist governments.

Both major parties have adopted a similar policy towards Europe. This is the case with regard to achieving economic convergence with the other member-states and fulfilling the criteria of the second phase of the Economic and Monetary Union (EMU). None of the major parties would like to be held responsible for having left Greece behind (in reaching the criteria of the second phase) in comparison with the other members of the EC or having left the country out of the EMU all together.

The role of the Ministry of Foreign Affairs has increased dramatically since 1987. Furthermore, due to the broadening of the scope of policies and activities of the Community in the daily life of the member-states, there is very good cooperation with the Ministry of Finance and the Ministry of National Economy. This is viewed as crucial for the Greek economy. The strategy of the country on the planning for and the channelling of funds from the EC for the needs of the country is decided in close collaboration among these three ministries. It is crucial to realize how important the resources available from the Community funds are for structural purposes in Greece. The financial assistance granted to Greece from the EC in 1992 represented about 5 per cent of the country's GDP and 11 per cent of the total investment in the country (Kazakos, 1994: 7–8).

Since accession in 1981, the role of the prime minister in Greece's relations with the EC and on the positions and the strategy that the country will follow in the multitude of EC affairs has been decisive. But still, the prime minister is in close contact and cooperates with the Ministry of Foreign Affairs, which plays the key role of coordination and representation of the country in the ministerial councils of the EU. The fact that Greece attributes such an importance to its relations with the EU is reflected in the institution of the junior minister of foreign affairs. The general direction of all EC affairs in Greece is exclusively assigned to this position. In this way, the Ministry of Foreign Affairs coordinates and supports the activities of the sectoral ministries.

As part of its strategic adaptation to the continuously increasing scope of the activities of the EU, the administrative apparatus and especially the representatives of the sectoral ministries have adapted the strategy they employ to exert influence on decision-making in Brussels. Since the signing of the SEA, they have started using techniques of lobbying in order to maximize the gains for the country's interests (Andersen and Elilassen, 1991). This is a technique that will be used more extensively in the future.

Greek views on the Intergovernmental Conference

The EU needs a vision and the member-states need to agree on specific common goals to establish whether to move further with the political union and how to achieve this. It remains to be seen whether the pending revision of the TEU will be limited to specific adjustments of the Maastricht Treaty to create the conditions for a further enlargement of membership. In order to assist in the timely and appropriate formation of the agenda of the IGC, the Greek presidency proposed and achieved the setting up of a reflection group for its preparation. This group proved to be the most appropriate body to draw up the annotated agenda for the IGC of 1996.

The Greek government, like other member-states, has not been in the position to find the answers to all the questions posed. It does, however, have a clear idea of the direction to follow. A new type of federal organization for the EU is an attractive option for Greece. This is attractive not only for reasons of philosophical preference, but also for reasons associated with the country's geography and its position within the Union (Kranidiotis, 1995).

The main objective for Greece is to promote the idea that the 1996 revision should and could achieve a better balance of rights and obligations for all member states. The role of the European Parliament should be strengthened. The EP must also have a greater say in the Common Foreign and Security Policy and in the Cooperation on Justice and Home Affairs.[4] The Parliament should also have greater control over the work of the Commission and should participate more actively in the appointment of its members.

With these measures, the status of the Commission would be strengthened, due to the fact that the involvement of the EP in its appointment would give more legitimacy to its power. This would enable its members to undertake a more active role, not only in the more traditional EC matters, but also in the CFSP as well as in the Cooperation on Justice and Home Affairs. The Greek government also feels that the field of competence of the EU should also be expanded. Culture, education, consumer protection, transport, tourism and energy are sectors that should be given more attention.

Greece feels that the protection of the territorial integrity of the EU is an issue to which more attention should be given through the building of the appropriate mechanisms for safeguarding and preserving peace. These mechanisms should be included in the objectives of the common foreign policy. Furthermore, the WEU should be incorporated into the framework of the common defence policy. This is a very important issue for Greece.

The Greek government is of the opinion that EU decision-making must be made more effective. Greece supports the principle of equality between member-states. While the representation of the member-states in the European Parliament should be proportionate to the size of their population, this criteria cannot apply to the Council to the same extent. To the extent that the traditional decision rule of unanimity is replaced by qualified majority voting, the Greek government does not discount the possibility that further integration will confront the country with some difficult choices and dilemmas regarding possible conflicts between the common European interest and the national interest for several years to come. In the field of foreign policy this may mean that Greece will be forced to invoke the principle of vital national interests. In order to promote these interests, Greece will need to search for allies and common ground among its partners in order to improve its position within the EU. The country's objective is to play a significant role in the upcoming IGC negotiations, and to contribute to the construction of the new Europe.

Conclusion

Greece is a member-state of the EU and, at the same time, a geographic part of the Balkans and the Mediterranean. These are the two main areas where Greece feels that it can play a political and economic role. Its participation in the EU is to serve as the point of departure for an active policy in the Balkans and the eastern Mediterranean. Here Greece's ultimate goal is, first of all, to integrate the Balkan countries into European institutions, and second, to enhance significantly the cooperation of the EU with the Mediterranean countries. A policy such as this requires that the country's leadership plan and take action on a new orientation regarding Greece's foreign policy.

Greece has gone through a process of slow adaptation in governmental, administrative, political and strategic terms to its membership of the EU. This process has slowly but steadily adjusted the state apparatus and the political and governmental mechanisms in Greece to fit better in a continuously changing environment in Europe.

The changes that were made in the principal ministries in 1988 and 1989 were due to the signing of the SEA. The signing of the TEU provided impetus for further adaptation. At the same time, the administrative bodies established in the Ministry of Foreign Affairs have achieved better coordination between sectoral ministries with considerable results for the country. The main concern still for Greece, and a thorny area for adaptation, is the country's foreign policy. Within the same context, the different subnational and national authorities have made great advances in organizing a good connection both with the Ministry of Foreign Affairs and with EU bodies.

Recent Greek governments have realized that the country's membership in the EC is indispensable and have embarked upon a long process of structural and behavioural change. This is taking place not only at a political, governmental and administrative level but at a social level as well. Greece has adapted faster politically than administratively.[5] Still, the interests of Greece are put first and they are followed by the interests of the EU. This is most apparent in the case of Greece's foreign policy which is strongly influenced by the problems that the country is facing in this sector with its neighbours. Nevertheless, there is a major effort to combine the interests of Greece and the EU in all other sectors.

With regard to the IGC, the country's target is to be able to play a significant role in the deliberations and decisions of the IGC and, in this way, to make a specific Greek contribution to designing the future of Europe. In return, the Greek government would like more support from its partners and allies regarding its interests, especially on the problems facing its external relations.

Notes

1. The IMPs were special EC programmes designed in 1985 to assist the poorer Mediterranean regions in France, Italy and Greece to face the competition from the accession of the Iberian countries to the EC in 1986.
2. From the interview with the ex-Minister of Foreign Affairs Yannos Kranidiotis, on 4 September 1995.
3. The first presidency was from July to December 1983, the second presidency was from July to December 1988 and the third presidency was from January to June 1994.
4. Greece has supported – and continues to do so – the conclusion of inter-institutional agreements on these issues.
5. This is exactly the opposite of the case of Britain, which adapts faster administratively than politically.

References

Andersen, S. and Eliassen, K. (1991) European Community Lobbying *European Journal of Political Research*, vol. 20, pp. 173–87.

Couloumbus, T. (1994) The Impact of EC (EU) Membership on Greece's Foreign Policy Profile, in P. Kazakos and P.C. Ioakimides, eds., *Greece and EC Membership Evaluated*, 189–198, (Guildford: Pinter).

Kazakos, P. (1994) Greece and the EC: Historical Review, in P. Kazakos and P.C. Ioakimides, eds., *Greece and EC Membership Evaluated*, 1–9, (Guildford: Pinter).

Kazakos, P. and Ioakimides, P.C. (eds) (1994) *Greece and EC Membership Evaluated* (Guildford: Pinter).

Kofos, E. (1995) The role of the specialised scientific advisor in the application of foreign policy, lecture at the Goulandris-Horn Foundation, Athens, 18 January 1995 (in Greek).

Kranidiotis, Y. (1994) *Foreign Policy and European Union* (Athens: Antonis Sakkoulas Publications).

Kranidiotis, Y. (1995) The Future of the European Unification Process: Perspectives on the Intergovernmental Conference of 1996, *Research Papers*, No. 31, Hellenic Centre for European Studies (in Greek).

Plaskovitis, I. (1994) EC Regional Policy in Greece: Ten Years of Structural Funds Intervention, in P. Kazakos and P.C. Ioakimides, eds., *Greece and EC Membership Evaluated*, 116–127, (Guildford: Pinter).

Stoforopoulos, T. and Makridimitris, A.P.C. (1996) The Greek Foreign Policy System: The Institutional Dimension, *Research Papers*, vol. 38, Hellenic Centre for European Studies (in Greek).

Wenturis, N. (1994) Political Culture, in P. Kazakos and P.C. Ioakimides, eds., *Greece and EC Membership Evaluated*, 225–237, (Guildford: Pinter).

Chapter 7

Spain: Modernization through Integration

FRANCESC MORATA

Introduction

The new Spanish democracy has had to face simultaneously two serious challenges which affected the very nature of the state: regional devolution and European integration. As regards the EU, membership has had a positive effect on Spain. The country has succeeded in breaking its centuries-long frustrating political isolation, and its democracy has become stronger in the process. Spain's entrance into the EC in 1986 was quite unanimously supported by political parties, interest groups and public opinion. For Spain, European integration has not only meant economic, social and political modernization; it has also allowed the country to recover its lost place in the European arena. Such a wide consensus allowed the country to face membership in the EC without serious problems of national identity. On the contrary, for a 'pluri-national' country like Spain, belonging to Europe has helped it to find a new 'common' identity. In addition, the EC has been perceived – at least until recently – as a source of benefits in terms of political stability, economic growth, regional assistance and foreign investments. However, such a consensus has also meant the absence of political debate about the real impact of Spain's incorporation into the process of European integration, including the Maastricht Treaty, which coincided with a phase of economic prosperity (1986–91). While the initial idyllic image of the EU has now given way to a more realistic, balanced evaluation, European integration, now defined in terms of monetary union, remains a top priority for Spanish authorities. Officially, the national interest continues to be identified with the Community, viewed as an emerging sovereignty, which will require wider political powers.

In what follows, we will examine some of the relevant aspects of Spanish political and administrative adaptation to the Community policy process. We will begin with a brief general overview of the Spanish institutional system and then assess the impact of European integration on it.

The impact of European integration on constitutional structure

According to the Spanish constitution of 1978, Spain is a parliamentary monarchy. National legislative power is vested in two chambers: the popularly elected Congress (Congreso de los Diputados) and the Upper Chamber (Senado), which provides a measure of territorial representation.

The cabinet, headed by the president of the government, consists of two vice-presidencies and thirteen ministries.[1] The president, or prime minister, conducts domestic policy, foreign relations, civil administration and national defence. During the last socialist cabinet, the vice-president entrusted with the management of the president's office was in charge of coordinating the several ministries in preparation for the weekly meetings of the Council of Ministers. The government that took office in May 1996 includes two vice-presidents responsible respectively for economic and presidency affairs.

The division of powers between central and regional institutions is the most controversial aspect of the Spanish constitution. A hybrid system has been established which is neither federal nor regional, but based on the somewhat contradictory principles of the 'unity of the Spanish nation' and 'the autonomy of the nationalities and regions that constitute it'.

Spain is a decentralized state divided into seventeen autonomous communities (regions). Most constitutional functions are shared between the central government and the regions. All regions are responsible for many policy areas such as education, industry, public works, communications and transport, environment, regional development, agriculture and tourism. In addition, the seven regions with full autonomy (Catalonia, Basque Country, Galicia, Andalusia, Valencia, the Canaries and Navarre) are responsible for public health, social security, local administration and police affairs. The central government is empowered to establish the basic legislative framework in most of these fields. Notwithstanding areas of political disagreement, there has been a massive transfer of functions and resources to the regional governments, which now dispose of 27 per cent of total public expenditure and almost 35 per cent of total public investment.

From 1982 until 1993, the Socialist Party (PSOE) enjoyed an absolute majority in the national legislature. As a consequence, the role of Parliament declined somewhat during this period, while the powers of the national executive and central administration became more significant. However, after the Socialist Party only received a relative majority in the general elections of 1993, the decision-making power of the central government, to a large extent, depended on political support from other parties, especially from the Catalan Nationalists (CiU). After the general elections of March 1996, the Popular Party became the ruling party, albeit only with a very small majority. The need for parliamentary support from other parties has created a situation in which the moderate nationalist parties (Catalan, Basque and Canary Islands) play a central role in Spanish politics, without assuming governmental responsibilities.

Membership of the EU has affected the internal distribution of functions in Spain, both horizontally and vertically. First, as a result of the prominent role that it plays at the Community level, decision-making functions have been concentrated in the hands of the central government which constitutionally belong to the national Parliament. This has occurred to such an extent that, as we will see below, Parliament does not play any significant role in the domestic decision-making process regarding Community affairs. Second, Spanish participation in the EU has had important consequences for the vertical distribution of functions. The constitutional position of the regions has been weakened by the transfer of internal competencies to the Community, as specified in the accession treaty, the SEA and the Maastricht Treaty. The loss of regional powers affects many areas: finance, agriculture and fisheries, regional policy, transport, research policy, the environment and consumer rights. At the same time, however, the regions are increasingly involved in the implementation of Community policies and in the management of structural funds. Some of them also play a role as independent political actors in the Community arena.

Governmental adaptation

The Spanish government has been quite active in adapting its behaviour to the requirements of Community decision-making. Even before joining the EC, Spain had to transpose into national legislation almost 800 Community directives related to the *acquis communautaire*.

The formulation of national positions: organizational setting and coordination

In Spain there is neither a central ministry exclusively responsible for EC matters nor a specific government committee. Since 1986, the Secretariat of State for the EC (SECE), which is lodged in the Ministry of Foreign Affairs, has been in charge of coordinating Spanish positions regarding the EU while the General Secretariat for Foreign Policy retains responsibilities for national coordination on specific issues. However, this formal arrangement for dividing responsibility has not prevented the other departments from exercising their own powers when they are affected by EU policies.[2]

The General Secretariat within the SECE is divided into two general directorates responsible, respectively, for technical coordination and judicial and institutional coordination. The first is entrusted with the monitoring of Community sectoral policies (agriculture and fisheries; economic, financial and social affairs; trade and customs; industry and energy; and transport and communications) while the second is in charge of coordinating judicial affairs and institutional relations within the central administration.

It has been argued that the coordination capabilities of the SECE could be improved by linking it to presidency of the government, as it is the case with the French Secrétariat Général du Comité Interministeriel or the British European Secretariat. However, the several actors involved seem to feel quite comfortable with the present arrangement: on the one hand, the absence of hierarchical relations allows the sectoral ministries to keep their decision-making autonomy; on the other hand, the regions prefer to relate informally to such a structure since it does not represent a threat to their autonomy (Dastis, 1995).

The SECE also chairs the Interministerial Committee for Economic Affairs related to the EC (CIEA-CE), which was created in September 1985 to improve intragovernmental coordination, mainly on an informal basis. Its main functions consist of:

- coordinating administrative actions related to EC economic affairs;
- discussing decisions related to the EC taken by the several ministries;
- assessing and resolving issues affecting more than one ministry;
- informing any member of the CIEA-CE (see below) on matters of interest.

In addition to the chairman, the CIEA-CE also includes two vice-chairmen, which are shared by the SECE and the Ministry for Economic and Financial Affairs, and a number of high-level representatives (ordinarily at the sub-state secretary or general secretary level) from the ministries of agriculture, industry, labour, finance, trade and fisheries. The committee usually meets once every three weeks in order to discuss the forthcoming EU Council agenda, relevant EU issues and decisions taken in recent Council meetings. Most of the CIEA-CE activity is devoted to exchanging information among the different ministries and trying to solve specific interdepartmental conflicts. In this regard, its main job is to try to achieve short-term consensus on pending issues, and not to define strategic positions (Zapico, 1995).

The fact that the members of the SECE have been recruited from the different ministries seems to have led to a high degree of coordination. High officials, representing the office of the president of the government and the several ministries involved in Community policies participate in the committee, which essentially coordinates economic affairs and disseminates available information on developments in Brussels. The SECE systematically evaluates the administrative implications of any Community document, including the impacts for the services specifically affected. Instructions from the CIAE-CE are binding for Spanish public officials participating in EU working groups, while they serve only as general guidelines for the ministries and state secretaries. This organizational set-up is intended to ensure that on Community matters Spain speaks with a single voice – the SECE – while recognizing the special competencies and political influence of the individual ministries. However, the work of the committee has not prevented interministerial conflict on major Community proposals.

Sometimes, the Interministerial Committee is unable to define Spain's position in relation to issues on the agenda of the COREPER and the Council of Ministries. In such cases, negotiation is mostly a matter of informal contacts between the Spanish PR, the SECE and officials of the ministries involved. If these actors are unable to reach an agreement on the position to be taken, the government-appointed Committee on Economic Affairs (CDGAE) or – as a very last resort – the national Council of Ministries makes the final decision.

In addition to the Interministerial Committee, there is a Monitoring and Coordinating Committee for Affairs relating to the European Court of Justice. This committee, which consists of representatives from the office of the president, the SECE, the ministries of justice and economy and, when appropriate, other affected departments, examines all pending cases brought against Spain as well as those cases that could affect the national interests of Spain.

Although most of the central ministries are at one time or another involved in Community policies, some are more active players in the Community arena. These have included the ministries of foreign affairs; economy and financial affairs; industry and energy; public works, transport and the environment; agriculture and fisheries; health and consumer affairs; justice; and home affairs. The different ministries are staffed with medium-ranking experts in European affairs – usually lawyers and economists. No special structures have been created to deal with European affairs, even though Spain had to assume the coordination and chairing of 250 committees and working groups at the EU level during the Spanish presidency of the Council of Ministers.

The Spanish PR in Brussels, which is made up of diplomats from the Ministry of Foreign Affairs (51) and experts directly appointed by the sectoral ministries (almost 100), mirrors the central government organization. Only four departments (public administration, culture, defence and the office of the president) are not represented in Brussels. Depending on the requirements of a particular EU negotiation process, it is not only the experts from the different sectoral ministries that travel to Brussels to participate in the meetings of the committees and working groups. The Permanent Representatives also attend, whenever it is necessary, the coordinating meetings in Madrid. However, this procedure has not been institutionalized and consequently it is not infrequent that, in absence of specific instructions, the Spanish position has to be formulated by the members of the PR (Dastis, 1995). It is worth noting, however, that due to its plural composition, the Spanish delegation is closely linked to the national ministries and thus itself is a kind of mechanism for informal interministerial coordination. In addition, coordination is strengthened by virtue of the fact that instructions from the central government to the PR are channelled through the SECE and not, as it often happens with the working groups, via the sectoral ministries.

In summary, the SECE – together with the PR in Brussels – plays a central role in the EC negotiating process since it channels information and communications with the several departments through the CIEA-CE or through other existing procedures of coordination, both formal and informal. As noted, the SECE systematically evaluates the implications of the draft Community proposals for the different ministries, including the determination of which central services are to be involved. However, problems still arise when jurisdiction for an issue is shared among several ministries. In spite of all the internal procedures for coordination, the final decision defining the national position on a concrete Community issue is usually taken by the ministry directly involved in the Council negotiations. Intra- and intergovernmental coordination has been technically improved in recent years. Since 1992, a telematic database and an E-mail service link to the PR and to the SECE provide direct Community information to the central ministries and to the regions. Again, however, it is worth noting that national positions are usually taken by the ministries involved in the Council decision-making process.

The implementation of EC policies

By 1994, Spain had adapted its internal legislation to conform with approximately 85 per cent of the EC directives then in force. Although Spain initially had no special problems in applying EC law, after its period of grace came to an end in 1988, there was a dramatic increase in the number of proceedings against the country with regard to failure to enforce EC directives. Since 1991, there is a growing concern among government officials regarding the implications of the internal market for transnational administrative competitiveness as well as for internal coordination on Community policies. A survey conducted in 1990/91 among 650 high public officials of central administration showed a clear degree of dissatisfaction regarding both the impact of European integration and the process of decentralization. The conclusions of this study stressed the need to improve the implementation structures for Community legislation, interministerial coordination and cooperation with regional governments. These results reflect the growing difficulties encountered in implementing Community directives in Spain, especially when they disrupt traditional procedures and require meeting higher standards of administrative performance. Public managers need to cope with such new principles as administrative transparency, and subsidiarity and partnership with the regions. Despite efforts made in recent years by both central and regional governments to improve the transposition of Community directives, serious doubts still remain regarding their effective application, as can be seen from infringement proceedings against Spain, some of which have reached the European Court of Justice, and from the warnings addressed to the Spanish administrative bodies by the Commission.

Community pressures have had a significant impact on Spanish administration. For example, in response to complaints by the Commission about the management of environmental policies in Spain, the central government has had to revise its organizational structure. First, the post of general secretary for the environment was created in 1990 within the Ministry of Public Works and Housing. However, this change was not enough. In 1991, renewed pressures from the Commission to provide it with a competent interlocutor led to the setting up of a new state secretariat responsible for water and environmental policy. In 1993 the government decided to give ministerial status to the environment by adding this policy field to the already existing Ministry of Public Works and Transport. Finally, in May 1996, most of environmental functions were brought together in a single ministry by the new conservative government.

With regard to the national transposition of Community directives, Spain now shows a quite respectable level of performance. It is ranked by the Commission as the fourth most reliable member state. As far as the implementation of the single economic market is concerned, by the end of 1995 almost 92 per cent of Community directives had been transposed by Spanish authorities. Usually, national proposals are sent to the Commission in order to have them checked for conformity with Community law. Spanish performance has been improved since 1990, when the cabinet decided to improve the transposition of Community directives with a monitoring programme. This includes a monthly report put together by SECE, which is intended to remind the different ministries of the directives still needing to implemented, especially when the specified date has passed. The CIEA-CE has been charged with monitoring the directives requiring some interministerial co-ordination or posing special problems (Dastis, 1995). This is the case with directives that have to be implemented through a national law like, for example, public contracts or private insurance regulations. As of April 1995, of the eight legal proceedings introduced by the Commission against Spain, six dealt with directives that required a national law for their transposition.

The national Parliament

The national Parliament is not directly involved in the EC decision-making process. However, over recent years a number of improvements have been introduced to improve its ability to control the executive more closely and to participate in the formulation of the Spanish positions on European issues. Nevertheless, its role has been mainly symbolic since the information it receives from the government usually arrives after the decisions on the Spanish positions have been already taken. A Joint Committee of the Upper and the Lower Houses, which was created in 1986, is in charge of monitoring EC policies. In its follow-up activity this committee looks at:

- legislative decrees presented by the executive to enact EC regulations and directives;
- government information about Community proposals which, according to the Spanish constitution, should be enforced through law;
- government information about Community activities affecting Spanish membership; and
- information about central government politics within the EC.

However, the committee does not monitor the decrees or any other administrative measure adopted by the executive, which is the usual way that Community legislation is implemented in Spain. In addition, the state secretary of the foreign ministry makes a bi-monthly appearance before the Upper House Budget Committee and the Joint Committee in order to answer questions regarding the implementation of Community policy.

More generally, the prime minister reports to the Congress after each Community summit and responds to questions from the leaders of the opposition. These EC debates produce general resolutions and special recommendations aimed at influencing the Spanish positions in Brussels. A proposal presented to the Chamber by the Conservative Popular Party in 1993 was intended to involve the Mixed Committee for European Affairs more closely in the preparation of the IGC responsible for reviewing the Maastricht Treaty. However, up until now there has been little evidence of such involvement. According to a law of 1994, the Joint Committee must be informed by the Ministry of Foreign Affairs about those European Commission proposals that are likely to have a special impact on Spanish interests. These reports are supposed to summarize the proposals and evaluate their legal, political and financial effects. This new regulation is intended to improve political debate within the committee and thus increase its ability to intervene in Community decision-making at an earlier point in the process. On the other hand, the Upper House does not participate in Community affairs except for questions addressed to the executive on EC issues affecting the regions, e.g. the Spanish representation in the Committee of the Regions. Recently, the Upper House decided to set up a special committee to report on regional participation in Europe. MPs do not generally have permanent channels of communication with EC institutions. Occasionally, however, delegations from the Spanish Parliament and regional assemblies pay official visits to the European Parliament or get in touch with Brussels when they need information and usually make contacts through SECE, MEPs or their own political parties.

The regions

According to the internal distribution of functions, the regions implement Community policies within their own areas of competence. Since joining the EC, only Catalonia and the Basque Country, because of their more extensive legislative powers, have had to adapt already existing regional legislation to Community rules (*acquis communautaire*). However, insofar as Community membership was taken for granted since the early 1980s, in both regions there had already been voluntary adaptation.

Up until now regional parliaments have in practice been excluded from both the processes of making and implementing EC policy, just as, at the central level, it is regional executives that, in the first instance, deal with Community policies. Parliamentary activity is mainly devoted to a debate on the impact of European integration at the regional level (SEM, EU, structural funds, etc.). This can result in the adoption of initiatives or recommendations designed to influence the behaviour of the executive (i.e. the regional administration response to the EC policies), including its relations with the national government. In most regional parliaments, permanent non-legislative committees have been set up to monitor European policies affecting the regions.

As regards regional participation in the preparation of EC decisions, faced with pressure from the regions the central government proposed in 1986 and in 1988 two agreements on intergovernmental cooperation in Community matters. However, in both cases negotiations became bogged down. The central government was not ready to accept direct representation of Catalonia and the Basque Country in Brussels. In 1988, regional demands led to the establishment of an IGC on Community affairs which was institutionalized in 1992. Following the German model, the conference is a cooperative arrangement which brings together representatives of central and regional governments. It concentrates on the following issues:

- exchanging information and discussion about the developments of European integration;
- regional participation in Community affairs; and
- stimulating and monitoring regional participation in the different areas of Community policy through the already existing sectoral conferences.

The conference, which has been set up at the ministerial level, is assisted by a permanent working group, the Committee of Coordinators on Community Affairs. The central executive is represented by the minister for public administration, who is not a permanent member of the CIEA-CE. The real – informal – partner of the regions at the central level is SECE with which they have developed regular bilateral contacts.

The 'political agreement for governance' signed by the Conservative Popular Party and the Catalan Nationalists in May 1996, as the basis for their cooperation in the present national government, provides for enhancing regional participation in Community decision-making. First, the agreement foresees strengthening the IGC on Community affairs, which in future will meet monthly in order to make more effective regional participation. Second, following the German model, a regional observer – and eventually a second – will join the Spanish PR in Brussels.

Despite such multilateral arrangements, Catalonia and the Basque Country have not stopped trying to establish an institutional presence in Brussels. Between 1994 and 1995, the Basque government negotiated with the central authorities a special status in the EU. The objective of the regional government was to establish a bilateral relationship with the EU which would cover such issues as tax policy, transport and infrastructures and police. The Basque proposal provides for regional participation in the negotiations on structural and cohesion funds, and in the Schengen and Trevi groups. It also includes the possibility that a regional minister could represent Spain in the Council meetings as far as issues falling under the exclusive jurisdictions of the regions are being discussed. The Catalan strategy on Community matters is much more pragmatic in that it is aimed at fostering close cooperation with central authorities (e.g. joint organization of the Euro-Mediterranean Conference) while developing direct contacts with EC institutions, especially with the Commission, as well as with other European regional partners.

In Catalonia, the Patronat pro-Europa, a public consortium established in 1982, takes care of organizing, promoting and coordinating activities linked to the EC. The Patronat, which is chaired by the president of the region, is made up of representatives of universities, savings and loans associations, the chamber of commerce, local government associations and the city of Barcelona. The Patronat's council provides for academic, parliamentary and employment-related representation, including Catalan representatives of EC lobbies and Brussels-based officials. When Spain joined the EC in 1986, the Patronat immediately opened an office in Brussels.

In general, regional administrations have adapted their organizational arrangements in order to carry out Community policies and acquire regional funds. The office of regional presidency assumes the political representation of the region at the European level. However, only in Catalonia is there a ministry specifically responsible for 'external relations', which include, of course, the EU.

In spite of the central government's initial reluctance, the regions have established regular informal relations with Community institutions. Their strategic position as policy implementers made it inevitable that they should have contacts with Commission officials interested in following up regional activities on the ground. Much like the German Länder, up until now fourteen Spanish regions have set up their own offices in Brussels to represent public and private interests.[3]

In preparation for the internal market and the EU, some regions and cities forged a network of inter- and transregional relations, including not only participation in Europe-wide organizations but bilateral or multilateral agreements as well. The Catalan government and the city of Barcelona have been the most active in this regard. Indeed, the president of Catalonia chairs the Assembly of European Regions (ARE) while the mayor of Barcelona heads the Council of Municipalities and Regions of Europe (CMRE). As the main representatives of regional and local governments in Europe, both politicians were involved in the negotiations leading to the constitution of the Committee of the Regions which was decided in Maastricht. As regards transregional cooperation, the 'Four Motors of Europe' set up by mutual agreement in 1988 by Baden-Württemberg, Catalonia, Lombardia and Rhône-Alpes covers different areas such as foreign economic relations, technology transfer, research and design policy, the environment and cultural exchange. By working together and acting as a public lobby, the four regions intend to play a major role in European integration. Another initiative promoted by the Catalan government was the creation, in 1989, of a trans-Pyrenean Euroregion which covers Catalonia, Languedoc-Roussillon and Midi-Pyrénées. The three regional governments combine forces to carry out joint ventures in some areas such as communications and telecommunications infrastructure; occupational training; research and technology transfer; culture, sports and tourism.

Political adaptation

According to a recent Eurobarometer (June 1996), Spaniards express a more positive attitude towards European integration than the average European (60 per cent as opposed to 56 per cent). In addition, in Spain a consistent majority (75 per cent) supports efforts leading to a unified Europe (European average: 69 per cent). When asked about their 'fears regarding European integration', most of the Spanish respondents did not consider it to be a real threat for the Spanish state in terms of language, national identity or culture. However, a majority of the people interviewed did express concern about more concrete items such as tax increases, the economic situation of small and medium-sized firms, the disappearance of the fishing industry, drug traffic and internationally organized crime, and the possibility of a 'deep economic crisis'.

Trust in European institutions is much higher in Spain than the European average. Indeed, it is even higher than trust in domestic institutions (see Table 7.1).

Table 7.1 Domestic Support for National and EU Institutions

	Spain	**EU-15**
European Parliament	51	39
European Commission	50	38
Council of Ministers	46	35
National government	38	39
National Parliament	45	42

Source: European Commission, 1996.

Belonging to the EU is considered as something both 'good and beneficial' for Spain by the whole sample, and a large majority supports continued participation by Spain in the EU. In addition, respondents stress the need to strengthen European activities in such areas as environmental, social and agricultural policy, the EMU, and the security and defence pillar. Further, 64 per cent of the Spaniards interviewed would support a European executive elected by the European Parliament, while only 57 per cent of Europeans are in favour of such a proposal. Asked whether 'the EU should be responsible for policies that national, regional and local governments cannot deal with', the overwhelming majority of the Spanish people interviewed responded affirmatively (65 per cent), with more enthusiasm than the European average (58 per cent), even though only a relative majority of the Spaniards (41 per cent) supports the idea of a federal Europe.

The institutional system of the EU enjoys a relatively high degree of acceptance in Spain. In general it can be said that Spain's entrance into the EC generated a positive attitude toward the institutions of Europe. As has been the case in almost all member-states, the majority of the Spanish population is not familiar with the structure of these institutions and how they function. Until very recently, these general impressions were supported by the coincidence of participation in the EU with the period of prosperity from the end of the 1980s and the beginning of the 1990s. In spite of the scarce interest in the workings of the EU, some policies, like environmental policy, agriculture and fishing and public assistance, have enjoyed a certain prominence in the media as well as in political debate. However, without doubt the topic at the centre of attention at the moment is the EMU since it will require the adoption of a lean budget and a readjustment of the welfare state in a country in which social policy is still in a phase of growth.

With regard to the institutions of the EU, the European Parliament is relatively well known although, in contrast, the Spanish public is not familiar with its functions. Nor is the public very interested in the EP. The MEPs also do not enjoy very much popularity, probably due to the fact that little attention is paid to their work by the mass media. On the other hand, the Council of Ministers and the European Council are more popular. The Commission is often perceived in ambiguous terms as a weak and distant 'European executive', champion of the common interests, privileged bureaucracy and victim of the governments of the large member-states.

While European integration and the institutions of the EU enjoy substantial support at the level of general principles and overall commitment, things are not as clear-cut at the level of more specific policies and outcomes. Since 1992 the Parliament and the Commission shared one characteristic in common: the slow decline in the degree of acceptance among the Spanish public. Perhaps the most important reason for this is the general dissatisfaction with respect to the products of this institutional system and the complexity of its functioning.

With the exception of the Spanish Communist Party, until now the process of integration has received the clear support of the principal political forces, even if the attitudes of these parties with regard to European matters has been quite reactive and their participation limited. Only quite recently did the Spanish political parties 'discover' Europe in connection with the negative impact that the Maastricht Treaty had on public opinion in various member-states. In the aftermath of these public debates and the close votes in the referenda, it was no longer possible to assume a general popular support for the EU and further integration in Spain. It became necessary for the political parties to play a more active role in organizing and participating in the discussion over the future 'meaning' of Europe for Spanish interests.

Spanish relations between business and government are not as close as the North European model. Participation by the private sector in the decision-making process is still seen as an obstacle to the achievement of the so-called 'public interest'. However, the growing impact of EC policies on the Spanish economy has encouraged the involvement of business associations as well as individual big public and private companies to become active at the European level. At the same time, ministries involved in the negotiation of Community policies increasingly tend to establish contacts with interest groups' representatives in order to get their input into the formulation of the Spanish position on pending issues, as well as to facilitate the smooth implementation of directives, especially those linked with the SEM. Banks, chambers of commerce and industry, the Spanish employer's federation, small and medium companies, as well as organizations representing farming and fishing interests are the most active private lobbies in Brussels. In addition, as already noted, regional governments act as promoters of public and private interests at the territorial level in Brussels.

Thus, since 1986, the presence of Spanish business and social organizations in Brussels has been increasing. Large companies and organized general and sectoral interests use a double-track strategy of lobbying, which combines action at both the national and European levels. On the one hand, they provide information, evaluative opinions and technical advice to national and regional civil servants, on both the formulation and implementation of Community policies and programmes. On the other hand, they work in Brussels through national delegations and Euro-federations in order to obtain information and to establish contacts with EC officials during the preparation of Community proposals.

Nevertheless, Spanish interests groups are still more reactive than proactive, making use of professionals when they try to deal with specific problems. The lack of efficient lobbying activities in Brussels is a serious handicap for some important sectors of the Spanish economy which are greatly dependent on Community decisions, like shipping and fishing. On the whole, private interests are still reluctant to establish contacts with MEPs, and the role of consultative bodies such as the Economic and Social Committee and the Committee of the Regions is seen as largely a formality. Worried about the increasing difficulties faced by national and regional administrations in enforcing Community acts, environmental groups try to exert pressure by, among other things, bringing complaints against the Spanish government before the Commission.

Strategic adaptation

Spain's entry into the EC coincided with the negotiation and the coming into force of the SEA. In January 1989, Spain fulfilled its first term of Community presidency;

this was soon followed by the two IGCs that paved the way to the TEU. Unlike the older member-states, which were accustomed to the unanimity rule, the Spanish government was able to adjust quite rapidly to the new procedures. Since becoming a member, Spain has worked within this institutional framework to realize three priority objectives:

1   To increase the weight of southern Europe – and particularly Spain – by getting more funding to promote economic and social cohesion within the Community and to gain recognition for this specific geographic area.
2   To secure more favourable treatment as a laggard country (e.g. more flexible deadlines for implementing certain directives on environmental protection, consumer rights, the customs union, the shipping and steel industries reconversion, free flow of goods and public markets).
3   To strengthen EC links with South Mediterranean and Latin American countries. (The European Council meeting in Madrid in June 1989 considered the Spanish proposal to establish a European guarantee fund for the Latin American debt.)

At the EC level, Spain has rather successfully employed a twofold bargaining strategy combining a commitment to far-reaching European integration and the claim for additional funds to enable it to close the gap with the big member-states. The Spanish government played the 'federal card' during the Maastricht negotiation since deepening European integration is seen as the best guarantee for the future of the country. At the Maastricht Summit the Spanish government succeeded in getting its proposal for European citizenship included in the treaty. In addition, Spain was one of the main supporters of the principle of subsidiarity, viewed as a principle to be applied in deciding how best to achieve Community objectives and not as a way of limiting what the Community could do. According to the Spanish memorandum on subsidiarity presented at the Edinburgh Summit: 'The EU Treaty does not create a federal structure and thus it is still too early to draw up a list of exclusive Community competencies . . . The real extent of subsidiarity, which only has to do with shared powers, has to be progressively established by the Court of Justice.'

The principle of cohesion, already included in the SEA in order to satisfy Spain's claims about financial compensations to counteract the potential disruptive effects of the single market on its less developed regions, reappeared once again in Maastricht. Spain vetoed the EC budget of 1988 until it got general agreement on doubling the Structural Fund as compensation for its acceptance of the SEM. Despite increasing internal economic difficulties, Spanish negotiators accepted the demanding targets of the EMU in exchange for the new Cohesion Fund and a doubling of the amount of financial aid to be made available to those countries whose economics experienced difficulties as a result of the completion of the single market.

During the IGC on political union, Spain strongly argued that 'the final objective of the Union should be to have inter-state compensation systems similar to and on the same scale as those existing in other Federal States (such as the Federal Republic of Germany, for example) which alleviate economic disparities among the Member States of the Union' (Laursen and Vanhoonacker, 1993). According to the Spanish position, the structural funds were no substitute for the achievement of social cohesion and had an exclusively regional focus. In fact, the central government was seriously worried about the possibility that Spain would become a net contributor to the Community in 1993. Receipts from the Community had been declining, relative to the money that Spain contributed to the European budget, reaching only 233 million ECUs (European Currency Units) in 1992. While the Spanish negotiators did not succeed in imposing their views on the need to establish a compensatory financial fund, they did convince Portugal, Greece and Ireland to support the demand for additional resources to compensate for economic differences among the member states.

In fact, Spain threatened to block the agreement on political union if the fund was not included in the EU treaty. In exchange for the agreement of the other member-states on the Cohesion Fund, the Spanish government was ready to accept majority voting for a number of environmental decisions. The Spanish strategy consisted in leading a winning coalition with three small member-states – Portugal, Greece and Ireland – even though Spain clearly expected to get 60 per cent of the fund when the time came to negotiate sharing the receipts among the four countries. It was also Spain's insistence that led to setting a price, in terms of limits to the amounts of grants and loans that would be available, that Norway, Finland, Sweden and Austria would have to pay in order join the European Economic Area. With regard to the EU enlargement, Spain feared that, as the EU got bigger, the centre of gravity would shift northwards, and that the Mediterranean countries would find it increasingly difficult to grab the lion's share of the EU's regional aid.

Together with Great Britain, Spain opposed increasing the votes needed, from 23 to 26, to form a blocking minority in the decision-making of the Council of Ministers as a result of the membership of these countries in the EU. After long and very complex negotiations, the then twelve member-states agreed, at the Ionian Summit, to fix the qualified majority at 65 votes (62 of 87 possible votes after Norway voted not to join) and the minority veto at 23 votes.

Following three 'weak' presidencies (Greece, Germany and France), the second Spanish presidency in the second half of 1995 was viewed with scepticism by Spain's European partners for different reasons: the country was wracked by political scandals, and the socialist government had but a narrow parliamentary majority. Nevertheless, Spain reached the main targets that had been set (España, 1995), such as the presentation of the conclusions of the Reflection Group – chaired by the Spanish state secretary for the EC – regarding the preparation for the IGC of 1996; the agreement to include employment policy as a political priority on the IGC's agenda; the organization of the Euro-Mediterrarean Conference in Barcelona; the fixing of the final deadline for the EMU; and the signing of trade agreements with Latin-American Mercosur and Mexico, and with the United States (the Transatlantic Declaration). The Euro-Mediterranean Conference was one of the main accomplishments of the Spanish presidency. To a large extent, the success of the Barcelona Conference was due to the persuasive strategy employed some months before, at the Cannes Summit, by the Spanish prime minister, Gonzalez, in order to convince his other partners, and the German government, to increase Community subsidies to twelve Mediterranean countries by 110 per cent.

In addition to the formal meetings of the European Council, the Spanish presidency also included a fruitful informal summit that led to agreement on the sharing of the costs of the military operations in the former Yugoslavia. It was also decided that the IGC on the reform of Maastricht would start its activities in Turin, in March 1996, and present its conclusions in mid-1997. The European agenda was fixed for the next four or five years, including the enlargement by the end of the century, to include Malta and Cyprus as well as eastern Europe.

Conclusion

In Spain democracy has meant a rapid process of modernization and adaptation to West European standards. During the last fifteen years, the longest period of democracy ever experienced in Spain, governments at all levels have had to face crucial challenges such as the consolidation of the new institutional setting, including the development of the welfare state, decentralization and European integration. EC membership has had a far-reaching impact on Spanish public administration, the structures and procedures of which have undergone a process of adaptation to the processes of decision-making at the Community level and to the requirements of Community legislation. As a result, administrative action at the domestic level has been shaped increasingly by decisions and events at the Community level. For example, Spain's entrance into the EC in 1986 has been a determining factor for the development of regional, environmental, R&D and free-market policies. In spite of the difficulties it has faced in enforcing Community legislation, Spain has developed a bargaining strategy, combining both a claim for special treatment, in keeping with the relatively less developed level of its economy, and a demand for additional funds to enable it to comply more effectively with Community standards.

Spain has been a pro-active Community partner which has been able to share some of the privileges of the big member-states and has itself been the leader of the cohesion policy coalition. According to the Spanish leader (Gonzalez, 1996):

> For Spain, the new emerging Europe . . . generates challenges and opportunities. Not only for the state, but for the whole Spanish society too. More integration in Europe, especially through the EU, suits Spain . . . both in functional and political terms. Two alternative scenarios can be imagined. The first one includes some important areas in which European integration would progress without a full Spanish participation. The second one is Europe backing down. Both would represent a real disaster for Spain.

In this sense, the country must be ready to play the European card for all it is worth.

However, EC membership has also laid bare a number of inadequacies in domestic institutional and policy-making structures of Spain. As in other member-states, MPs are almost excluded from EC decision-making. Nor, until 1992, did the regions participate in the formulation of national positions. Opportunities for such participation have recently been improved through a political agreement for national governance established between the new conservative executive and the nationalist parties of Catalonia, the Basque Country and the Canary Islands. At the same time regional and local governments play an increasing role in the European arena. This includes both individual lobbying in Brussels through regional offices and joint lobbying with other territorial partners through interregional and transregional cooperation.

Notes

1. Some of the following material appears in an earlier version in Morata (1996).
2. Vice-presidencies: Presidential Office and Economic and Financial Affairs. Ministries: Foreign Affairs; Interior; Justice; Public Works and Transport; Environment; Education and Research; Defence; Industry and Energy; Agriculture and Fisheries; Labour and Social Security; Public Administration; Health and Consumer Affairs; Culture.
3. Before Spain's entry into the EC, the negotiation process was effectively managed by a small group of high officials belonging to the Ministry of Foreign Affairs and the rest of the ministries directly involved in negotiations. In 1986, they joined the Spanish PR in Brussels or returned to their own ministries. This negatively affected the availability of trained personnel for dealing with and coordinating European affairs.
4. In 1992, the constitutional court stated the constitutional right of the regions to be represented in the EU provided that such activity does not interfere with the defence of national interests.

References

Commission of the European Communities (1996) La opinión de los españoles sobre la Unión European, *Eurobarometro Magnum*, Julio.

Dastis, A. (1995) La Administración española ante la Unión Europea, *Revista de Estudios Europeos*, vol. 90, pp. 223–350.

España (1995) Prioridades de la Presidencia Española del Consejo de la Unión Europea, *Presidencia Española del Consejo de la Unión Europea* (*Comité Organizador*) (Madrid: Presidencia del Gobierno).

Gonzalez, F. (1996) Pilotar Europa hacia su rumbo, *Politica Exterioe*, vol. 48, pp. 14–21.

Laursen, F. and Vanhoonacker, S. (eds) (1993) *The Intergovernmental Conference on Political Union* (Maastricht: IEAP).

Morata, F. (1996) Fundamentals of Spain in EU Affairs, in W. Wessels, (ed.), *The European Union and Member States Towards Institutional Fusion?* (Manchester: Manchester University Press), pp. 134–54.

Zapico, E. (1995) La adaptación de la Administración española a la Unión Europea: un proceso de evolución y aprendizaje permenente, *Gestión y Análisis de Políticas Públicas*, vol. 4, pp. 37–46.

Chapter 8

Austria: Adaptation through Anticipation

PAUL LUIF

Introduction

The relations with the EC/EU have been an important element of Austrian politics for a long time. After being part of a multinational empire for centuries, its place on the geopolitical map of Europe was not well established subsequent to the break-up of the Austro-Hungarian monarchy. In the aftermath of the Second World War, Austria's political élite strove to secure the country a place as part of western Europe. The main reasons for this change from the former more central European orientation were, on the one hand, the reduction of (economic) contacts with its neighbours in the East, due to the Iron Curtain; on the other hand, the communism of east central Europe had no attraction for the large majority of the élite and population. They wanted the country to be anchored in the democratic and economically successful western part of the continent.

But to become a full member of the institution that organized western Europe in a new way, the EC/EU, took more than 40 years. Membership was achieved at a time when the rigid East–West frontier had already disappeared. This chapter starts with a short look back at the history of Austria's integration policy and how the country finally joined the EU. The adaptation to membership, in particular the development of the decision-making structures, will receive close attention. A discussion of political and strategic adaptation concludes the chapter.

The road to EU membership

Already in the early 1950s, when the country was still occupied by the four Allies, Austria's government tried to secure a special relationship with the new European Coal and Steel Community. Its large trade with western Europe (in particular with West Germany) warranted secure access to the markets of the ECSC countries. Austria gained its full independence through the State Treaty from May 1955 and its Constitutional Law from October 1955. In spite of its newly acquired international status, politicians of the grand coalition government started to talk about joining the ECSC – which would most probably also have led to membership of the emerging EEC. The Community side seems to have indicated interest as well. Somewhat surprisingly in view of their later position that joining the Common Market was inconsistent with its neutrality, Austria was apparently felt by some West Europeans to be a useful 'land-bridge' between Italy and the rest (Luif, 1995: 185).

The Soviet criticism of Austria's (verbal) behaviour during the Hungarian uprising made its politicians more cautious and curbed their interest in ECSC/EEC membership. There were also domestic reasons. The small and medium-sized companies, an important clientele of the conservative Christian Democratic People's Party (ÖVP), feared increased competition from the EEC countries. The Socialists (SPÖ), after being the champions of integration with western Europe, changed their attitudes in the late 1950s and started to oppose a liberalization of the markets which would reduce their political influence by decreasing the power of the nationalized industries and the trade unions.

The way out for these politicians and interest groups was to counterbalance the EEC by the creation of the European Free Trade Association (EFTA) in 1960 together with six other non-EEC states. The EFTA member-states retained their independent economic policy. In 1972, Austria and the other EFTA states not joining the EC signed free trade agreements (for industrial goods, but not for agricultural products) with the EC.

An intensive debate on EC membership first started in the mid-1980s, earlier than in the other EFTA countries. The reasons were, on the one hand, the relatively bad economic performance of its industry (especially its nationalized part) at that time; on the other hand, several scandals led to a general decline of confidence in the 'island of the blessed' image that the country had, in particular during the rule of the charismatic Bruno Kreisky (SPÖ), Austrian chancellor from 1970 to 1983.[1] Just at that time the 'new dynamics' of the EC (completion of the internal market and implementation of the SEA) was in full swing. First big business, but then also the small and medium-sized companies, pushed for EC membership. Accession to the EC became very popular and the ÖVP jumped on the EC train to become the 'party of Europe'. The trade unions and particularly the SPÖ were more reluctant, but finally also accepted application for membership.

Inside the EC, many voices were raised against an early enlargement, 'deepening first' being the slogan. It was Jacques Delors who in January 1989 proposed the creation of an European Economic Area (EEA) as an alternate route for a very close relationship between the EFTA states and the EC. The Austrians, like all the other EFTA members, accepted this offer. But most Austrian officials did not see the EEA as an alternative to EC membership, only as a further step toward accession. On 17 July 1989, Foreign Minister Alois Mock (ÖVP) delivered the Austrian membership application in Brussels. It contained a neutrality clause. At that time it seemed that this clause would cause problems for the Austrians. But the geopolitical changes in Europe in connection with the fall of the Berlin Wall on 9 November 1989 made the neutrality clause of little relevance for attaining membership.

The rather difficult negotiations on the EEA proved the Austrian politicians right. The EC could not offer full participation in the internal market for outsiders, as the optimists from the EFTA side had hoped for. A ruling of the EC Court of Justice and a negative referendum in Switzerland led to a postponement of the ratification of the EEA Treaty. It finally came into force on 1 January 1994, at a time when Austria as well as Finland, Norway and Sweden were in the final rounds of their membership negotiations with the EU.

The adaptation process

The period before membership

In January 1987, a new grand coalition government of SPÖ and ÖVP replaced the small coalition government which had consisted of the SPÖ and the increasingly nationalistic Freedom Party (FPÖ). The new government declared that intensifying Austria's relations with the EC was a 'central objective' of its foreign policy.[2] Foreign Minister Alois Mock (ÖVP) conceived the global approach for Austria's participation in the internal market of the EC. In this way, Austria would aim to take part in the total substance, the four freedoms of the internal market. The previous pragmatic and sectoral approach, whereby Austria would participate only in some aspects of the internal market, was not deemed satisfactory.

In connection with this global approach, the Working Group for European Integration was created by the government. This group carried out the first in-depth analyses of the compatibility of Austria's legal order with the EC rules. All ministries, except the defence ministry, participated in this endeavour. In typical Austrian fashion, officials from the Liaison Office of the Austrian Provinces, the Austrian National Bank and the social partners (the Federal Chamber of Commerce, the Council of the Chambers of Labour, the President's Conference of the Chambers of Agriculture and the Federation of Austrian Industrialists)[3] participated in the meetings of the working group and its subgroups as well.

Up to then few parts of the administration had any systematic contact with the EC, the exceptions being the foreign ministry and the foreign trade ministry (since April 1987 called the Ministry of Economics). The final report of this first broad review of Austria's relations with the EC hinted more or less clearly that only EC membership would enable full participation in the internal market.[4] The next step in contacts with EC matters were the negotiations with the EC on the EEA. All ministries (again except the defence ministry) and the social partners as well as representatives of the provinces were involved in these negotiations. Since all rules concerning the internal market (excluding agriculture) would be part of the EEA, the negotiators had to go through the relevant *acquis communautaire*. It was during this time period that Austrian civil servants for the first time acquired the relevant know-how and expertise.[5] Practically all federal ministries set up EC departments which have since been in charge of the horizontal coordination of EC matters in their respective ministry.

In March 1992, at the end of the negotiations on the EEA, the federal government concluded an agreement with the nine Austrian provinces on their participation in integration matters, in particular concerning decisions on the EEA.[6] In addition, the provinces reached an understanding among themselves on how to implement these decision-making powers. For this purpose, they created an Integration Conference of the Provinces where the provincial governors (*Landeshauptleute*) could decide unanimously on the position of the provinces in integration matters.[7] In October 1992, Chancellor Franz Vranitzky and the provincial governors signed a Political Agreement on the Reorganization of the Federal State. The intention of this agreement was to give the provinces new powers as a compensation for the eventual losses of

Table 8.1 The results of the EU referenda in the EFTA applicant countries (percentages)

Date	Country	'Yes'	'No'	Turnout
12 June 1994	Austria	66.6	33.4	82.3
16 October 1994	Finland	56.9	43.1	74.0
13 November 1994	Sweden	52.7	47.3	83.3
27/28 November 1994	Norway	47.7	52.3	88.6

Notes: The results for the Swedish referendum were calculated like the results in the other countries, i.e. the blank votes were excluded from the calculation of 'yes' and 'no', but included in the turnout. When calculating the 'official way', the results in Sweden were 52.3% 'yes', 46.8% 'no' and 0.9% blank votes.
Source: Luif (1995), p. 320.
Reproduced by kind permission of Wilhelm Braumüller.

competencies that an EC/EU membership would bring for Austria's provinces (Schaller, 1996: 191–4).

Even more intensive contacts with EC/EU matters took place during the negotiations on EU membership which started on 1 February 1993 and ended on 1 March 1994. The Austrian negotiators had to admit that the EU side was much better versed in the bargaining that these negotiations involved.[8] After the signing of the Accession Treaty on 24 June 1994, representatives of Austria could participate in all meetings of EU bodies as 'active observers'. But only a short time was left to get acquainted with the EU political and bureaucratic system and its working traditions.

On 1 January 1995, Austria, together with Finland and Sweden, became a member of the EU. The Austrian public was very favourable to EU membership, as expressed in the EU referendum. According to Table 8.1, it had by far the highest percentage voting for EU membership, compared to the other applicant countries.

The decision-making processes at the level of the federal ministries

Austria joined the EU in a quite advanced phase of integration, at a time when the Union's structures had already been developed for more than 40 years. From the start of its membership, which practically involved no transitional periods,[9] almost all areas of Austria's domestic politics were immediately affected.

There already existed several models for organizing an EU member-state's participation in EU decision-making, basically either the very centralized model of France (or Great Britain) or the much more decentralized model of Germany. For the choice of Austria's adaptation, its domestic structure had a decisive influence. First, Austria is one of the smaller EU countries. Second, it has a federal structure of government, but one that is somewhat more centralized than Germany's. And finally, Austria possesses a, for various reasons weakened but still viable, consensus-oriented political and administrative system based on the grand coalition government and on the close cooperation of the social partners (Morass, 1996: 81).

One expression of this political system was the huge delegations on the Austrian side during the membership negotiations. Not only ministers and high-ranking civil servants participated in these delegations, but also representatives of the provincial governments and from the social partners. Austria's PR is one of the largest in Brussels, since it houses, besides people from the foreign ministry and most other ministries, officials from the provinces and the social partners under one roof. In addition to that, all Austrian provinces (except Vorarlberg) now have their own representations in Brussels. At the same time, most provinces reduced or even closed their representations in Vienna.

For each issue area to be debated and decided in Brussels, the competent federal ministry has been put in charge of preparing Austria's position in Brussels, be it for the preparatory groups of the Commission and of the Council or for the decision-making in the Council itself. Many issues discussed in Brussels often cut across the competencies of several ministries in Austria and thus involve more then one ministry. To ensure coordination, a list of responsible federal ministrie (*federführende Bundesministerien*) had to be established (Morass, 1996: 81).

The responsible ministry is in charge of the Austrian preparations for the decision-making processes in the EU Council. The first step in this procedure is coordinating the Austrian position for the working groups in the Council. These preparations are usually made through so-called interministerial meetings which should take place at least once a month in the responsible ministry.[10] Interministerial meetings have a long tradition in Austrian bureaucratic life and have been the instrument for various coordination processes in the federal ministries. The responsible ministry usually invites officials from other relevant ministries, from the Liaison Office of the Austrian Provinces, the social partners (including frequently the Federation of Austrian Industrialists) and in some cases officials from the Austrian National Bank, the Austrian Court of Auditors and other institutions. The decisions in these interministerial meetings are normally made by consensus; the officials of the responsible ministry, who in theory could decide on their own, almost never do so in practice.

There exists a wide variation for the procedures followed in the preparations of the Council working groups. The decision process in the economics ministry follows a clear schedule. There the interministerial meetings for preparing, for example, the Article 113 Committee, take place every week on Thursdays. The Ministry for Work and Social Affairs also regularly convenes interministerial meetings. If the social partners cannot agree on a common approach, the Austrian representative will not take position in the Council working group or will do so with a reservation (*ad referendum*). In contrast to most other ministries, the finance ministry usually readies its positions for the Council working groups internally and contacts other ministries and the social partners only informally (Karlhofer and Tálos, 1996: 147–8).[11]

Most of the time, Council working groups matters are regarded as routine affairs. In such routine (technical) matters, after the ministry officials have made up their mind through the interministerial meetings (or in other ways), an instruction is sent by the responsible ministry to the Austrian representative in the Council working group (usually a person from the PR in Brussels). A copy of the instruction is also to be sent to the Federal Chancellery (the prime minister's office) and the foreign ministry.[12] In non-routine matters (e.g. matters where more than one ministry is legally responsible), the appropriate way is to send the instruction to Brussels via the foreign ministry, with a copy to the Federal Chancellery.

The next level of Council decision-making, the COREPER meetings, are jointly prepared by the Federal Chancellery and the foreign ministry. Every week on Tuesdays, starting at 2pm, officials from all ministries,[13] representatives from all social partners, the Liaison Office of the Austrian Provinces and if necessary officials from other institutions meet for the so-called *jour fixe*. Before, two groups were involved in the coordination of integration matters: the already mentioned Working Group for European Integration (headed by an official from the ÖVP-dominated foreign ministry) and the Working Group for Integration Questions which was created in 1989 by the federal chancellor from the SPÖ. At the end of 1992, these two groups started to meet together for preparing the membership negotiations. Since this arrangement proved to be too cumbersome, the *jour fixe* was created in May 1993 for the preparatory meetings during the membership negotiations (Itzlinger, 1996: 63–4; Morass, 1996: 82). At the *jour fixe*, most of the time only a 'finishing rub' is called for since about 80–90 per cent of the issues have already been decided; problems still remaining usually concern more political questions. The *jour fixe* is generally used as a coordination forum. For the social partners it is also a kind of 'control' forum where they can check whether their requests in the interministerial meetings have been adhered to. The meetings are alternately presided over by high officials from the Federal Chancellery and the foreign ministry. At the end of the *jour fixe*, the instructions for the upcoming COREPER meeting are sent via the foreign ministry to the Austrian Permanent Representative in Brussels.

The EU Council meetings are again prepared by the responsible ministries in interministerial meetings (with the participants already mentioned above). They usually take place one or two weeks before the respective EU Council; preferably before the last COREPER meeting preparing the Council meeting. The result of the interministerial meeting has to be recorded in a 'result report' (*Ergebnisbericht*) which must be sent to the concerned authorities as well as to the Federal Chancellery and the foreign ministry. Important questions could also be debated and decided in the cabinet. To improve the coordination of the government's positions in the EU bodies, the cabinet now discusses Austria's EU policy regularly at its weekly meetings. This new coordination effort was introduced by the new government in March 1996. It can be regarded as an answer to the demands for better coordination of Austria's EU policies.

The meetings of the European Council are jointly prepared by the Federal Chancellery and the foreign ministry. The federal chancellor is the Austrian representative at the European Council, accompanied by the foreign minister. After some quarrels with the chancellor, the president, who is directly elected by the population in Austria, abandoned his request for regular participation in the European Councils and only takes part on ceremonial occasions and without any political mandate.

For the Commission expert groups no such formal decision procedures exist. Here the Commission itself decides who will participate; the experts in these groups do not get instructions from the member-states.

All participants agree that the road to EU membership and in particular EU membership itself entailed wide-ranging adaptation processes for the Austrian federal ministries. One important impact not yet mentioned has come from the very short time-frame for the preparation of decisions concerning EU matters. The civil servants in the ministries must decide EU questions much more quickly than they were used to in domestic matters. This has called for more flexible structure and behaviour, and less formal file handling in formal – legalistic bureaucratic procedures. Modern means of communication (*e-mail, fax*) are used extensively. The civil servants employed in the EU departments of the ministries are usually younger, have better knowledge of foreign languages and possess more management skills than the average Austrian civil servant.[14]

These decentralized and informal decision-making processes generally fit well with the Austrian system of social partnership (the Austrian variant of neo-corporatism). Social partnership has always meant informal, consensus-oriented cooperation – very similar to the way that EU matters are now basically handled in Austria. The lack of time for decision even strengthens the need for consensus. It is also the best way to bolster Austrian interests in Brussels. Still, as we will see, problems continue to exist.

Before membership, a debate raged among specialists over whether the system of social partnership could survive accession to the EU. After more than a year of membership, specialists think that the Austrian system of cooperation between business and trade unions will remain – albeit with significant modifications. The social partners were heavily involved in paving the way for Austria's EU accession. On several occasions they supported with common platforms the endeavours of the government. Acknowledging their assistance for attaining EU membership, the social partners have been intensely involved in Austrian EU decision-making. To help them in preparing their participation in EU matters, they obtained the legal right to get all the relevant information from the Austrian government.[15]

But Austrian social partnership has already lost its formerly comprehensive influence on almost all ways of life in Austria. Therefore it is expected that the social partners will concentrate on specific issues in the future, concerning in particular economic policy, incomes policy, social policy and environmental questions. On questions to be decided in Brussels, they will have to act as a (quite forceful) lobby, but only as one among fifteen member-states (Karlhofer and Tálos, 1996: 179).

The participation of the provinces and the federal Parliament in EU decision-making[16]

The Austrian provinces (*Bundesländer*) and the federal Parliament can influence the EU decision-making process in Austria directly. It was mentioned that representatives of the provinces sit in the preparatory groups. But their influence goes beyond this informal method. In connection with Austria's impending membership in the EEA, an agreement was concluded between the federal government and the provinces concerning the provinces' participation in the decision-making regarding integration matters (see above). These rules were adapted for EU membership. The reform of the federal state, also intended in connection with accession to the EU, was not achieved. The offer made by the federal authorities was rejected by the provinces as being insufficient and too costly (Schaller, 1996: 194).

The new Article 23d of the federal constitution regulates the participation of Austria's provinces in determining the behaviour of the Austrian representatives in the EU Council. The federal government has to inform as soon as possible the provinces and municipalities of all 'plans' (*Vorhaben*)[17] of the EU that touch upon the legislative powers and important interests of these regional and local entities. When the provinces agree on a common position (*einheitliche Stellungnahme*), the Austrian representative is bound by this position and has to adjust his or her (voting) behaviour in the Council accordingly.[18] The Austrian representative can deviate from the provinces' common positions only in case of 'compelling reasons concerning foreign or integration policy'.[19]

The federal government can transfer the right to participate in the EU Council (but not in the European Council) to a representative nominated by the provinces for issues where the provinces have the power to legislate.[20] The representative has to exercise this right in coordination with the competent minister of the federal government. The power of the Austrian *Bundesländer* in EU matters, which resembles the influence of the German *Länder* on EU decision-making, is a clear expression of Austria's federal structure.

The federal Parliament's control of the Austrian representative in the Council is regulated in Article 23e of the federal constitution. The competent minister of the government has to inform both houses of Parliament as soon as possible of all plans concerning the first, second and third pillar of the EU. The Nationalrat (the lower and more important house of Parliament) can take a position at any time on a matter that concerns the planned adoption in the Council of a regulation, a directive or a decision with legislative effects and which in domestic matters would pertain to the competencies of the Austrian federal authorities. These decisions are not made in the plenary session of the Nationalrat, and the specialized committees of the Nationalrat are not involved in decisions on EU matters. Article 23e(5) of the federal constitution puts the Main Committee (*Hauptausschuß*) of the Nationalrat in charge of this task. The Main Committee meets behind closed doors. The positions it takes are not published since, in general, documents concerning the work of the EU Council are not publicly available. The Main Committee plays an important role in the decision system of the Nationalrat and is involved in the execution of various Austrian laws. The addition of EU matters to its agenda has enormously increased its workload.[21]

The Austrian representative (the competent minister of the federal government) is bound to the position of the Main Committee during the negotiations and at the voting in the EU Council. Once again, the representative can deviate from positions of the Main Committee only in the case of 'compelling reasons concerning foreign or integration policy'. But the minister may deviate from the position only after the Main Committee has again considered the matter. If the planned legislative act of the EU would mean a change of the Austrian federal constitution, the minister can only deviate from the position of the Main Committee if the committee does not oppose this deviation within a reasonable period of time.[22] In case a position was taken by the Main Committee, the minister has to inform the Main Committee after the vote took place in the EU Council. In particular, he or she must explain the reasons for any deviation from the position of the Main Committee.

If the minister (or other representative) does not act in the Council according to the position of the Main Committee or the common position of the provinces, he or she can be brought to trial before the constitutional court by a simple majority of the plenary session of the Nationalrat or by majority decisions in all parliaments of the provinces (Article 142(2)c of the Austrian constitution). This legal control of Austria's representative in the Council is supplemented and in practice most probably superseded by the political responsibility of the minister in the federal Parliament. According to Article 74 of the Austrian federal constitution, a minister has to resign if a vote of 'no confidence' is passed by a simple majority of the Nationalrat.

The most controversial part of the Parliament's participation in Austria's EU decision-making is without doubt the question of how far the Austrian representative can deviate from the position of the Main Committee (or the common position of the provinces). The room for manoeuvre depends on the interpretation of the escape clause, the 'compelling reasons concerning foreign or integration policy'. The federal government commented in its bill that such a need for deviation could arise 'when this is irrefutable for the protection of important Austrian interests'.[23] This rather vague definition leaves the door open for all kinds of interpretations. The legal and political responsibility lies with the Austrian representative when he or she wants to deviate from the position of the Parliament/provinces. Concerning the legal aspects, in the final instance it will be up to the constitutional court to interpret this clause.

The experience with using this right to give instructions, which goes further than the influence of, for example, the Danish Parliament, has been mixed. At the beginning, the Nationalrat wanted to give detailed instructions to the Austrian minister in the EU Council. It turned out that such tight rules for behaviour left no leeway for negotiations. Since many decisions in the Council are part of a package deal, the bargaining power of the Austrian minister was actually weakened. Therefore, the positions of the Nationalrat are now less strictly formulated and give the Austrian minister some room for manoeuvre. Since the Main Committee meets only every other week to discuss EU matters, it can concentrate only on a few topics that will be discussed in the coming EU Councils.[24] The handling of EU matters in the Nationalrat is still disputed among the political parties. On several occasions, the Greens complained that other parties blocked the discussion of relevant topics in the Main Committee.

Political adaptation

An example for political adaptation: neutrality policy

Besides these adaptations in decision-making, the Austrian authorities had to make far-ranging adjustments to align Austrian law to the *acquis communautaire*. As already mentioned, this process had started in the late 1980s and gained speed with the ratification of the EEA Agreement. One important aspect of adjustment, which was not touched directly by the efforts of the 1980s or the EEA, was Austria's neutrality status.

Here the basic problem was a rather paradoxical effect of the EU's three-pillar structure. In the supranational first pillar, legal acts (directives and regulations) of the EU have direct effect in the member-states and supersede all national law, even constitutional law. Therefore decisions in the first pillar would also supersede the Austrian neutrality law; no domestic adjustments would (in theory) be necessary. But since the EU's foreign policy pertains to its intergovernmental second pillar, Austria's neutrality law would have priority over decisions taken in the EU's Common Foreign and Security Policy; they would have no effect in Austria if they contradicted Austria's neutrality. The new Article 23f(1) of the Austrian federal constitution takes care of this problem: Austria participates in the CFSP of the EU on the basis of Title V of the TEU. This includes participation in measures with which economic relations with one or more non-EU countries are interrupted or in part or completely reduced.[25]

The government's comments on the bill stated that there existed no contradiction between participation in the CFSP and the core elements of Austria's neutrality. The wording of Article 23f(1) was a compromise between the reluctant Social Democrats and the ÖVP, which wanted as few restrictions for Austria's EU policy as possible. The comments of the government affirmed that this article allowed Austria to participate in sanctions decided in the framework of the CFSP and named economic sanctions as the 'most important example'.[26] Article 23f of the federal constitution annuls all Austrian laws in contradiction with it, but the range of its effects would finally depend on the interpretation of the constitutional court which can rule on the constitutionality of ordinary law.

Some critics have written that the words of Article 23f 'lack clarity'; they have apparently been chosen to make the changes of Austria's neutrality status not too obvious (Zemanek, 1994: 9). The comments of the government added that the bill 'focuses on the law in force in the European Union' at this time. If there were a change of the EU's legal order in the future, a decision on an 'appropriate revision of the domestic legal situation' would then have to be made.[27]

Strategic adaptation

Since the discussions on EC/EU membership started in the mid-1980s, Austrian authorities had a longer time to contemplate their country's position in the EU, compared to the other new members. But several factors have hampered Austria's strategic adaptation to membership.

The competencies of the Austrian ministries do not conform to the distribution of tasks among the EU Councils. Therefore tight coordination among the ministries is indispensable to present a common position in Brussels. But Austria's federal constitution gives each minister full responsibility for the ministry. The chancellor, as head of the cabinet, is only *primus inter pares*; he or she has no formal power to give guidelines or instructions to the ministers. In this respect, the position of the Austrian chancellor is even weaker than that of the German chancellor. In practice, the Austrian chancellor can influence the ministers, because usually he or she is the head of the most important party in government; but this power extends only to the ministers of his or her own party (Mueller, 1992: 121). The system of 'responsible ministries', which should have made EU coordination easier, is far from perfect. Therefore it is often hard to create an 'Austrian profile' for EU matters. In addition, the Austrian legal system puts a tight rein on the authorities. All state behaviour has to be based on written law. In its extreme form this principle forbids behaviour that cannot prove its legal foundations. The pragmatic decision-making processes in connection with the EU often find their limit in legal constraints.

Before Austria's accession, the government had to avoid any resemblance of too close a relationship with Germany, since some EU members would have resented a strengthening of the 'Germanic bloc'. Because of language, geographical location and comparable political and economic systems, Austria and Germany often do have similar positions in EU matters. This does not impede the existence of important differences as well, e.g. Austria's transit traffic policy is often criticized by German (in particular Bavarian) politicians. But a tight cooperation with Germany would not always be helpful in advancing Austrian interests. However, Austria does not have any natural partners like, for example, the Nordic or the Benelux countries have inside the EU. A partnership among the EU's four neutral members (or among its non-WEU members, which would also include Denmark) is not possible for domestic political reasons. Whereas the SPÖ would favour such a grouping in CFSP matters, the ÖVP is strictly against the creation of a neutral bloc since it wants Austria to abandon its neutral status and to become full member of the WEU (and NATO). In general, neutrality would be of little relevance for most areas of EU politics.

This problematic situation has been recognized by the Federal Chamber of Commerce. Its basic idea is that EU membership entails a permanent negotiation process. Therefore Austria should develop a 'comprehensive strategy' to succeed in asserting its interests. This should be secured by 'creating *alliances with like-minded partners in the Union*'. But to implement this strategy, an '*extensive coordination of the Austrian interests*' has to be set up early on, which would support and expand the coordination already instituted in preparing the COREPER and the EU Council meetings. Fundamental positions should be decided – after discussions with the social partners – by the cabinet.[28] The demands of the Federal Chamber of Commerce clearly put the finger on the sore spot of Austria's EU adaptation. It lacks a strategic approach in EU matters. The IGC, Austria's presidency in the second half of 1998 and the impending enlargement toward the east could be occasions to rethink and improve Austria's strategic position in the EU.

Conclusion

To make the country, in contrast to the other new members, part of the EU's 'hard core' could be regarded as an attempt at a more strategic outlook for Austria's EU policy. Already in January 1995, Austria joined the ERM of the European Monetary System (EMS). In April 1995, it signed the Schengen Agreement. Austria plans

Table 8.2 Implementation of the EU directives concerning
the internal market (15 May 1996, percentages)

Denmark	99.5
Netherlands	97.7
Sweden	96.8
Luxemburg	95.5
Great Britain	95.0
Spain	94.5
Portugal	94.5
France	94.1
Ireland	93.2
Italy	91.8
Greece	90.4
Belgium	90.0
Germany	90.0
Finland	84.5
Austria	80.4

Source: EU Commission, taken from *Der Standard*,
31 May 1996, p. 25. Reproduced by kind permission of
Oscar Bronner GmbH, Austria.

to abolish the border controls for persons (the controls for goods were abolished the day Austria became an EU member) *vis-à-vis* the Schengen states in mid-1997. This intention of the government can be also recognized in the positions that Austria has taken at the IGC. Here the country is among those members that want a further deepening of the EU structures.[29] Federalism has no negative connotation in Austria.

But one can doubt whether Austria really is a 'good European'. Table 8.2 is an example of Austria's sloppiness concerning its obligations to carry out EU rules. In fact, it implemented fewer directives for the internal market than any other EU member-state by May 1996, almost one and a half years after accession. In defence of Austria it could be argued that federal states (among the bottom four EU member-states of Table 8.2, three are federal states) have particular problems in implementing EU rules because more than one level of government is involved.

Among the general public, the early euphoria about EU membership has gone (cf. Table 8.1). Recent public opinion polls show that a majority of Austrians would now vote against EU membership.[30] It seems that various quarrels that the Austrian authorities have had and still have with Brussels have negatively influenced the attitudes of the Austrians. One of the most glaring examples in this respect has been the issue of the 'anonymous savings accounts'. In Austria, any person can open an account without providing any information on his or her identity. Formally there is a limit on the monetary amount for opening such an account. This practice breaks EU rules and has been used to whitewash illegal money. In practice, this rule is not heeded. Although the Commission has demanded a change of Austrian law, the government indicated that it wants to defend the anonymous savings accounts, even if this would bring Austria before the EU Court of Justice.

When the EU Commissioner from Austria, Franz Fischler, defended the position of the Commission, he was strongly criticized in the media, but also by the leaders of practically all political parties for not supporting Austrian interests. It seems that the adaptation process, as far as the minds of the Austrians are concerned, still has a long way to go.

Notes

1. In January 1985, the Austrian defence minister welcomed Walter Reder, a Nazi war criminal, back to Austrian soil. The 'wine scandal' gained international notoriety in July 1985. The discussion about Kurt Waldheim's behaviour during the Second World War started in March 1986. In spite of his evasive answers about his past, Waldheim, candidate of the ÖVP, was elected president of Austria in June 1986.
2. Erklärung der Bundesregierung vor dem Nationalrat von Bundeskanzler Dr Franz Vranitzky, 28.1.1987, Vienna: Bundespressedienst, pp. 32–3.
3. In the official terminology, the 'social partners' in Austria consist of four 'peak' organizations: Federal Chamber of Commerce, Council of the Chambers of Labour (now Federal Chamber of Labour), the President's Conference of the Chambers of Agriculture, and the Austrian Trade Union Federation. The Federation of Austrian Industrialists is not part of this group, but is often also involved in consultations.
4. See Bericht der Arbeitsgruppe für Europäische Integration an die Bundesregierung, Vienna, 20.6.1988, mimeo.
5. Except for the foreign ministry and the economics ministry, which already had extensive contacts with the EC.
6. Vereinbarung zwischen dem Bund und den Ländern gemäß Artikel 15a B-VG über die Mitwirkungsrechte der Länder und Gemeinden in Angelegenheiten der europäischen Integration, Bundesgesetzblatt 1992/775, reprinted in: Kodex des österreichischen Rechts. Verfassungsrecht, Stand 1.9.1995, Vienna: Orac 1995, pp. 46–9.
7. Vereinbarung zwischen den Ländern gemäß Artikel 15a B-VG über die gemeinsame Willensbildung der Länder in Angelegenheiten der europäischen Integration; the version from the Official Journal of Vienna is reprinted in Kodex, note 7, pp. 53–4.
8. On the membership negotiations, in particular the final phase, see the eyewitness account by Woschnagg, 1996: 129–42.
9. Important exceptions concerned transitional periods in environmental matters (four years), the legislation regarding secondary residences (five years) and transit traffic (a system involving three times three years). However, EEA membership (lasting only one year, from 1 January 1994 to 31 December 1994) could be regarded as some kind of general transitional phase.
10. This is demanded by the Federal Chancellery and the foreign ministry in their position on the legal and organizational questions of Austria's EU membership; see Bundeskanzleram/ Bundesministerium für auswärtige Angelegenheiten, Rechtliche und organisatorische Fragen der EU-Mitgliedschaft, Rundschreiben, Vienna, 19 January 1996, mimeo, p. 10.
11. Information on the ministries' preparations are from Karlhofer and Tálos (1996), pp. 147–8.
12. This information could be used for coordination purposes, but also for political control – since in the grand coalition government the federal chancellor has always been a Social Democrat and the foreign minister a member of the ÖVP.
13. Officials of the defence ministry take part only when matters concerning security (as regards the EU's second pillar) are discussed.

14. Several of them have also graduated or worked at the College of Europe in Bruges, the European Institute of Public Administration in Maastricht, as *stagiaires* in the EU Commission or the European Parliament, etc.

15. Their right to information is similar to that of the Austrian provinces and the federal Parliament; see below.

16. This and the next section are partly taken from Luif (1995: 333/334).

17. There exists no comprehensive definitions of what *Vorhaben* means, but one could list among them, in particular, proposals of the Commission and reports of the Austrian PR in Brussels. There is an incomplete list of such 'plans' in the Vereinbarung zwischen dem Bund und den Ländern (see note 7).

18. The municipalities do not have this right.

19. This wording has been taken from a German law implementing the SEA; see Bundesk-anzleramt/Bundesministerium, note 15, p. 6.

20. Article 146 EC Treaty, as amended by the TEU, allows the participation of 'a representative of each Member State at ministerial level' in the EU Council. Previously, Article 2 of the Merger Treaty had stipulated that '[e]ach Government shall delegate to it [the Council] one of its members'.

21. Article 23e(5) allows the creation of a subcommittee of the Main Committee for EU matters. So far, this has not been done.

22. This further restriction was added at the insistence of the opposition parties in the Parliament's Constitution Committee.

23. See Regierungsvorlage: Bundesverfassungsgesetz, mit dem das Bundes-Verfassungsgesetz in der Fassung von 1929 abgeändert und das EWR-Bundesverfassungsgesetz aufgehoben wird. 27 der Beilagen zu den Stenographischen Protokollen des Nationalrates, XIX. Gesetzgebungsperiode, November 1994, pp. 9–10.

24. For a detailed analysis, see Luif (1995: 343–6).

25. Translation Paul Luif; the second sentence of this paragraph closely follows parts of Article 228a, EC Treaty.

26. Regierungsvorlage (note 23), p. 7.

27. Regierungsvorlage (note 23), p. 8. New developments in the EU could mean, for example, that the WEU would be included into the EU's framework and the EU would thus become a military alliance. Since the report only talks about a domestic adjustment and does not mention a change in Austria's international legal situation, it has practically accepted the thesis that there exists no international legal obligation for Austria to maintain its neutrality status.

28. These theses were published in a paper putting demands to the new government; see Österreichs Zukunft sichern. Das Forderungsprogramm der Wirtschaftskammern für die neue Legislaturperiode, Vienna: Wirtschaftskammer Österreich, January 1996, quotes from p. 35, emphases in the original.

29. See, for example, the editorial in *Le Monde*, 31 March/1 April 1996, p. 12, where Austria is put with the six founding members and Spain among the *pays de consensus*.

30. In one poll from early May 1996, 53 per cent of Austrians said that they would now vote against EU membership and only 42 per cent said that they would vote for membership; OGM opinion poll, N=1,000, quoted from *Die Presse*, 31 May 1996, p. 7.

References

Itzlinger, A. (1996) Österreichs Vorbereitungen auf die Europäische Union. In A. Rothacher, M. Zemanek and W. Hargasser (eds) *Österreichs europäische Zukunft. Analysen und Perspektiven* (Vienna: Signum), pp. 51–69.

Karlhofer, F. and Tálos, E. (1996) *Sozialpartner und EU. Integrationsdynamik und Handlungsrahmen der österreichischen Sozialpartnerschaft* (Vienna: Signum).

Luif, P. (1995) *On the Road to Brussels: The Political Dimension of Austria's, Finland's and Sweden's Accession to the European Union* (Vienna: Braumüller).

Morass, M. (1996) *Österreich in der Europäischen Union. Strukturen der Mitwirkung in den EU-Institutionen,* Informationen zur Politischen Bildung, no. 10 (1995/96), pp. 77–92.

Mueller, W.C. (1992) Regierung und Kabinettsystem. In Herbert Dachs *et al.* (eds) *Handbuch des politischen Systems Österreichs,* 2nd edn (Vienna: Manz), pp. 118–33.

Schaller, C. (1996) Die österreichische EG/EU-Diskussion in den Ländern. In A. Rothacher, M. Zemanek and W. Hargasser (eds) *Österreichs europäische Zukunft. Analysen und Perspektiven* (Vienna: Signum), pp. 183–234.

Woschnagg, G. (1996) Die EU-Beitrittsverhandlungen Österreichs. In A. Rothacher, M. Zemanek and W. Hargassner (eds) *Österreichs europäische Zukunft. Analysen und Perspektiven* (Vienna: Signum), pp. 129–42.

Zemanek, K. (1994) Österreichs Neutralität und die GSAP, *Österreichisches Jahrbuch für Internationale Politik,* pp. 1–17.

Chapter 9

Sweden: The State Joins the European Union

MAGNUS EKENGREN AND BENGT SUNDELIUS

Introduction

In this chapter the Swedish experiences in dealing with the administrative and political–strategic changes resulting from its new and formalized West European involvement will be analysed. The adaptations of national institutions, policies and strategies undertaken in the face of the revitalized European integration phase of the late 1980s and early 1990s will be outlined. Second, the demands of full membership from 1 January 1995 on material and human resources for governance at home, and on the personal involvements in a myriad of intensive European collaboration networks across multiple sectors will be traced. Constitutional issues, administrative structures, policy processes, the prevailing logic of appropriate procedures, policies and state strategies have been greatly affected by the requirements of membership.

The initial year of membership was devoted to keeping the Swedish head above the steadily rising EU water level. At the same time, however, some new ideas were articulated within the relevant ministries on how to improve the administrative and technical capacity for a more proactive and potentially influential posture in prioritized policy areas. After all, a primary argument for membership had been that only through that formal step could Sweden move beyond a series of national adjustments to Brussels toward having an impact upon European policy in the making. The strategies for influence on EU decisions considered within the government machinery will be noted, although the record is still vague on this more elusive aspect of adaptation. The practical results of this new Europe-focused strategic thinking within the Swedish foreign relations élite remains to be seen.

National traditions, dogmas and practices disbanded

The Swedish form of government conforms to the West European pattern of pure parliamentarianism. The executive functions of government are handled by the cabinet, whose authority rests on the support of a majority in the Parliament. During most of contemporary Swedish political history, the Social Democratic Party has formed majority or minority governments. Exceptions to this reign by the left were in 1976–82 and 1991–94, when non-socialist coalitions governed the nation. The Social Democratic Prime Minister Ingvar Carlsson, who brought Sweden into the Union, resigned in March 1996 and was followed by the former Finance Minister Göran Persson.

In Sweden the management of foreign relations rests firmly in the hands of the executive branch of government. The role of Parliament is primarily formal in most foreign policy questions not involving any legislative elements, such as treaty ratification or appropriations. Typically, parliamentary control of foreign policy is conducted *ex post facto*. A select group of senior parliamentarians from the major parties serve on the Advisory Foreign Affairs Committee, created in 1921 and chaired by the monarch. A parallel Advisory Committee for European Union Affairs has been established for weekly briefings by the ministers prior to the meetings of the Council of Ministers. This procedure of regular consultation outside the cabinet prior to any major policy initiative accords with the Swedish tradition of building consensus around foreign relations.

National referenda have not been typical of Swedish political history. Instead, the virtues of indirect representation through parliamentary enactments have been emphasized in the constitutional tradition. Exceptions occurred in 1980 over the future of nuclear power and on the EU in November 1994, when a slim 53 per cent majority favoured membership (Björklund, 1996; Gilljam and Holmberg, 1996). In 1996 proposals were made for holding a referendum also on membership of the planned EMU. So far, the government has resisted these overtures. A pattern of polling the public on vital steps in the European integration process, as has developed in Denmark, may be emerging. This would represent a new dimension in Swedish political history.

During the post-war period of East–West conflict in Europe a widely shared sense of loyalty to the official national security doctrine of neutrality was evident. Traditionally, Swedish neutrality was conceived as an instrument by which the state sought to remain outside any armed confrontation in its vicinity. One vital aspect became the credibility of this articulated will and demonstrated ability to remain neutral even under crisis pressure. Swedish involvements with other states or commitments to international organizations were carefully assessed with regard to the implications for this credibility fixation.

In the domestic setting, the requirements of credible neutrality were used as the primary reference point in political debate and in inter-bureaucratic rivalries over national security policy. The Ministry of Foreign Affairs served as the only legitimate interpreter of this doctrine within the state. The dominant Social Democratic Party was its primary protector against potential deviations to the left or to the right. A domestic decision regime for foreign policy, based on the notion of credible neutrality, developed over time (Sundelius, 1989). This domestic control device was reinforced during the tense years of the so-called new cold war of the early to mid-1980s.

During the recent rapid transformation in Europe, the cognitive foundations for this well-entrenched national problem definition began to crumble. Swedish policy-makers only slowly picked up on the new developments. These did not fit well with their schemata for understanding world politics or the Swedish role in superpower relations. After the critical German settlement and the collapse of the Soviet Union, it became obvious that a new mode of dealing with the classical dual Swedish problem formulation of prosperity and security was required. One had to find a revised policy formula for achieving the still important joint objective of continued prosperity and adherence to the deeply entrenched security posture (Sundelius, 1994).

National adaptations to a revitalized European integration phase

The 'step-child' institutional relationship

For Sweden, the forward-looking governmental bill of 1987 on the new dynamics of West European integration (Proposition 1987/88: 66) and the initiation of the negotiations for a European Economic Area in 1989, formed the first phase of the institutional adaptation of the central governmental structures. On the basis of the 1984 Luxemburg declaration and following the political acceptance of the January 1989 invitation by Commission President Delors to a more structured form of collaboration between the EC and EFTA, Sweden launched a number of administrative reforms. Over twenty permanent working groups covering different policy sectors were established to undertake a massive adjustment of national laws and directives to conform with the ensuing harmonization effort inside the EC. This adaptation machinery was comprehensive across policy sectors and unified under the direction of a cabinet-level committee, chaired by the prime minister. A council of representatives for various corporate interests was also attached to this new structure.

A high-ranking official in the trade division of the foreign ministry was appointed to spearhead this highly exceptional coordination and adaptation process. At his disposal was placed a specially created unit for European integration coordination with far-reaching authority. This administrative reform implied a new centralization of the public administration's relations with the Community: the foreign ministry aspired to control the contacts with the EC of the other levels of government by means of 'co-participation' in a growing number of meetings (Ekengren, 1996).

During the EEA negotiations, the political department of the foreign ministry was not directly involved in the comprehensive process toward adjustments of national policy and procedures to conform with EC standards. A special working group for foreign and security policy was chaired by the head of the political department, but this committee was not very highly profiled. Similarly, the Ministry of Defence did not take part in this adjustment process. Except for the then still axiomatic neutrality posture in the security policy area, there was a clear administrative and judicial drive in Sweden already under way before the 1991 application to become fully integrated into the envisioned European internal market (Danielsson, 1988; UDH, 1992a).

Critics of the so-called EFTA track either did not believe that these multilateral negotiations would result in anything concrete, or they feared that the resulting treaty would make EFTA a powerless 'step-child' of Brussels. In this view, the promised European Economic Area was not a sufficient base for competitive Swedish business involvements in the anticipated economic dynamics of the 1990s and beyond. The question of how to secure some influence on EC decision-making concerning the rules for this internal market was left ambiguous until the final phases of the negotiations in 1991. At that time, some judicial problems appeared after the EEA treaty text was reviewed by the European Court.

The reluctant political transformation from being apart to taking part

The image of turning into a small, marginalized nation on the northern fringe of a dynamic European continent haunted most political groups and business leaders as the Delors internal market target of 1992 approached (Hamilton, 1987; Sundelius, 1990). Nevertheless, the Swedish government declared repeatedly during 1989/90 that it was not seeking membership in the Community. Several arguments were presented for this restrictive official position. The supranational character of the EC which by limiting state sovereignty also impacts on neutrality, was a factor. The security and defence policy aspirations of the Community were viewed as incompatible with a neutrality posture. Further, it was argued that the Swedish international role as mediator and bridge-builder in various global conflicts would become less credible if the government were to subject itself to the collective will of the Community. The visible foreign policy profile of Sweden, including its unique development assistance programme, would be eroded through membership (Proposition 1987/88).

After a season of academic exchanges and newspaper debates on the subject, Prime Minister Ingvar Carlsson in May 1990 set in writing the parameters for involvement by the Swedish state in the EC. In contrast to the direction of this authoritative statement, the Swedish government's position on the issue of adaptation to and involvement in European integration processes evidenced a clear forward slide ever since. This relatively speedy departure from the traditional dogma that credible neutrality would be incompatible with membership was made possible through an increasingly positive interpretation of the European security setting. At the opening of the annual parliamentary session on 2 October 1990, the prime minister presented a vision of an evolving Europe, 'with a new peace order and where the bloc divisions have disappeared'. In this security setting, it would be possible to 'combine Swedish EC membership and continued neutrality policy'.[1] Later the same month, in an economic reform package to forestall further balance of payments problems, the government articulated an even clearer ambition to begin negotiations for membership. This statement of intent was followed by a request to Parliament for an official declaration supporting a Swedish application for membership (Skrivelse, 1990/91: 50). In early December 1990, such a parliamentary resolution was passed. It stated that membership with retained neutrality was in the Swedish national interest.

During the spring of 1991, a high-level foreign ministry working group drafted versions of a public declaration favouring membership with retained neutrality.[2] An application was formally submitted by Ingvar Carlsson to the presidency of the EC Council of Ministers in The Hague on 1 July. Following the September 1991 Social Democratic election defeat, the Conservative Party leader, Carl Bildt, assumed the position of prime minister. In the autumn of 1991 he experimented with a catchy phrase to capture the new commitment to European integration. In the words of Carl Bildt, neutrality no longer properly described Swedish foreign policy. Instead, Sweden was to pursue a foreign policy with a European identity (Luif, 1995: 246).

The traditionally important neutrality term was erased from official speech even before Sweden officially became a party to the Maastricht Treaty and to its second pillar through its membership. The change of terminology can be seen as an adaptation to the sceptical view of this notion by the Commission, as expressed in its July 1992 pre-negotiation review statement (*Bulletin of the European Communities*, Supplement 5, 1992). The transition from an image of Sweden as the committed neutral to a committed European seemed to have been fully completed well ahead of the beginning of the membership negotiations, at least at the top of the government. Later political developments have clearly indicated, however, that the nation of Swedes has not followed the early lead by the cabinet in this fundamental identity shift (Karvonen and Sundelius, 1996).

Another significant step in the political adaptation process was the removal of legal and administrative barriers to the international flow of capital, a traditional small-state tool for financial control of industry and banks. In 1989 significant financial deregulations were enacted without any serious debate over their long-term implications. It was seen as part of the necessary adjustment to the emerging internal market. Already in October 1990 Sweden faced a serious balance of payments crisis, which led to the surprise announcement to initiate the process toward membership. In May 1991 the national currency was pegged to the ECU in a multilateral parity index. This politically non-controversial step was regarded as an informal link to the EMS. Swedish financial participation in the European integration effort thus preceded its membership, indeed even its application for membership.

The symbolically significant ECU link came to an abrupt end as a result of the 19 November 1992 crisis decision to float the currency. This dramatic step was forced upon the Bildt government by the international market and it was labelled a policy fiasco by the prime minister. The government, as well as the Social Democratic leadership, had wanted to build the krona into one of the hard currencies of Europe, a member of the economic inner core of the Union (Stern and Sundelius, 1997). In fact, the unwanted Swedish devaluation in November had been preceded in September by an equally dramatic, temporary 500 per cent interest rate level in defence of the fixed currency value.

The steps taken in the financial sector were the most obvious examples of the pre-membership trend toward adaptations of national institutions, governing norms and public policies to the evolving European integration scene. Similar movements were visible also in other policy sectors. The political drive toward liberalization reached its peak during the 1991–94 Bildt government, when various domestic structural changes were introduced as elements of the necessary adaptation to the EC-based internal market.

Parallel to the negotiations for membership, several official commissions examined how various national institutions and existing policy arrangements would have to be rearranged in light of the pending membership (e.g. SOU, 1993: 80; SOU, 1994: 8). Experts agreed that a possible membership would require amendments to the Swedish constitution to allow for the transfer of some sovereign powers to the

Community level for supranational decision-making. A debate developed in 1994 over how best to accomplish this necessary revision of the legal foundation for the parliamentary democracy. Political science professor Olof Ruin chaired the relevant public commission on this subject. In his view, the most elegant and practical solution would be to introduce a preamble to the constitution, whereby all subsequent paragraphs should be considered secondary to a primary legal obligation of adherence to Community laws and directives. Such an overriding constitutional amendment would facilitate other, more specialized legal changes in the future without requiring a cumbersome political and judicial process. Critics saw this expert proposal as the ultimate establishment expression of a flat acceptance of all conceivable directives coming out of the Brussels-based joint decision-making process. The critics claimed that such a constitutional preamble would, in a democratically questionable way, relinquish Swedish national sovereignty for the sake of judicially smooth, continuous adjustments to the legal requirements of membership. The proposal by the independent expert commission was withdrawn from further consideration by the government following this heated public controversy. The final choice on how to amend the constitution was the insertion of a new paragraph into Article 5 of Chapter 10 dealing with relations with other states. This amendment sets a formal limit to the transfer of sovereign legislative power to the supranational EU level (Luif, 1995: 340).

The 'flat-on-our-backs constitutional proposal' of 1994 represented the high point of a series of pre-membership national adjustments to the EC. These adaptations had already begun before the application for membership was submitted in July 1991. The ambition behind this comprehensive adjustment drive was that Sweden would already become a more fully integrated state before entry than many members had achieved after years in the Community. The Swedish government aspired to belong to the inner core, together with Germany, France and Holland, and would not accept a position as one of the many peripheral members. The image of a European *Musterknabe* in the making could facilitate positive results in the ensuing negotiations, it was also argued. Others saw this accommodating style as demeaning to the national heritage of being qualitatively distinct from the traditionally less progressive countries of the European Continent.

Adaptation to membership

National democracy and central coordination

The Swedish government has repeatedly stated that the democratic legitimacy of the EU is ultimately based on the democratic processes within the member-states (e.g. Ministry for Foreign Affairs, 1995). EU cooperation should strengthen democracy in the member-states, not erode it. A stronger European Parliament 'may . . . imply a corresponding weakening of the indirect influence of national parliaments through the Council' (*ibid.*: 36). In the Swedish view, democracy has to be secured through special arrangements between the executives and the national parliaments. The information exchange and dialogue between the Swedish Parliament and government precede decision-making in the Council and take place in the Advisory Committee on European Affairs (Riksdagens EU-nämnd) (Konstitutionsutskottets betänkande 1994/95: KU22).

This committee was modelled on the former Danish Market Committee (Markedsutvalget, today the European Committee). In Swedish eyes, this select parliamentary body had managed to strike a proper balance between, on the one hand, democracy and openness, and on the other, the demands stemming from the executive as a legislator in the EC. Democratic accountability is exerted through weekly briefings by cabinet ministers in the committee. They then account for the Swedish positions in up-coming Council deliberations. The government has no legal obligation to follow the advice of the committee, however.

Some controversies have disrupted the effectiveness of this committee for parliamentary supervision. The limited interest by some cabinet members in its meetings and deliberations – the minister of finance, for example, only participated in four out of nine meetings during 1995 (Sverdrup, 1996: 9) – together with the fact that no votes are taken in the committee, has prompted the anti-EU environmental party to threaten to boycott its proceedings (DN, 7 May 1995). It has been the practice to release the discussion minutes from the committee two weeks after each session to enable the media to follow the deliberations. An internal dispute arose when the committee, in spring 1996, decided not to make public its recorded discussions concerning the IGC negotiations until the IGC is concluded in 1997 (*Riksdag och Departement*, 16 1996; *Dagens Nyheter*, 21 June 1996).

For Sweden, previous trends toward a decentralization of foreign relations and growing difficulties in political and administrative coordination of the national foreign policy posture have been accentuated by membership. All government decisions are formally taken collectively by the cabinet, previously the King in Council, in the Swedish constitutional tradition. The preparation of EU issues prior to membership always included the cabinet office, the Ministry for Foreign Affairs and the Ministry of Finance. In the new membership situation with a vast array of questions to cover, the domestic ministers have direct responsibility for their respective areas. EU issues are seen as extensions of their domestic policy-making authority.

At the same time, traditional calls for central coordination for the sake of a unified external posture have returned to the forefront of the political and technocratic debate over how best to maximize national influence in the competitive European decision-making arena. Advocates of central coordination have noted its value in forging a strong negotiation position in intergovernmental bargaining. National coordination of prioritized policy positions is presented as a substitute for material resources and political weight for a small but ambitious member state. The balance struck between central coordination and sector-based autonomy will vary among policy areas and between issues of higher or lower political salience. Significant differences are already notable between the workings of the wide scope of internal market aspects and the interactions within the second pillar.

The EU Coordination Secretariat at the Ministry for Foreign Affairs is the link between the Swedish PR in Brussels and the various ministries. It has the responsibility for ensuring that Swedish standpoints are prepared for all items on the agendas prepared by the EU presidency, and for finalizing and transmitting official instructions to the representatives in COREPER and in Council meetings. The final collection of official instructions to Brussels is made at the weekly meeting of the committee of EU coordinators of each ministry, chaired by the head of the pivotal EU Secretariat. Moreover, this secretariat has the responsibility for coordinating relations between the ministries and the Swedish Parliament, in particular the dialogue with its advisory committee on EU affairs (Nilsson, 1996).

The main body for political-level coordination of EU relations and policy positions is the Coordinating Group for EU Relations (EU-beredningen). This permanent committee is composed of the state secretaries of the cabinet office, the Ministry for Justice and the Ministry for Finance, and is chaired by the state secretary for European affairs in the Ministry for Foreign Affairs. The role of this senior-level coordinating group is to settle questions that have not been resolved by the civil servants. The under-secretaries of other ministries participate as needed, when the unresolved issue falls under their competence. These institutional arrangements and regularized procedures obviously give a very influential role to the Ministry for Foreign Affairs, being the core of this government-wide web for national EU coordination (authors' interviews). The foreign ministry can still claim exclusive authority in forging a nationally unified position in the area of the Common Foreign and Security Policy (CFSP). However, to achieve even that more limited coordination end, significant reorganizations have recently been made within this ministry. Basically, the functionally defined, bilateral departments have been rearranged into a desk system with geographical jurisdictions. The objective is to bring together better the often competing aspects of political relations, commercial and legal matters, and the global development assistance profile. The up-grading, already in August 1995, of the position of the small CFSP coordination unit was a direct result of the experiences of the first half year of membership. The fact that almost every unit in the foreign ministry is affected by CFSP was not realized until one worked inside this network. Initially, this small unit was part of the West European division, but it is now placed directly under the head of the political department, who participates in the political committee of CFSP. This closeness would give it a better position to pursue the general CFSP responsibility across the jurisdiction of other ministry units.

This institutional adjustment in the Ministry for Foreign Affairs reflects well the Swedish learning process of the first membership year. Earlier, the EU was seen as only an 'extra' question, which could be added to the organizational chart. EU coordination concerns quickly became an overarching priority for the ministry as a whole. Contrary to what could be expected, it was here and not in the domestic ministries that one found the greatest surprise over the scope and scale of the process changes required after the membership. The EU was not merely another international organization, as the traditionally trained diplomats had to learn quickly on the job (interviews 1995/96; Ministry for Foreign Affairs, 1996).

Clashing administrative traditions

The initial administrative planning for EU membership was based on the prediction that this new experience would not fundamentally affect the Swedish governing model (SOU, 1993: 80). In this tradition, a clear delineation is made between relatively small ministries serving the cabinet members (*departement*) and a large public administration composed of constitutionally autonomous authorities (*ämbetsverk*). This expectation of no basic change had to be reconsidered after the first year of working within the EU. In public reports it has been suggested that a considerable redistribution of human resources from the public administration to the central ministries is necessary. An expansion of the ministries by up to 30–40 per cent in the long-term perspective has been mentioned. This was also reflected in the spring 1995 government budget bill, where additional parliamentary funding for the central ministries was requested amidst a number of public austerity measures.

The need for increased personnel at the ministerial level is said to be quite urgent (*Dagens Nyheter*, 21 March 1996). The main reason for this administrative concern is the initial inadequacies in the coordination of Swedish actions in various EU institutions. The ministries have not been able to formulate clear and timely instructions to all Swedish representatives negotiating in Brussels. The ministries are too small to function both as cabinet offices for the daily preparation of Swedish positions and as more forward-orientated policy-shaping units (Ds, 1995: 21). Expansion is needed in order for the Swedish ministries to work in a more 'strategic' and 'problem-orientated' way, at the same time as they must cope daily with an increased overall workload due to membership.

The negotiation culture of the EU has created certain adjustment problems for the traditional Swedish civil servant. In a public report (SOU, 1996: 6) on the experiences after one year with the EU, it was concluded that the 'overall picture is that the [Swedish] administration functions relatively well in EU, but that there are some clear shortcomings in the EU administration'. The weaknesses of the EU were considered as particularly detrimental for a state with a relatively small civil service. The main reasons for the inefficiency of the EU were concluded to be lack of sufficient resources, weak coordination and an 'excessively hierarchic administrative culture' within the Commission and the Council secretariat. Swedish officials complained that they had difficulties in adapting to the 'legalistic environment'. Many of the meetings were seen as 'inefficient', but 'important'. The working difficulties were compounded as Swedish translation services had not been available at many meetings. The civil servants also called for reforms of the Union toward a 'flatter administrative organization'.

These personal experiences of the first year of participation reveal a clash between the EU style and Swedish administrative culture. Proper performance in the Swedish civil service is based on an attitude of time-orientated fulfilments: the timetable for rule-making and implementation has to be followed. The means to achieve this in a rational manner is through a pragmatic, 'non-hierarchic' handling of issues. In Swedish eyes, efficiency was lost when a time schedule, including dates for implementation, could not be achieved. The task-orientated attitude of the EU negotiation culture, in which much time for verbal declarations of intent and lengthy compromise producing deal-making are seen as unavoidable parts of collective decision-making, was perceived by the Swedes as wasteful.

The positive reaction of EU colleagues to the Swedish way of working has been that the Swedes are 'rational' and 'get things done'. The less benevolent perception is that they try to play *Besserwisser*, arriving at the meeting with a project plan which is presented as 'the' best solution even before hearing the views of their colleagues. Another peculiarity with the Swedes is their self-perceived high level of ambition: 'they have an opinion, present a position, and interfere in almost every question', as described by diplomats from other EU member-states (*Dagens Nyheter*, 24 December 1995). The value of keeping a high profile across a wide range of questions has also been questioned by Swedish officials as being overly ambitious.

The short time spans between EU meetings have challenged the Swedish logic of appropriate procedure. The high pace of decision-making in the Council has created difficulties for the strong Swedish tradition of securing wide support for every decision, both within and outside the administration. There is simply not time for officials to discuss Swedish actions in the EU thoroughly with affected groups and individuals at home. One consequence of the high-speed decision race is that officials have been forced to take official positions independently without consulting Stockholm. The short time for preparation has been particularly acute in budgetary questions. Many officials have complained about the short notice given to attend meetings, despite the fact that the rule for Council working groups is 48 hours (SOU, 1996:6: 65).

Moreover, there is a general frustration among public administrators over the difficulties of planning, foresight and predictions of EU colleagues' actions. One senses a loss of control over the policy process as a whole. The response has so far been proposals aimed at enhancing civil servant 'preparedness' and 'diplomatic skills' in order to function better in the unfamiliar EU rhythm of constant negotiations and changing conditions for the preparation of decisions (Ds, 1992: 96; SOU, 1996: 6).

The externalization of domestic policy aims

A major pro-membership argument in the 1994 referendum campaign was that only through this pivotal step could Sweden gain influence on the formation of those EU policies and directives that would, with or without membership, affect developments inside the country. Thus active participation in European policy-making was necessary to shape future domestic conditions in Sweden. In addition, a missionary zeal could be discerned in the referendum campaign. From a social democratic point of view, the task ahead was to infuse the rest of the Union with the progressive values and positive experiences of the time-tested Swedish version of the good society. The domestic record of achievements in many areas could be externalized upon the wider European scene, to direct benefit for other countries and indirectly also of value to the Swedish people.

Areas of particular concern included full employment, consumer protection, equality between the sexes, public openness, environmental standards, pan-European cooperation and global solidarity. In his cabinet declaration upon taking office in October 1994, Prime Minister Carlsson declared that one purpose behind joining the EU was to help turn it into a 'progressive force in world affairs'. Thus the Swedish government was bent on having an influence upon European policy-making in many issue areas. In this sense, Brussels was approached with considerable enthusiasm and optimism.

The Swedish government has declared that openness and the principle of public access to EU documentation is one of the three fields given priority in the IGC. Yet the handling of confidential EU documents has not been considered problematic by the Swedish civil servants, as was feared before membership. The Swedish PR in Brussels has experienced many requests for public releases, many of which were seen as 'test cases' by the press for adherence to the constitutional principle of public access to official records (SOU, 1996:6: 72). Swedish journalists have been surprised over the great difference between the formally restrictive rules for access to EU materials and the actual openness of the joint institutions. One journalist described the situation as a 'closed policy of leaks' (SOU, 1995:130: 12). The national press debate about democratic accountability and openness in the EU has been intensive. One proposal is to include into the Treaty the principle of public access to official records, with Swedish legislation on this freedom-of-information issue as a model (SOU, 1996:19: 29–31).

A high priority issue has been the effort to include in the revised Treaty a section on a union of full employment parallel to the planned monetary union. The first Swedish head of a directorate-general in the Commission, former Social Democratic Finance Minister Allan Larsson, was entrusted with the employment issues. So far, little progress has been made on this major policy initiative. Sweden has not been joined in this effort by any of the leading states, such as the Conservative governments of France, Germany or Britain. The Santer Commission picked up on the idea, however. It fits with an earlier Delors initiative for a large-scale programme for economic growth through investments in European infrastructures. Funding for this joint investment in new work opportunities for the construction sector has been uncertain thus far, also from Sweden. It seems unlikely that the suggested revision of the Treaty will be included in the draft IGC text.

The traditional cooperation structures among the five Nordic nations have been significantly affected by membership. A potential for coalition-building exists among the often like-minded nations of the north. This has paid off in the joint emphasis on the plight of the Baltic states and in the Baltic Sea Area initiative. The Nordic connection is also at work in the joint troop contingents, first to Macedonia and later to Bosnia. Nordbat was in place already before membership was formalized. In the security policy field, the former neutrals Sweden and Finland have launched a few joint initiatives on the future direction of the second pillar of the Union. A Nordic demand for joining the Schengen Agreement has been that Norway would also be included. A nation that twice has rejected membership must then be accepted by the Union members as one significant protector of the common Schengen border.

The government has placed a high priority on the enlargement of the EU, which is seen as necessary for pan-European security and order. In particular, Sweden has advocated the inclusion of the three Baltic states in the first round of expansion. Some progress can be noted on this priority issue as these small states were included on a par with the other eastern applicants. Also here, Sweden joined forces with Denmark and Finland in a continuation of support, which had already begun before the enlargement issue was raised.

The Baltic Sea Area was brought forward immediately as a priority region on equal standing with the previous Mediterranean programme. The high point of that early Swedish initiative was the May 1996 Visby Summit. This fringe area to the northeast was then recognized by the EU leaders and by Russia as an important focus for more intense cooperation. Sweden continues to spearhead this work of economic, environmental, cultural and security significance. One Swedish objective is to draw into the region the official interests of the larger European partners, as well as the US. Prime Minister Persson in August 1996 visited the White House as a US show of support for the Swedish leadership role in the Baltic Sea Area.

With regard to other foreign policy areas, the opinion of most Swedish diplomats is that there has been very little difference between traditional Swedish views and the content of the CFSP decisions taken since Sweden joined. The main difference has been that Swedish officials in CFSP are forced to make their policy more concrete than before. Also they have had to formulate positions in international controversies, where Sweden traditionally did not articulate an official view. Areas where Swedish influence on CFSP has been particularly discernible are cooperation with Russia and the Baltic States, the Baltic region policy and human rights questions (interviews, 1995).

Party rivalry and dissension

Public interest in the EU has been modest, as could be witnessed in the low participation in the European Parliament elections of September 1995. This grassroots neglect has been explained by many observers as a result of a widespread feeling that the EU is something 'far away', not affecting everyday lives. The parties opposed to membership have continued their active opposition even after the Swedish entry into the Union. The Left Party and the Environmental Party have gained considerable support in the opinion polls from their strong anti-EU profile. The Centre Party's position was always ambiguous and it has remained so due to internal divisions on many questions regarding the future of the EU. This party was a strong supporter of the traditional, neutrality-based security policy and it remains critical of initiatives to depart from the time-tested path of no alliances. The recent decision by the party congress to say 'no' already to EMU was preceded by a harsh open debate between the party leader and other prominent members (*Dagens Nyheter*, 18 June 1996).

The Social Democratic Party has been deeply split. Strong sections of the party have seen the EU as a threat to full employment, to the Swedish active labour market policy and to the welfare programmes. The split was already obvious at the time of the 1994 referendum. It was only accentuated in the campaigns for the European Parliament elections the following year. However, at the March 1996 party conference, the EU critics in this ruling party experienced a decisive defeat. Almost all of their resolutions on EU policy were opposed by the party establishment and voted down. The media conclusion was that 'the Social Democratic Party now has joined the EU' (*Dagens Nyheter*, 18 March 1996). The Conservative, Liberal and Christian Democratic parties have continued their pro-EU profiles after being placed in roles opposed to the Social Democratic government.

Towards a pro-active strategy for influence

At the strategic level, the neutrality dogma traditionally served as a unifying element of a fairly effective national coordination mechanism aimed at defining the parameters for permissible external engagements. The members of the foreign relations community of the state learned through informal socialization procedures where these outer boundaries were drawn. When in doubt, they could informally consult the neutrality high priests of the political department of the Ministry for Foreign Affairs. One of the most significant consequences of abandoning the neutrality doctrine as a guiding dogma for Swedish security policy has been the erosion of this core of the domestic decision regime for foreign policy. The rationale for the normatively privileged position of the traditional diplomat was then also undermined.

Considering this loss of domestic legitimacy after the end of the cold war, it is not surprising that the foreign ministry, as an institution in search of a politically central position, has become a strong advocate of the necessity of central coordination of external relations as a means toward enhancing Swedish influence in the EU. It is argued that an effective membership requires such a centralizing process, unless the national leadership is willing to accept a segmentation of the state into sector-defined and autonomously pursued interactions with the Brussels-based networks.

Some tension quickly developed between this foreign ministry-based coordination ambition and other ministries and agencies involved in EU affairs. It was not apparent, for example, why the finance ministry, with responsibility for Swedish positions would not be given an equally important role in shaping them. The work in the EU concerns most parts of the government apparatus and a strong coordinating position is not easily upheld by a ministry without any real control mechanisms, like budget authority. Following a year of tug of war on this delicate issue, the new Prime Minister and former Finance Minister Göran Persson, upon taking charge in March 1996, emphasized the importance that each ministry takes responsibility for its own EU affairs. He also noted the value of cabinet-level coordination of EU matters and suggested that its political direction could be elevated into his own office.

The emerging new dogma justifying EU coordination and counteracting Swedish difficulties in adapting effectively to the EU negotiation culture has been characterized by the term 'common outlook' (*samsyn*). The rationale behind this unifying concept is that formalized and regularized central coordination is very difficult in the EU context. The aim of national coordination should instead be to form 'common outlooks' that can guide Swedish representatives in the complex and decentralized European policy-making processes. A new government institute responsible for shaping such 'common outlooks' across the many policy sectors of EU relations has been proposed. It would bring together diverse societal and corporate interests and prepare national directives for long-term strategy priorities (Ds, 1995: 21). Due to prevailing political sensitivities over further large-scale governmental adjustments in the name of EU adaptation, this expert proposal has not yet led to any concrete result. However, considering the strongly felt need for improved national coordination and the corporativist tradition of consensus formation across sector interests, the proposal will probably generate some notable institutional reform in the near future.

It is hoped that at least the Ministry for Foreign Affairs will be able to speak in Brussels with one voice, even if the Swedish state as a whole would be unable to do so. At the same time, the permanent delegation in Brussels has grown to almost one hundred persons representing all parts of the government. In the future, one may very well expect coordination problems between this mini-cabinet office in place and the home-based senior officials in the ministry. A further problem has been the serious staff shortages. Many of the most knowledgeable, mid-level officials were quickly recruited into EU institutions. It will require some rebuilding of staff resources before a sufficient number of qualified officers can fill the growing ranks needed to deal in a competent manner with the fast-moving, multifaceted EU agenda. If the foreign ministry is unable to keep ahead of the pack of national Eurocrats, other ministries will surely pick up the slack in expertise and experience. The institutional arrangements for national EU coordination are still in a formative phase, where ambitious government players can position themselves as future activists or gate-keepers.

A major lesson after one year in the EU has been that tacit understandings exist among the member-states as regards 'special interests'. These base lines are recognized by the other members as areas where the country in question has priority, and where it is difficult to pursue an assertive policy line. The dispersion of Swedish efforts and resources across many EU fields has, in addition to placing a great strain on the diplomats and civil servants, had the effect of making Swedish bargaining priorities appear unclear. Therefore, the initial wide-scope approach has increasingly been regarded as being counterproductive to the Swedish interest in affecting specific outcomes (authors' interviews, September 1995).

After the initial shock of confronting the massive information flow and slow-grinding bureaucracy in Brussels, Swedish officials have pursued several initiatives, but with mixed success. In the preparations for the IGC many of the core contestable issues of the Union had to be addressed early. One such problem concerned whether to identify with the small states of Europe, as one had traditionally defined the Swedish position in global politics. This role choice would mean to insist on retaining all the formal privileges of equal state sovereignty in decision-making, following the planned enlargement of the Union.

The national veto, the use of native language, the right to a Commissioner and other quotas were all presented initially as Swedish IGC demands. The fear of being outvoted or simply ignored in the new working arena left its mark during the first year of membership. The maintenance of the veto right was particularly underlined in the discussion of CFSP reform. However, with regard to certain foreign policy questions such as preventive diplomacy, peace-keeping and humanitarian aid, the government has upon some reflection become 'willing to consider whether it might be possible to modify the principle of unanimity' (Skrivelse, 1995/96: 30).

Over time, one can note a gradual slide away from a formalistic, small-state fixation. Many participants in the Brussels-based policy-making committees have testified to their surprise over the informal character of these meetings, as compared to other international fora. The potential for wielding influence based on superior knowledge and negotiation skill was regarded as a very positive, and unexpected, feature of this continuous working process. Swedish participants learned by experiencing the

Union at work, rather than by observing it on display from a distance. Increasingly, high-level government officials have recognized the advantages for a state, with limited resources but with an activist profile, of strong joint institutions and shared norms for analytically grounded compromise solutions (SOU, 1995: 132).

Typical of this more recent Swedish attitude, Prime Minister Persson at his first meeting of the European Council in Florence in June 1996 sharply criticized Britain for violating the crucial EU norms for consensus formation in the 'mad cow' crisis. He argued that the assembled statesmen must not condone or excuse such myopic behaviour by a single government, as that would undermine the entire cooperative enterprise. Persson here articulated a holistic perspective often used in Swedish domestic politics to undercut sector-defined interest advocates. Coming from the leader of a nation with a known affinity to many British positions in the EU, this critical statement on proper procedure caused some headlines and a sharp public rebuttal by John Major. Also Persson's declaration of a similarity of views with the conservative French President Chirac on the social dimension was interpreted by observers as a very conscious Swedish move towards a 'mainstream' position in EU deliberation (*Dagens Nyheter*, 20 June 1996). Like his domestic rival, former Prime Minister Carl Bildt, Göran Persson has quickly shown his ability to interact forcefully with his fellow statesmen in the European Council.

State adaptations versus national adjustment

The recent record of Swedish adaptations to European integration can be depicted in terms of the classical divide in the study of national politics between state and society. In short, the Swedish state joined the European Community almost a decade ago, while only parts of Swedish society have done so as of 1996. The discrepancy is quite notable between the comprehensive and speedy movement toward adaptation at the governmental level from the late 1980s, and on the other hand the steadily high public opinion figures rejecting Swedish membership well beyond the mid-1990s. According to recent surveys, some 60 per cent of respondents would, in 1996, have voted against membership. State and society appear to be out of touch with each other on an issue of fundamental importance to the future identity of the nation. A northern people of committed neutrals have not yet been transformed into committed Europeans, if by that one means supporters of the evolving EU (Sundelius, 1995).

Certainly Swedish industry, investors and most of the city élites joined the European bandwagon as the Berlin Wall crumbled, Germany was reunited and the internal market emerged as the promised land. The state apparatus was soon thereafter driven forward through a social democratic initiative for a comprehensive national adaptation programme. This push from above toward becoming more European in procedures, regulations and normative outlooks was accentuated during the non-socialist interregnum headed by Carl Bildt. Following a divisive national referendum, the kingdom of Sweden acquired membership status in January 1995. It became evident then that the people in the vast outlying areas of the country did not want to join Europe, as manifested in the Union. Investments in grassroots information campaigns about the true meaning and possible benefits of the new partnership intensified following this close call for the pro-membership establishment. A political centre–periphery gap over the EU connection exists in Sweden, as in Norway, where the periphery in 1972 and 1994 formed majorities against membership.

The September 1995 elections to the European Parliament reinforced the societal pattern of stubborn grassroots resistance to the state-sponsored notion of a deepening involvement in the work of the Union. The voter turnout was exceptionally modest by Swedish standards – around 40 per cent. The parties and candidates opposed to the EU fared very well, capturing half of the twenty-two Swedish seats in Strasburg. The deep resistance within the governing Social Democratic Party became glaringly evident as it received only 28 per cent of the votes, as compared to 45 per cent in the elections to the national Parliament a year before. The prospects of another referendum in a few years' time over membership of the EMU appear like a cruel nightmare to many leading establishment figures in Sweden.

In a deeper sense, the Swedish nation has not adapted to the requirements of EU membership or even to the wider movement toward a transnationally defined human existence. While the officials of the state machinery have adjusted rapidly to the demanding conditions of a non-territorially defined European space and are also trying to grasp the emerging realities of the new time frameworks of action, the Swedish public at large appears to exist in a cognitive frame out of tune with the rapid transnationalization of Europe. To many voters, the immediate and very visible costs associated with the Europeanization of Sweden far outweigh the potential but diffused benefits of membership, as professed by various establishment figures.

The people of Sweden were inspired by their political authorities to turn their backs on the Continent of Europe some fifty years ago. In spite of the best efforts by the new generation of leaders to draw public attention back to this traditional focus of interest, most Swedes (across party lines, but more so the young and women than the middle-aged and men) tend to remain sceptical. State and society at large are out of touch on the issue of how best to deal with the inevitable slide forward in the territorial and temporal redefinitions of European policy-making. Governmental (and large business) adaptations are well under way, but more fundamental national adjustments to the requirements of EU membership lay far ahead. This unique experiment in transnational and multi-layered, democratic governance does not yet play well in places like Svedala.

Notes

1. *Documents on Swedish Foreign Policy 1990*. 'Should the EC choose to proceed toward such a far-reaching goal?' *Dagens Nyheter*, 27 May 1990).
2. See statement to Parliament by the Prime Minister Ingvar Carlsson on Sweden's application for membership of the EC (14 June), in *Documents on Swedish Foreign Policy 1991*. Also see the statement by the parliamentary foreign affairs committee on 28 April 1992, 'Säkerhet och nedrustning'. The Parliament stated that 'Sweden's policy of non-alliance with the possibility of neutrality in the case of war in its vicinity remains' (Utrikesutskottets betänkande, 1991/92:UU19).

References

Björklund, T. (1996) The three Nordic 1994 referenda concerning membership in the EU, *Cooperation and Conflict*, vol. 31, no. 1, pp. 11–36.

Carlsson, I. (1991) Statement to the Parliament on Sweden's application for membership of the European Community (14 June), *Documents on Swedish Foreign Policy 1990–91* (Stockholm: Government Printing Office).

Danielsson, Christian (1988) Europafrågorna i regeringskansliet, *Aktuellt i handelspolitiken*, vol. 3, pp. 35–41.

Ds (1992): 96 *Statsförvaltningens Europakompetens – Om behovet av kompetensutveckling hos myndigheterna inför integrationen*, Cabinet Office (Stockholm: Government Printing Office).

Ds (1995) *Samsyn och alliansförmåga – Hur regeringen, näringslivet, intresseorganisationer, regionala intressen och forskarvärlden behöver samverka för att stärka Sveriges position i EU*, Ministry of Finance (Stockholm: Government Printing Office).

Ekengren, M. (1996) Statsförvaltningens europeisering i tid och rum – En studie av den politiska tidens förändring till följd av EU-samarbetet, Research Report 25 (Stockholm: The Swedish Institute of International Affairs).

Gilljam, M. and Holmberg, S. (1996) *Väljarna och folkomröstningen 1994*, Norstedts Juridik.

Hamilton, C. (1987) *Europa och Sverige – EG-frågan inför 90-talet* (Stockholm: SNS förlag).

Karvonen, L. and Sundelius, B. (1996) 'The Nordic neutrals entering the EU'. In Lee Miles (ed.), *The North Joining the European Union* (London: Routledge).

Konstitutionsutskottets betänkande 1994/95:KU22. Samverkan mellan riksdag och regering med anledning av Sveriges anslutning till Europeiska unionen (Stockholm: Parliament Printing Office).

Luif, P. (1995) *On the Road to Brussels: The Political Dimension of Austria's, Finland's and Sweden's Accession to the European Union*, Austrian Institute for International Affairs (Vienna: Braumüller).

Ministry for Foreign Affairs (1995) *Svenska principiella intressen inför EU:s regeringskonferens 1996*, July (Stockholm: Regeringskansliet).

Ministry for Foreign Affairs (1996) *Det nya utrikesdepartementet-Information om omorganisationen*, Meddelande Nr 1–19 (Stockholm: Regeringskansliet).

Nilsson, J. (1996) The Council of the European Union in theory and practice: a report on the actors and power-instruments of the EU in relation to the organisation of the Swedish government, unpublished thesis, Department of Government, Uppsala University.

Proposition (1987/88) Regeringens proposition om Sverige och den västeuropeiska integrationen (Stockholm: Parliament Printing Office).

Proposition (1994/95) Regeringens proposition om Sveriges medlemskap i Europeiska unionen (Stockholm: Parliament Printing Office).

Skrivelse (1990/91) Regeringens skrivelse om åtgärder för att stabilisera ekonomin och begränsa tillväxten av de offentliga utgifterna, 26 October 1990 (Stockholm: Parliament Printing Office).

Skrivelse (1995/96): 30 Regeringens skrivelse om EUs regeringskonferens 1996, 30 November 1996 (Stockholm: Parliament Printing Office).

SOU (1993) *Statsförvaltningen och EG* (Stockholm: Government Printing Office).

SOU (1994) *Historiskt vägval. Följderna för Sverige i utrikespolitiskt hänseende av att bli, respektive inte bli medlem i Europeiska unionen* (Stockholm: Government Printing Office).

SOU (1995): 130 *Sverige i EU – makt, öppenhet, kontroll* (Stockholm: Government Printing Office).

SOU (1996): 6 *Ett år med EU-Svenska statstjänstemäns erfarenheter av arbetet i EU* (Stockholm: Government Printing Office).

Stern, E. and Sundelius, B. (1997) Sweden's twin monetary crises of 1992: rigidity and learning in crisis decision making, *Journal of Contingencies and Crisis Management*, **5**, 1, 32–48.

Sundelius, B. (1989) Das Primat der Neutralitätspolitik: building regimes at home, *Cooperation and Conflict*, vol. 23, no. 4, pp. 163–78.

Sundelius, B. (1990) Neutralitet och konfliktfylld interdependens. In U. Nordlöf-Lagerkranz (ed.), *Svensk neutralitet, Europa och EG* (Stockholm: Swedish Institute of International Affairs), pp. 123–46.

Sundelius, B. (1994) Changing course: when neutral Sweden chose to join the European Community. In W. Carlsnaes and S. Smith (eds), *European Foreign Policy* (London: Sage), pp. 177–201.

Sundelius, B. (1995) Sveriges säkerhet i sekelskiftets Europa. In I. Neumann (ed.), *Ny giv för Nordisk samarbeid?* (Oslo: Tano Förlag), pp. 52–75.

Sverdrup, U. (1996) Europeanisation of the heavy rhythms of the nation state: the emerging temporal order in Europe, paper presented at the CORE Seminar on the Study of European Integration: Domestic and International Issues, Humlebaek, Denmark.

Utrikesdepartementets handelsavdelning (1992a) *Information om EES-avtalet*, Bakgrundsfakta (Stockholm: Regeringskansliet).

Utrikesdepartementets handelsavdelning (1992b) *Agreement on the European Economic Area: EES-avtalet – I. Huvudbestämmelser och Protokoll. II. Bilagor*, (Stockholm: Regeringskansliet).

Utrikesutskottets betänkande (1991/92) Säkerhet och nedrustning, 28 April 1992 (Stockholm: Parliament Printing Office).

Chapter 10

Norway: An Adaptive Non-Member

ULF SVERDRUP

Introduction

Norway has been invited to become a member of the European Community/European Union twice, but both times a bare majority turned down the proposal in national referenda. The voters are deeply divided on the question of European integration, and the governing Labour Party is split in half on the issue. In spite of the political conflict on European issues, during the last decade the Norwegian government has made major efforts to adapt the organization and orientation of the Norwegian political system toward increased European integration. New organizations have been established and new procedures for securing sufficient coordination and control have been developed. Cross-border contacts between domestic Norwegian institutions and institutions at the European level have increased in scope and importance. European contacts and regulations are considered as important within most national policy fields, even in the fields traditionally totally dominated by domestic considerations. Furthermore, increased attention, time and energy have been devoted to European issues, and Norway has developed shared decision-making institutions with the EU.

As this listing indicates, the Norwegian political system is in a process of becoming Europeanized. The term 'Europeanization' is understood as a process in which Europe, and especially the EU, become an increasingly more relevant and important political community for the Norwegian political system. Moreover, the process of Europeanization is understood as a process of gradually increasing homogenization across European states. This does not necessarily imply standardization, but should rather be interpreted as a process that reduces the variance between, and within, different European states with regard to how political processes are perceived and how they organize in order to solve problems (Olsen, 1996a). The Norwegian political system is not responding to the process of Europeanization by exploring radically new solutions. Responses reflect historical experiences and stem largely from endogenous dynamics of the Norwegian political system. Existing routines and capabilities are considered to be effective and appropriate for coping with the new challenges and possibilities. Europeanization of the Norwegian administration is therefore best understood as an incremental process of gradual adaptation, rather than a dramatic break with the past (Farsund and Sverdrup, 1994; Christensen, 1996). This way of step-wise learning and incremental adaptation is consistent with previous analysis of attempts to reform and change the political institutions in Norway (Olsen, 1996b).

Why should we pay any attention to the developments in a non-member state? Truly, the Norwegian case has limited relevance in understanding some of the functioning of the European policy. Scholars in the field of Europeanization have traditionally focused upon adaptations in member-states, but this approach is too narrow. Only comparative analysis has the potential to examine critically the distinct characteristics of Europeanization. Without the comparative dimension it is impossible to isolate changes related to Europe from the more general processes of administrative modernization and internationalization. Such comparisons of member-states as well as non-member-states are currently lacking. Thus investigating the Norwegian case gives us a unique opportunity to shed light on the significance of formal membership of the EU.

Two propositions could be put forward. The first proposition suggests that formal membership of the EU implies a strong pressure for administrative adaptation (Andersen and Eliassen, 1993). Increased European integration will lead to reorganization and destabilization of the domestic political and administrative system (Toonen, 1992). It is assumed that non-member-states are less affected than member-states, and therefore have more leeway in organizing their political and administrative system. According to this proposition, membership is a significant parameter in understanding the current administrative changes in Europe. The second proposition suggests that differences between member and non-member-states are of less importance. Non-members are affected by decisions in the EU, but they have less influence and control of decisions than the member-states, thus non-members experience a higher level of uncertainty in relation to the EU. In order to reduce uncertainty and increase their legitimacy, non-members undertake extensive adaptations in their political and administrative systems. As Prime Minister Gro Harlem Brundtland suggested a short time after the referendum: Norway must act more or less as if it were a member (Brundtland, 1995).

Furthermore, the concept of membership is problematic. A wide range of informal and formal linkages exist between Norway and the EU. And the 'variable geometry' character of the EU makes it hard to draw a clear distinction between member- and non-member-states. In addition, there are considerable variations between different policy sectors in the density and strength of these linkages. For instance, in a field like science and research policy Norway is probably as affected by European integration as the member-states. Moreover, isolating the effect of membership is difficult since administrative changes in Norway were part of a pre-accession process undertaken together with some other EFTA countries. It is therefore too early to assess whether the referendum was the first step in a series of choices which in the long term will represent a dramatic break, or whether other dynamics and linkages will make the result of the referendum less relevant. So far, the development in Norway is ambiguous, and it seems to vary from one political field and sector to another.

In order to comprehend the adaptations that have taken place in Norway, we have to take into account the country's historical background. It is only possible to explain the Europeanization of political institutions through an analysis of historical roots, routes and internal dynamics (Olsen, 1996a). In the following section I will therefore

briefly outline Norway's historical relationship with the EU, and the gradual internationalization of the political and administrative system. I will also include a brief
presentation of the Agreement on the European Economic Area, which currently is
the core institution regulating the relationship between Norway and the EU. Then
I turn to a detailed analysis of how Norwegian administration and political leadership adapted to the challenges and possibilities raised by increased European integration. Since Norway is less involved in influencing the decision-making processes
in the EU than the member-states, I will primarily focus on national adaptation and
implementation. I argue that increased European integration has led to a considerable
reorganization of the relationship *between* Norwegian and European institutions, as
well as in the relations *within* the Norwegian political and administrative system.

Popular resistance against formal membership

Norway is larger than Italy and is almost the size of Germany in terms of total land
area. However, with only 4.2 million inhabitants it is still a small state. Its unique
topography and geography has influenced the political and economic development
of the country. The key to growth and development has been the effective explora-
tion and exploitation of natural resources. Especially important are the resources of
the sea, through the industries of shipping, fishing and, more recently, oil and gas.
Norway is therefore probably more dependent upon the resources of its territory
and thereby its territorial boundaries than most continental European states.

Norway has a tradition of isolationism, due to historical experiences. Political
leaders have often felt little in common with the larger and more powerful states of
the continent. This is particularly true regarding the idea of creating pan-European
cooperation. European political integration has never received strong support, and
most Norwegians have expressed scepticism about any attempt to develop supranational political institutions in Europe (Løchen, 1993; Urwin, 1995). The sceptical
attitude is illustrated by a remark made by Jørgen Løvland, the first Norwegian minister of foreign affairs after Norway's independence from Sweden in 1905. He stated
that his prime task was to keep Norway out of the 'combinations and alliances that
can drag the country into belligerent adventures together with any of the European
warrior states' (cited in Røhne, 1991: 4).

However, isolationism is not a good description of Norwegian policy and polity.
The opposite has been the case. Norway has been an active participant in a wide
range of international cooperation during the post-war period. Norwegian foreign
policy developed from the interplay between three separate pillars: the Atlantic
pillar, the Nordic pillar and the continental European pillar (Riste, 1991). Norwegian membership in NATO in 1949 paved the way for close contacts with Britain
and the United States. In the period since the end of the 1940s, the Atlantic pillar
dominated the Norwegian foreign policy orientation (Riste, 1995). The Norwegian
political and administrative system also became increasingly internationalized in
other policy areas, such as foreign trade, development aid and the petroleum industry.
The administration participated in a growing number of international organizations
and a number of international departments were established in the ministries during

the 1970s. Already by the end of the 1970s, scholars conceptualized the Norwegian political system as having a fourth level of government (Egeberg, 1980).

In spite of increased internationalization, Norway's relation to the EEC/EC remained ambiguous. Norway applied for membership for the first time in 1961, and a decade later a second time. Norway's first referendum was held in 1972, and a majority of 53.5 per cent voted against membership. The campaign created, and unveiled, deep cleavages within the Norwegian society, cutting across and within political parties. Some of the controversies represented a troublesome break with the political tradition of consensus and low levels of conflict (Furre, 1991). When preparing for membership in 1972, the administration made some adaptations in order to prepare for membership, but they were all minor and temporary (Underdal, 1972). Since most of the bureaucrats supported the pro-membership side, the referendum resulted in reduced legitimacy for the administration, especially for the Ministry of Foreign Affairs (Gleditsch, Østerud and Elster, 1974).

After the first referendum the issue of European integration was removed from the political agenda, and Norway's relationship with the EC became a non-issue. Interest in European politics declined, and thus knowledge of the development in the EC decreased in every part of society. During a period of fifteen years the relationship with the EC was not subject to any political debate in the Parliament; neither did any political party show interest in the issue. Memories of the referendum and political conflicts in 1972 prevented them from taking any steps. However, external changes in the mid-1980s brought an end to this silence. The decision to create the single market in the EC created a window of opportunity for political initiatives. The government drafted two White Papers on the country's relation with the EC and European integration in 1987 (St. meld. no. 61, 1986–87, St. meld. no. 63, 1986–87). Neither of them suggested membership, but both recommended that Norway should pay increased attention to the development of the EC. The documents resulted in the establishment of a permanent Norwegian delegation in Brussels, and an invitation to the EC to establish a delegation for the European Commission in Oslo. These two administrative changes were the first step in building a stronger institutional framework for the Norwegian process of adaptation.

The European issue was reintroduced to the political agenda with great care, and it was primarily motivated by economic concerns. The small and vulnerable EFTA members were afraid of possibly being excluded from the single market. In order to resolve the 'EFTA problem', President of the European Commission Jacques Delors suggested increasing the integration between EC and EFTA. He considered it as a natural extension of the slowly moving Luxemburg process, which had started in 1984, aiming at developing further the linkages between EFTA and the EC (Delors, 1989: 18). Negotiations between the Commission and EFTA representatives started in June 1990. After intense and complicated negotiations, both within EFTA and between EFTA and the EC, an agreement was signed in May 1992. In January 1994 the European Economic Area Agreement was implemented.

Already during the EEA negotiations major changes dramatically altered the situation. First, the political map of Europe changed. The dramatic transformation of central and eastern Europe challenged the fundaments and borders of Europe, and called for reorganization. What used to be an issue of integration of western Europe became an issue of integrating Europe. Exogenous changes and the EC's response to these challenges led some neutral EFTA states to reinterpret their political situation (Luif, 1996). Second, it became increasingly obvious during the negotiation that the EFTA pillar would be weak and have a built-in democratic deficit. The EFTA countries would have limited access and control over decisions which would have considerable impact on the domestic political and administrative system. Hence, a growing number argued that only full membership would give sufficient influence and democratic control. These two developments led to the applications for membership. Austria applied in 1989, Sweden in 1991, Finland in 1992 and finally Norway at the end of 1992. Through the sequence of applications a self-enforcing loop was created. When the EFTA countries applied for membership, the EFTA pillar in the EEA was further weakened. This snowball effect explains the timing of the Norwegian application. Of particular importance in triggering the Norwegian application were the changes in the Swedish attitude and policy towards the EC. The political leadership in Norway wanted initially to slow down the process and stick to the gradual and careful approach, in order to reduce the level of domestic conflicts and gain sufficient popular support.

The negotiations on the agreement on membership proceeded at an even higher speed than the EEA negotiations. Since most of the issues had been resolved during these negotiations, it was possible to complete the negotiations on membership during a period of barely two years. The most difficult fields were related to fishing quotas, agriculture subsidies and the food industry. Important and controversial issues related to the Economic and Monetary Union, and the development of a Common Foreign and Security Policy did not receive much attention, nor did they create any major obstacle in the negotiations (St. meld no. 40, 1993–94).

In the aftermath of the European Council meeting in Crete in June 1994, the new applicant countries were invited to participate as observers in the EU with the right to speak. During the so-called 'interim period', from June until the day after the referendum in November 1994, Norway acted as if it were a full member. Norwegian politicians and bureaucrats participated in meetings in the European Commission, under the auspices of the Council and in COREPER. The Norwegian administration participated in more than 430 committees in the Council. The interim period functioned as an eye-opener for the Norwegian administration, and during this period the traditional mode of organizing the public administration was challenged (Trondal, 1996). The dramatic increase in participation, flow of information, deadlines and meetings created major difficulties in coordinating activities. The interim period unveiled that the Norwegian administration lacked sufficient competence and knowledge of the actual working of the EU system, and that the relatively small administration lacked administrative capacity (Christensen, 1996; Trondal, 1996).

As the date of the referendum approached, the debate became increasingly more intense. The issue had the priority of the political leadership and overshadowed all other issues. Prime Minister Gro Harlem Brundtland argued in general terms and with a long-term perspective. Her concern was the future role of Norway in post-cold war Europe (Ringdal, 1995). In spite of the transformation in eastern and central Europe and the developments within the EU, the topics debated, as well as the pattern of voting, showed a striking similarity to the pattern of 1972. During the campaign the dominating issues were: supranational vs. national control; economic growth vs. unemployment; security policy and the right to self-determination of natural resources (Ringdal, 1995). The strong counterculture and centre–periphery dimensions in Norwegian politics, which had been so important in 1972, were rediscovered and reconstructed in 1994 (Todal Jenssen *et al.*, 1995). In general, the voters in the rural areas – along the coast and in the north – voted against membership. A majority voted in favour of membership in the southeastern part of the country.

However, it was the strong ability to mobilize voters from all over the country and across the whole spectrum of political life that made the referendum into a victory for the opposition. Farmers, fishermen, public employees and blue-collar workers organized a large coalition against the political and economic establishment. The mobilizing capacity of the popular movement Nei til EU (No to EU) was tremendous. The organization received its financial support from members and the organizations for the farmers and fishermen. At the time of the referendum they had 145,000 members, 470 local organizations and 19 regional organizations (Nei til EU, 1994). In contrast, the leading organization on the fragmented pro-membership side, Europabevegelsen (The European Movement), had only 33,000 members. Their financial support, which was at approximately the same size as the 'No' side, came primarily from the industry and various business interests.

After the Danish referendum in 1992, the Norwegian opinion polls continually reported a majority against membership, and the Swedish and Finnish referenda had little impact on the voters. Hence, it came as no surprise that a majority voted 'no' on 28 November 1994. Approximately 52 per cent voted against membership, with a record high turnout of 89 per cent.

Rapid implementation within the EEA framework

Norway's relationship with the EU is at present formally organized through the EEA Agreement. The wide scale and scope of the EEA Agreement increased Norway's integration and relations with the EU. Through the EEA Agreement, Norway committed itself to transpose most of the *acquis communautaire* related to the free movement of goods, capital, services and persons, as well as the EU competition rules into its national legislation (Sejersted *et al.*, 1995). Within the framework of the EEA Agreement there has also been an increase in cooperation in fields such as environmental protection, the social dimension, consumer protection, research and development, education, training, culture, company law, measures for small and medium-sized enterprises, audio-visual services, tourism, statistics, information services and disaster preparedness (European Commission, 1995).

The EEA Agreement created a complex set of joint institutions to control and monitor political, legal, social and cultural cooperation. The EEA Council is the highest-ranking organ, and it holds two meetings per year. The EEA Council consists of members of the Council of the EU, members of the Commission and one member of the government from each EFTA member of the EEA. The EEA Joint Committee is made up of bureaucrats from EFTA and the Commission and they meet every month. This organ is supposed to update the Agreement continuously by incorporating recent additions to the community legislation. Decisions are made under the rule of unanimity, with a formal right to veto for all parties. Norway, Iceland and Liechtenstein have a formal possibility to veto any new proposal coming from the EU, but the political consequences of such action are rather uncertain. The political leaders have so far showed limited interest in using the 'exit' or 'voice' option laid down in the Agreement (Brundtland, 1995). Finally, a Joint EEA Parliamentary Committee was established. Here MPs from the EFTA countries meet MEPs. In addition to these joint institutions, EFTA created its own European Surveillance Authority (ESA) and a separate EFTA court (St. prp. no. 100, 1991–92).

The agreement is dynamic. That is, when new legislation is developed within the EU in a field covered by the agreement, it is also incorporated into the legislation in the EEA countries. Through the agreement Norway is formally linked to the stream of decisions that flow from the EU system. In addition, the EEA Agreement is based upon a homogeneous interpretation and enforcement of the legislation. Naturally, in most cases this implies that the legislation is interpreted in Norway as it was originally interpreted in the EU. The continuous and automatic transposition of newly elaborated EU legislation into the Norwegian legislation imposes a strong, continuous, direct effect on the Norwegian legislation. In addition, the EEA Agreement has led to changes in legal reasoning and in some legal principles (Sejersted, *et al.*, 1995). Furthermore, through the setting of agenda and deadlines, the dynamic aspect of the EEA Agreement has had a strong indirect effect on the distribution of the attention of the decision-makers. The EEA legislation has so far been transposed into the Norwegian legislation on a large scale and at a high speed (Sollien, 1995). During the first stage of ratification a total number of 1,300 legal acts were transposed. When the EEA II, covering the legal acts developed in the EC during the negotiations on the EEA Agreement, was passed in March 1994, an additional 500 acts were transposed. Since these two major packages, a total of 107 decisions were made in the EEA committee, 44 in 1994 and 63 in 1995 (European Commission, 1995). The Norwegian administration had transposed 94 per cent of the legislation related to the internal market by the end of 1995, which is a high proportion even compared to the figures of the member-states (ESA, 1995). Consequently, the legal framework laid down by the EEA Agreement contributes to create opportunities and constraints for decision-makers and thereby shapes the day-to-day policy in a number of fields and at all levels of governance. However, few studies of implementation of the EEA legislation in Norway go beyond the simple understanding of implementation as legal transposition.

The rapid implementation of the legislation was a result of a process of gradual convergence and a good match between the two systems. Norway made multiple step-wise approximations of legislation prior to the application for membership or the implementation of the EEA Agreement, creating a relatively high degree of similarity between the two sets of legislation (Farsund and Sverdrup, 1994). The gradual process of convergence stemmed from different and partly independent processes. First, it was a result of the changing perceptions of what was to be considered technically superior solutions, for instance in the case of changing the currency exchange control. Second, EC legislation had been imitated in order to reduce the complications and transaction costs of applying a different kind of legislation. An example of this can be found in the gradual development of the financial legislation (Skogstad Aamo, 1995). Third, convergence of the legislation stemmed from bureaucratic anticipation of the preferences held by the political leadership. The Norwegian political leadership stressed the importance of a changing attitude towards the EC in the Norwegian administration. In a letter from the prime minister sent to all ministries in 1988, a formal procedure for harmonization of legislation was laid down (Statusrapport, 1989). According to this procedure, the administration had to analyse how each new change in the legislation differed from the *acquis communautaire*. If it was necessary to make legislation that differed from the *acquis*, such deviations should be given an explicit basis. Political statements like this indicate the strong political will to reduce differences in legislation, and to smooth the integration process. Fourth, the implementation could proceed rapidly due to procedural characteristics. Since most of the adaptations of the EEA law were considered as regulations, and thereby delegated to the administration, there was no reason for the Parliament to pass this as an act, which normally is a more time-consuming process (Sejersted, 1996). Both the internal dynamics of the institutions involved and the strong will of the political leadership created a platform for rapid and efficient transposition of EC legislation into Norwegian legislation. Consequently, in transposing the EEA Agreement, with some exceptions, primarily minor adjustments were made in the Norwegian legislation (Sollien, 1995). Changes were perceived as a matter of minor technical adjustments, rather than any dramatic change in content of policy or shape of the polity.

Administrative flexibility and adaptation

For a small state with a relatively small administrative capacity, preparation for membership was a critical test of Norway's ability to adapt and cope with new challenges and opportunities. In terms of the size of the administration, Norway is a small state compared to other European states. However, Norway had experienced considerable growth in public sector spending during the last decades, even in the 1980s, when most OECD (Organization for Economic Co-operation and Development) countries tried to reduce their spending (Olsen, 1996b). A total of 3,940 persons were employed in the Norwegian ministries in 1990 (St. meld no. 35, 1991–92). The exact number of ministries varies from time to time, depending upon the match between the political traditions, the workload of the ministries and various political priorities and trade-offs. There are currently sixteen ministries, including the Prime Minister's Office. The Ministry of Foreign Affairs has traditionally played the key role in coordinating, developing and managing Norway's international relations (Christensen, 1996). However, the process of gradual internationalization of the administration challenged its role as a monopolist. Domestic institutions became increasingly internationalized, and participated in the shaping of Norway's relations to other countries and organizations (Egeberg, 1980).

Increased European integration did not lead to a dramatic increase in resources to the administration (Sverdrup, 1994). The objective of the Ministry of Finance reflected its standard attitude towards expenditure: new tasks stemming from increased European integration should not result in a corresponding increase in resources to the ministries (St. meld no. 35, 1991–92). The ministries, which held the budgetary responsibility for the directorates, gave the same instruction. Consequently all institutions had to give priority to European affairs without expecting budgetary compensations for increased spending. In general the initial objective was achieved. Few new resources were given to the administration, and most of the additional resources distributed in relation to European integration had a temporary character. The underlying rationality was more the one of a fire department preventing immediate crisis, rather than strengthening the capabilities of the administration permanently.

The number of bureaucrats in the ministries increased, with a total of 104 positions earmarked for European issues. Some ministries, first and foremost the Ministry of Foreign Affairs, experienced a considerable increase in their resources (Christensen, 1996). In addition, some of the directorates received a significant number of new positions. Approximately two-thirds of all new positions were temporary, and a major share of them were related to the translation of documents and legislation from various EU languages into Norwegian. Since more than 15,000 pages of legislation had to be translated during a short period of time, translation was one of the most resource-demanding tasks. However, budgetary figures do not provide us with an accurate picture of the resources spent on European issues. Figures from a survey undertaken by a governmental agency indicated that more than 400 labour years were used to handle European issues in the ministries during the interim period (Statskonsult, 1995: 15). More than 130 labour years were spent by the Ministry of Foreign Affairs, which at the time had a total of 630 positions. The figures varied between the ministries; less than ten in the Ministry of Education, Research and Church Affairs and in the Ministry of Health and Social Affairs; between 10 and 15 in the Ministry of Finance, Ministry of Fisheries, Ministry of Justice, Ministry of Local Government and Labour and the Ministry of Cultural Affairs. The highest relative number was found in the Ministry of Fisheries, where approximately 20 per cent of their labour years were occupied with European issues.

Increased European integration imposed a considerable strain on the capacity of the small-sized Norwegian administration. The gap between new resources and actually spent resources cannot be understood without analysing the dynamics of capabilities. First, since the institutions had to meet the new tasks without any additional resources, they were forced to alter their priorities and attention. European issues had top political priority and issues with less political priority were delayed (Farsund and Sverdrup, 1994). For instance, in one section in the Ministry of Finance the number of ordinary tasks older than three months increased by 50 per cent during this period because of altered priorities. Second, institutions compensated for limited capacity by increasing the workload on the personnel. The highly technical and specialized character of the European issues prevented mobility between tasks and persons. A high level of specialization made the administration increasingly dependent upon a relatively small group of key bureaucrats. Consequently, the very experienced personnel, who were experts in their respective field and also had experience from other international cooperation, became the 'Eurocrats' of the Norwegian administration. Third, some institutions were able to cope with the new challenges simply because they could reduce organizational slack. For instance, in the Ministry of Finance a unit had capacity to cope with the new tasks, since previous liberalization of exchange regulations had reduced their workload (Sverdrup, 1994). Institutions are often considered as inflexible arrangements with considerable inertia; however, the Norwegian case illustrates that institutions often have a wide repertoire of action and are able to show considerable flexibility within fairly stable institutional boundaries.

In order to adapt to increased European integration and to coordinate the Norwegian positions, an interministerial coordinating apparatus was established in June 1988 (Statusrapport, 1989). The reason for the rapid build-up of this apparatus was the need to prepare and coordinate the negotiations on the EEA Agreement. A slightly modified version of the apparatus was later used in the negotiations on membership, and after the referendum this apparatus remained more or less unchanged. The apparatus did not have any formal legal status, and it did not alter the distribution of political and legal responsibility between the ministries. The formal responsibility for handling EU issues was placed in the respective sector ministries. All of the ministries were involved, in addition to a great share of the directorates. However, the coordinating role of the Prime Minister's Office was considerably strengthened during the process. Only to a modest degree did the reorganization challenge the traditionally strong coordinating role of the Ministry of Finance in budgetary matters, the Ministry of Justice in legal affairs, and the Ministry of Foreign Affairs in foreign policy. In this respect, the newly built apparatus represented a continuation of the administrative tradition of Norway.

There are three different levels of coordination of European issues in the Norwegian government. First, at the political level the cabinet is the superior organ for political coordination. If the issue at stake has limited relevance to other ministers, coordination takes place in a smaller European committee within the cabinet, *Regjeringens Europa-utvalg*. Before a minister can bring an issue to the cabinet, he or she must brief the Ministry of Foreign Affairs in advance, and it is given the opportunity to state its opinion. Second, at the highest administrative level is the Coordinating Committee, *Koordinerings-utvalget*. The Ministry of Foreign Affairs is responsible for chairing the committee, as well as running the secretariat. All ministries are allowed to participate in the committee with one representative, but only if they are affected by the issue on the agenda. However, the Ministry of Finance and the Prime Minister's Office are obliged to participate in every session. A total number of 21 bureaucrats, at the level of permanent under-secretary of the state or deputy secretary, participate in these monthly meetings. Third, there is a number of various expert committees that take care of the day-to-day administration in a more technical way. There are in total twenty *spesial utvalg*, with some more active than others. The guiding principle for the administration is that Norwegian positions should be elaborated and negotiated as early as possible and at the lowest possible administrative level. A ministry holding the formal responsibility in a certain field is also responsible for chairing the relevant expert committee. The Ministry of Finance and the Ministry of Foreign Affairs as well as the Prime Minister's Office have the right to participate in any of the expert committees.

Corresponding to this institutional arrangement, the political leadership laid down a standard operating procedure for securing an effective adaptation of legislation. The standard procedure is based upon the initial instruction to the administration from Prime Minister Gro Harlem Brundtland in 1988, a long time prior to the start of negotiations on the EEA (Statusrapport, 1989). According to a letter sent by the Prime Minister's Office in April 1995, each Ministry has to write a 'framework document' for each new piece of legislation. This document accompanies the dossier of the case as it moves through the interministerial apparatus. The document is supposed to describe the background and the legal status of the EEA legislation, and, in addition, to give an overview of the current Norwegian legal position. Furthermore, the document must contain an analysis of the Norwegian interests, a description of the status of the negotiations within the EU, presentation of the view of interest groups and a short analysis of the consequences if Norway vetoes the proposal. In addition, the responsible ministry is also obliged to indicate how, why and with what budgetary implications a piece of legislation should be implemented in the Norwegian legislation. A comparison with other international treaties and the status in the other Nordic countries should also be made. Finally, the responsible ministry should draw an inference and recommend an official Norwegian position.

It is still too early to tell whether or not this very ambitious standard operating procedure is actually followed in the day-to-day work of the administration. It seems that some ministries and some *spesial utvalg* are operating according to the procedure, while other institutions give less priority to European issues. The way that the administration is affected by increased European integration differs considerably in terms of volume and task. Some institutions perceive the development as a serious threat to their traditional tasks, while other institutions see new opportunities and possibilities for increasing their influence or autonomy.

The high level of political conflict over the issue, combined with the vital national interests at stake, makes the Prime Minister's Office (PMO) a key institution. The prime minister and her advisers played the role of the initiator, coordinator and controller of the process. Tasks traditionally handled in the Ministry of Foreign Affairs were governed by firm instruction from the PMO. Thus the PMO increased its importance and influence substantially. Although this was strongly related to increased European integration, this development also had historical roots. In Norway, the prime minister has traditionally been *primus inter pares* without any privileged position, and there have been disputes on the role and strength of the PMO. Until 1939, the prime minister was even responsible for operating a ministry at the same time as being the head of the cabinet.

The PMO was first established in 1956 after a major parliamentary dispute. Carl J. Hambro, the Conservative leader of the opposition, argued that this was the 'most revolutionary proposal forwarded for the Parliament in fifty years' (St. forh. 1955 s. 3417). In the 1960s the PMO gained a coordinating role in international issues related to the Nordic Council, and became increasingly influential in international affairs (Bloch, 1963: 50). However, there were several reasons for the increased role of the PMO in relation to increased European integration. First, according to the formal procedures, it had the responsibility for preparing the weekly meetings in the cabinet. Consequently the PMO became predominantly occupied with European issues simply because so many of these issues were discussed in the cabinet. Second, the strong role of the PMO was considered as important in order to manoeuvre in an area with considerable domestic political conflict and possible tension between different administrative institutions. Participation by the PMO signalled the political priority devoted to the issue. Third, as long as the leading politicians considered membership of the EU as the important political objective, it was viewed as appropriate that the prime minister, in fulfilling her role, should play a key role and take responsibility in this important issue. Nevertheless, we should not overestimate the importance of the role of the PMO. The PMO had few resources. In 1991 a special position for the coordination of EFTA and EC matters was established; however, its international department still has only four positions. Thus the PMO has played the role of a competent commentator providing deadlines and coordination of the 'national interest', rather than the active role of analyst or executor.

Another institution that gained considerable influence on the development of the Norwegian policy towards the EC/EU was the PR in Brussels. During the negotiations on the EEA and EU membership, the PR was strengthened and played an important role in developing the relationship between the EU and Norway (Mathiesen, 1996). At present, 35 bureaucrats work at the PR, with a majority of experts coming from ministries other than the Ministry of Foreign Affairs. After the referendum, their main tasks were to report on the activity of the EU, to participate in meetings, and to try to influence decision-making (*ibid.*).

The Europeanization process has not only changed the *mode* of coordination, but also the *extent* of coordination within the administration, with the latter changes probably more significant. Institutions with a traditionally high level of autonomy were put under pressure to obey an increasing number of instructions and guidelines. Through extensive use of deadlines, guidelines and political signals the political leadership was able to coordinate traditionally autonomous institutions. It is likely that the transitional character, the clear objective of the political leadership and the political importance of the issue contributed to easing the conditions for deliberate design and political leadership. However, the extent of the coordination varied in relation to certain stages of the process. In the early, initiating stages the level of coordination was high, while in the later stages the general level decreased. The political leaders had limited capacity and paid sequential attention to some particular fields that were considered to be of vital importance, such as fishery, energy and agriculture. When the Norwegian institutions became increasingly involved in highly specialized technical issues, the amount and character of the information and documentation increased (Engen, 1995). This information overload led to sequential attention and thereby reduced the possibility and ability of political coordination within some fields.

Of particular importance in reorganizing the relationship between different governmental bodies were the changes made in the state-owned monopolies. The EEA Agreement imposed a clear distinction between operators and regulators of the market, two tasks that previously had been performed within the same organization. Some of the state-owned monopolies – for instance the Norwegian Medicine Control Authority, the import monopoly for wine and the monopolies in postal and tele-services – lost their privileges. New formal–legal means replaced the traditional trust-based and informal way of governing and regulating political life. For a small state the informal system had worked efficiently, but as the country became integrated in a larger political community it became increasingly formalized and regulated. A majority of these developments did not create political or administrative problems. Rather, the EEA Agreement gave further momentum to, and was a codification of, already ongoing processes of change, and the adaptations fitted well with the general conceptions of good and effective administration.

Increased European integration challenged and altered the relationship between different units within particular governmental bodies. In general, the formal structures of the ministries remained unchanged. Since it is often harder to change existing structures than to establish new ones, new problems are often resolved by creating new units (March and Olsen, 1995). For instance, in the 1970s, planning departments had been created, and during the 1980s administrative units were established. During the preparation for membership, the political leadership did not give any general guidelines for a preferred way of handling or organizing European issues within the respective ministries, and neither did the Ministry of Government Administration suggest one preferred standard model (St. meld no. 35, 1991–92). Consequently, different institutions had a considerable degree of discretion in choosing their own model which reflected their traditional way of solving problems and standard procedures of the organization. Few new special units were established within the administration. However, one major exception was the rapid build-up of a secretariat for European issues in the Ministry of Foreign Affairs. But even this was based upon the already existing structure of the former Ministry of Trade (Christensen, 1996). A few, among them the Ministry of Fisheries, had their own coordinating unit in a specialized international or European department. Other institutions, like the Ministry of Government Administration, distributed the coordinating role to the generalists within the administrative units. But in most institutions, like the Ministry of Finance, the coordinating role was carried out by the experts in the most affected unit. Setting up special units for handling these issues was simply not considered an appropriate solution. European issues were interpreted as integrated and natural parts of the normal tasks of the institutions, and the formal organizational structures were never really changed when facing these challenges (Farsund and Sverdrup, 1994).

Increased European integration also challenged the mode of vertical coordination between different institutions within the Norwegian administration. Like the ministries, the directorates went through a gradual process of internationalization during the 1970s and 1980s (Holberg, 1994). Some institutions had considerable experience and were involved in different European and international networks, which they operated with considerable skill and a high degree of freedom. Others had less experience. Since the Europeanization processes involved such a high degree of coordination, and had such political importance, many of the directorates were controlled, and instructed by their respective ministry to an unusually high degree and in untraditional ways. One example is the Directorate of Fisheries, which lost some of its traditional autonomy to the Ministry of Fisheries when they prepared for increased European integration (Engen, 1995). A relatively small number of all the directorates was given the possibility to participate in the Norwegian coordination apparatus, or in any of the working groups at the European level. These tasks were primarily handled by the ministries.

European integration also challenged the boundaries and relationship between government and non-governmental organizations. The tradition of giving legitimate access and participatory rights to organized interests in public policy-making had been exposed to considerable critique during the last decade. From being regarded as an extension of democracy and a complementary channel for representation in the 1960s and 1970s (Rokkan, 1969), participation of interest organizations gradually came to be considered as a hindrance to reforms and administrative modernization during the 1980s (Olsen, 1996b). In spite of the change in the normative environment, the traditional way of participation from the interest organizations was exploited when the Norwegian political system faced the European issues (Farsund and Sverdrup, 1994). Organized interests participated in the policy formation in specialized reference groups within the inter-institutional apparatus. Their participation was perceived as an effective method of distributing information and increasing the level of competence in various aspects of European politics within Norwegian society. However, the process of negotiating and creating the Norwegian national interest was still the domain of the public administration and the political leadership. In general, the interest organizations took only a modest part in formulating the negotiating positions. Nevertheless, this varied across sectors and segments. Ministries with well-established routines and long traditions of collaboration with interest organizations considered it appropriate to include them in the process of Europeanization. Other institutions with less tradition for including interest organizations did not invite such participation. Within the agricultural sector the relationship between government and non-governmental bodies became increasingly difficult. In this sector there has traditionally been a strong history of mutual support and cooperation between government and interest organizations. Still, opposing views on the Norwegian positions and the quality of the negotiations created a high level of conflict between the Ministry of Agriculture and the organizations of the farmers. The conflict between the parties escalated and ended in reduced contact and cooperation during the campaign. Nevertheless, a short time later the traditional relationship seemed to be more or less re-established.

The significance of membership

It is hard to assess the significance of formal membership of the EU. The time since the latest referendum is short, and the distinction between members and non-members is not easily drawn. As the discussion above shows, the Norwegian political and administrative system has made substantial changes in order to cope with the challenges and opportunities raised by European integration. However, Europeanization of the Norwegian administration is best interpreted as a process of a series of incremental and step-wise adaptation, rather than a dramatic and rapid break with the past. The Norwegian political system did not respond to the process of Europeanization by exploring or inventing radically new solutions – rather the opposite. Solutions that were found appropriate reflected historical experiences and traditional principles and methods of organizing political life in Norway. Existing routines and capabilities were considered effective and appropriate. In addition, the Norwegian administration had a considerable endogenous dynamic, and increased European integration gave further momentum to ongoing processes of modernization. Since the Norwegian legislation had gradually converged prior to formal membership in the EEA, it was possible to make rapid changes without any delay or any major conflicts within the administration. In addition, the political priority given to the issue made it easier to initiate changes and to adapt smoothly.

After the referendum in Norway the situation is different. There is uncertainty on the degree of discretion for strategic adaptation for the Norwegian government. The asymmetry in the relationship between EFTA and the EU increased substantially. EFTA has been reduced from being an important trading partner with the EU to consisting of only Norway, Iceland, Liechtenstein and Switzerland, with the latter not a member of the EEA. Shortly after the referendum the Norwegian government made efforts to reduce uncertainty related to the EEA Agreement. During 1995 it became clear that it was not necessary to renegotiate the EEA Agreement (European Commission, 1995). Moreover, the political leadership interpreted the result of the referendum as a 'no' to full membership of the EU, but as a 'yes' to as close a connection with the EU and European countries as possible (Brundtland, 1995). This interpretation increased the degree of discretion for the government and the position held has received remarkably little criticism from the voters.

With this mandate the political leadership has made attempts to deepen and widen both the formal and informal linkages between the EU and Norway. This development followed three different routes. First, changes have been made to develop the EEA Agreement further. Towards the end of 1995 decisions were taken to extend the cooperation to the social and cultural fields (European Commission, 1995: 315–17). Second, Norway has played an important role in the reorganization of Nordic cooperation. Since Sweden, Finland and Denmark are members of the EU, the Nordic countries are more strongly linked to the EU than ever before. In order to cope with the new tasks, Nordic cooperation and its political institutions have been reorganized. The underlying idea is that European issues, and particularly issues related to the EU, should have a more important role on the Nordic agenda (Lindström, 1996). Strengthened Nordic cooperation could give Norway better access to, and possibly more influence in the EU decision-making process. Third, the Norwegian political leadership has tried to strengthen the linkage to other European institutions and agreements that are more loosely coupled to the EU, such as NATO. Norway is currently an associated member of the WEU and an applicant to the Schengen Agreement.

The discussion of the Norwegian case has demonstrated some of the difficulties of assessing the significance of formal membership. In some fields it seems that non-members are affected, and have even adapted more or less as member-states. However, in other areas non-members are far less affected. In analysing Europeanization of small states it is therefore not very fruitful to start with a mono-causal analysis of member-states versus non-member-states. Nevertheless, participation in the regular political and administrative cooperation has been reduced since the referendum. Naturally, the EU is paying increased attention to the ongoing internal reforms and preparations for the future enlargement to central and eastern Europe. In addition, the capability of EFTA has been reduced. EFTA was left as an organization with considerably less influence and capabilities when the formerly important EFTA countries – Sweden, Finland and Austria – became full members of the EU. The staff of the EEA institutions and the EFTA secretariat has been reduced by about half. Furthermore, Norwegian policy has changed from being in a pre-accession period with rapid changes and clear political goals, to a situation with less clear political objectives or long-term visions.

We can identify three possible future developments in the relationship between Norway and the EU. First, Norway might continue its policy of adaptation, which would most likely lead to increased homogenization and convergence with the EU in a wide spectrum of fields. This was the strategy of the Norwegian political leadership shortly after the referendum, and it presupposes that the national institutions are able and willing to make and implement changes. Second, Norwegian administration might gradually alter its priorities and start to benefit from some of the positive effects of being a non-member on a small state with a small administration. Less participation in EU institutions means less meetings, fewer deadlines and less documents to read. Figures from the PR in Brussels indicate that this is the development. While more than 3,200 people visited the PR in 1994, this decreased to 2,300 in 1995. The number of national bureaucrats visiting the PR decreased by 68 per cent during the same period (Aftenposten, 1996). De-coupling from the flow of information has already reduced the strain on the Norwegian administration and made it possible to increase the attention and energy devoted to other and possibly more important fields. However, in relation to first-pillar issues the EEA Agreement created a fall-back position, which links Norway tightly to the permanent flow of decisions made in the EU. Third, it is possible to imagine a complicated mixture of these two models. The linkages and pattern of contact will most likely vary according to different sectors and different institutional traditions. In some fields Norwegian politicians and administration will be out of sight and out of mind as far as the decision-makers in the EU are concerned. In other fields, those with strong formal and informal linkages, it is likely that Norway will participate in one way or another. In this latter model we will probably witness increased segmentation and fragmentation, which in the long run could make overall democratic and political governance of Norwegian policy more difficult.

References

Aftenposten (1996) Fœrre norske besøker Brussel, June.

Andersen, S.S. and Eliassen, K.A. (eds) (1993) *Making Policy in Europe: The Europeification of National Policy Making* (London: Sage).

Bloch, K. (1963) *Kongens råd* (Oslo: Universitetsforlaget).

Brundtland, G.H. (1995) *Europas videre utvikling – Hvordan berøres Norge?*, ARENA Working Paper No. 12, Oslo.

Christensen, T. (1996) *Adapting to Processes of Europeanisation: A Study of the Norwegian Ministry of Foreign Affairs*, ARENA Report No. 2/96.

Delors, J. (1989) Erklæringer om retningslinjerne for Kommissjonen for de Europæiske Fælleskaper, 17 January, Bulletin for the European Communities, *Supplement* 1/1989, Office for Official Publications of the European Communities, Luxembourg.

Egeberg, M. (1980) The fourth level of government: on the standardisation of public policy within international regions, *Scandinavian Political Studies*, vol. 3, pp. 235–48.

Engen, R. (1995) Fiskeridepartementet – en aktør med ambisjoner på egne vegne?, unpublished thesis, University of Bergen, Bergen.

ESA (1995) *European Surveillance Annual Report* Brussels: European Surveillance Authority.

European Commission (1995) *General Report of the Activities of the EU* (Office for Official Publications of the European Communities, Luxembourg).

Farsund, A. and Sverdrup, U. (1994) Norsk forvaltning i EØS-prosessen – noen empiriske resultat, *Nordisk Administrativt Tidsskrift*, vol. 75, no. 1, pp. 48–67.

Furre, B. (1991) *Vårt hundreår – norsk historie 1905–1990* (Oslo: Det norske Samlaget).

Gleditsch, N.P., Østerud, O. and Elster J. (eds) (1974) *Kampen om EF* (Oslo: Pax forlag).

Holberg, U. (1994) *Direktoratenes internasjonalisering*, ARENA Working Paper no. 4, Oslo.

Lindström, G. (1996) Nordisk samarbete i en ny tid, *Nordisk Administrativt Tidsskrift*, vol. 77, no. 2, pp. 121–30.

Løchen, E. (1993) Norges møte med Europa 1950–1964, *IFS Info*, vol. 6, Oslo.

Luif, P. (1996) *On the Road to Brussels: The Political Dimension of Austria's, Finland's and Sweden's Accession to the European Union* (Vienna: Braumüller).

March, J.G. and Olsen, J.P. (1995) *Democratic Governance* (New York: Free Press).

Mathiesen, G. (1996) *Innenfor EU – en innføring i EUs beslutningsproseser* (Oslo: Universitetsforlaget).

Nei til EU (1994) *Annual Report*, Oslo: Nei til EU (No to the EU).

Olsen, J.P. (1996a) Europeanization and nation state dynamics. In Sverker Gustavsson and Leif Lewin (eds), *The Future of the Nation State: Essays on Cultural Pluralism and Political Integration* (London: Routledge), pp. 245–85.

Olsen, J.P. (1996b) Norway: slow learner – or another triumph of the tortoise? In Johan P. Olsen and B. Guy Peters (eds) *Lessons from Experience: Experiential Learning in Administrative Reforms in Eight Democracies* (Oslo: Scandinavian University Press), pp. 180–213.

Ringdal, K. (1995) Velgernes argumenter. In Anders Todal Jenssen and Henry Valen (eds) *Brussel midt imot – folkeavstemmingen om EU* (Oslo: AdNotam Gyldendal), pp. 45–64.

Riste, O. (1991) Isolasjonisme og stormaktsgarantiar: norsk tryggingspolitikk 1905–1990, *Forsvarsstudier*, vol. 3, Oslo.

Riste, O. (1995) Forord. In Narve Bjørgo, Øystein Rian and Alf Kaartvedt (eds) *Selvstendighet og union, Fra middelalderen til 1905*, Norsk utenrikspolitikks historie bind 1 (Oslo: Universitetsforlaget), pp. 5–9.

Røhne, N.A. (1991) Norwegian attitudes towards the Briand Plan, *IFS Info*, vol. 8, Oslo.

Rokkan, S. (1969) Norway: numerical democracy and corporate pluralism. In Robert A. Dahl (ed.) *Political Opposition in Western Democracies* (New Haven: Yale University Press), pp. 70–115.

Sejersted, F. (1996) The Norwegian Parliament and European integration: reflections from medium-speed Europe. In Eivind Smith (ed.) *National Parliaments as Cornerstones of European Integration* (London: Kluwer), pp. 124–56.

Sejersted, F. and Arnesen, F. *et al.* (eds) (1995) *EØS-rett* (Oslo: Universitetsforlaget).

Skogstad Aamo, B. (1995) Tilpasninger til EUs regelverk – problemer eller muligheter for finanssektoren, unpublished manuscript, presented at the National Conference of Norwegian Economists.

Sollien, T.H. (1995) EØS-avtalens betydning for norsk lovverk og den nasjonale beslutningsprosessen: en kartleggingsstudie, unpublished thesis, University of Oslo, Oslo.

Statskonsult (1995) EU/EØS arbeidet i departementene – en analyse av organisering of arbeidsformer, Report 1995:15, Oslo.

Statusrapport, (1989) Norges tilpasning til EF's indre marked Utgitt av Regjeringsutvalget for EF saker, October, Oslo.

Sverdrup, U. (1994) Nytt Europa – ny forvaltning?, LOS Report no. 9411, Bergen.

Todal Jenssen, A., Listhaug, O. and Pettersen, P.A. (1995) Betydningen av gamle og nye skiller. In Anders Todal Jenssen and Henry Valen (eds) *Brussel midt imot – folkeavstemmingen om EU* (Oslo: AdNotam Gyldendal), pp. 143–64.

Toonen, T.A.J. (1992) Europe of administrations: the challenge of '92 (and beyond), *Public Administration Review*, vol. 52, no. 2, pp. 108–15.

Trondal, J. (1996) Tilknytningsformer til EU og nasjonale samordningsprosesser – en studie av norske og danske departementer, unpublished thesis, University of Oslo, Oslo.

Underdal, Arild (1972) Forhandlinger om norsk medlemskap i EF – en studie av rammebetingelser, unpublished thesis, University of Oslo, Oslo.

Urwin, D.W. (1995) *The Community of Europe: A History of European Integration since 1945*, 2nd edn (London: Longman).

Chapter 11

Switzerland: Adjustment Despite Deadlock

STEPHAN KUX

Introduction

Switzerland is not and, in the foreseeable future, will not become a member of the EU. The case is nevertheless interesting because it shows that institutions of non-member countries are also adjusting to the changing requirements of bilateral relations with the EU. Moreover, the experiences of other small European states in the integration process can provide a useful lesson for the current discussion on reforming the Swiss political system. This chapter examines the administrative, political and strategic adaptations that Switzerland has experienced in the course of its evolving relationship with the EU. It is based on an analysis of the existing literature, a study of official documents and a series of interviews with government officials. The conclusion is that while Swiss integration policy remains in a deadlock, a substantial adaptation of the institutional system can be observed over the last five years. The challenges of non-integration have profoundly transformed the political discourse and have helped to promote institutional reforms of the Swiss system.

Switzerland's relationship with the EU is at a turning point. For decades, the country pursued a policy of participation without integration. Membership of the EFTA and bilateral agreements with the EC offered the economic advantages of participation without requiring political integration or a transfer of sovereignty to supranational institutions. European integration was a non-issue. The free movement of goods alone, however, could not satisfy the requirements of an increasingly differentiated post-industrial economy. In the 1980s, improved access to the emerging Single European Market became an important objective of Swiss integration policy. Jacques Delors' project for a European Economic Area was tailor-made for Switzerland (Sciarini, 1992). The agreement was based on a comprehensive, multilateral approach to economic integration, extending the *acquis communautaire* to the EFTA countries, offering the four freedoms, excluding the ever sensitive agricultural sector and establishing a loose form of institutionalized policy coordination. The EEA was only viewed as a first step toward full EU membership. In May 1992, even before the EEA was ratified, the federal government submitted Switzerland's membership application.

Yet on 6 December 1992, the Swiss electorate voted against EEA membership. Some of the main concerns included the loss of sovereignty, concessions on trans-Alpine transport, unrestricted freedom of labour and a general uneasiness toward the EC, which at that time experienced a severe crisis in the European Monetary System (Goetschel, 1994; Huth, 1996). This verdict put a halt to the government's plan to integrate gradually and left the country politically divided. There is probably no other political decision during the post-war period that has had such far-reaching implications for the Swiss polity than that of the EEA referendum. In order to overcome the deadlock in Swiss integration policy, the Federal Council decided to return to the pre-EEA strategy of bilateral sectoral agreements without integration. In the summer of 1993, the government submitted a list of sixteen policy areas concerning which it wanted to negotiate with the EU. On 8 November 1993, the Council of Ministers agreed to start bilateral talks with Switzerland in seven of these areas, namely air transport, land transport, agriculture, free movement of people, public procurement, research and technical barriers to trade. On 20 February 1994, however, the Swiss people voted in favour of the so-called Alpine initiative, introducing an article into the federal constitution which bars all trans Alpine road transport after the year 2004. This unilateral decision was perceived as an open violation of the 1992 EC–Swiss transit agreement. As a consequence, the Council of Ministers postponed the start of bilateral negotiations. Only after the Federal Council was able to convince the EU member-states that the Alpine initiative would be implemented in a non-discriminatory way and in line with existing commitments did bilateral talks begin in late 1994. The initial target to reach an agreement by 1995 – before the beginning of the 1996 IGC – was missed. Disagreements on the freedom of labour and road transport are the main reason for the delay.

The Federal Council is still committed to full EU membership as a 'strategic' (i.e. long-term) objective of Swiss integration policy. The membership application, however, has been put on hold, in order to relieve the domestic political debate of an additional, premature controversy. In the meantime, the Swiss government is pursuing a policy of gradual harmonization through 'unilateral transposition' of EU legislation. Eurolex, the package of legal amendments to EEA rules, has been implemented as Swisslex, despite the negative EEA vote. New laws are scrutinized for their compatibility with EU legislation. The *acquis communautaire*, in general, has become the point of reference for Swiss legislation. Moreover, on 1 July 1995 Switzerland became a member of the World Trade Organization (WTO). The world trade rules help to alleviate some of the negative impacts of non-integration and contribute to institutional adaptation. In comparison with the EEA members Iceland, Liechtenstein and Norway or the associated countries in central and eastern Europe, the degree of Switzerland's integration remains low. The failure of bilateral negotiations would deal another serious blow to the government's strategy and would further isolate the country in the dynamic process of European integration.

Governmental and administrative adaptation

Changes in foreign policy-making

In the Swiss post-war political system, the processes of domestic and foreign policy formulation were clearly separated. Domestic issues were subjected to an elaborate, direct democratic process of consultation and decision-making. The conduct of foreign policy in turn was restricted to a small élite in government, administration and Parliament. In 1977, however, a constitutional amendment was passed which required that permanent, irreversible international agreements, treaties implying multilateral harmonization of law and decisions to join international organizations should be put to a referendum. This new provision thus gives the people the final say in important foreign policy decisions. Suddenly, foreign policy became subject to direct democratic instruments (Kreis, 1995). Initially, this democratization posed few problems for relations with the EC. Until the 1980s, Swiss integration policy was limited to the free-trade agreements. Negotiations were mainly conducted in a bilateral framework and focused on specific aspects of the free movement of goods. In the framework of its foreign policy powers, the Federal Council had a clear mandate to deal with foreign trade issues. The Office of External Trade of the Ministry of Economy and the foreign ministry were in charge of integration policy. Since the sectoral agreements only required parliamentary approval and were not subjected to a referendum, no consultation process was necessary.

The situation started to change in April 1984 when the foreign ministers of the EC and EFTA member-states issued the so-called Luxemburg Declaration, which introduced the idea of creating a European Economic Area. Multilateral consultations started in order to examine the adaptation of the free-trade agreements to the single-market project. On 19 January 1989, Commission President Jacques Delors proposed the creation of the EEA, a more formal association between EC and EFTA covering most aspects of the *acquis communautaire*. In June 1990, the Council gave the Commission a formal mandate to negotiate an agreement with the EFTA states. A high-level negotiation group and several negotiation groups consisting of Commission representatives and high-ranking officials from the seven EFTA countries were established. The EFTA countries coordinated their positions toward the EC and presented a common point of view to the Commission. The year 1989 was thus the turning point in Switzerland's relations with the EC. Multilateralism replaced bilateral negotiations; a global approach covering most aspects of the single market replaced sectoral negotiations. Switzerland was about to add a fourth level of government to its political system.

This has had major repercussions on the conduct and the domestic politics of Swiss integration policy. First, the Federal Council as a collective assumed responsibilities for negotiations. The foreign ministry and the Ministry of Economy had to include other sectoral ministries and offices in the negotiation teams. Integration became an interdepartmental task. Second, the government had to seek parliamentary support for its negotiation position. Thus a closer interaction between the executive, the Parliament's two foreign affairs committees and the political parties became necessary. Third, since the EEA affected a broad range of political, economic and societal interests, the federal government had to consult organized interests, non-governmental organizations and social movements. And finally, the EEA covered policy areas such as education, health and public procurement, which fall under the exclusive domain of the cantons. For the first time in the history of the Swiss federation, non-central governments became involved in international negotiations, which previously had been a prerogative of the central government. The EEA negotiations required a substantial adjustment of the institutional and political frame-work of Swiss integration policy-making. Switzerland pursued a pre-accession strategy of adaptation. Even more important changes followed after the rejection of the EEA in the 1992 referendum.

Government

As with other democratic states, the Swiss constitution puts foreign policy into the hands of the executive. The Federal Council forms the collective government of the Swiss federation. It consists of seven members which are elected by Parliament. Over the last 30 years, a stable four-party coalition has been in power, currently holding over 70 per cent of the seats in Parliament. Several smaller parties form a relatively weak opposition. According to the voluntary power-sharing formula, the so-called 'magic formula' (*Zauberformel*) agreed on in 1959, the Christian People's Democratic Party (CVP), the Social Democratic Party (SPS) and the Radical Democratic Party (FDP) each hold two seats, and the Swiss People's Party (SVP) one seat in the seven-member Council. There is no permanent head of state. For a period of one year, one of the federal councillors acts as formal president of the federation. This rotation creates problems of representation towards the outside and problems of coordination towards the inside. Each of the federal councillors is head of a ministry. The consociational Federal Council takes collective responsibility for the conduct of Swiss foreign policy and decides by unanimity. Traditionally the councillor in charge of foreign affairs or the councillor in charge of the economy reports to the Council, which then takes a consensual decision. Negotiations on the EEA put an end to this division of labour. The EEA package directly affected the responsibilities of most of the seven ministries. Five councillors were directly involved in the negotiations.

The intensification of international cooperation in general, and of integration policy in particular, revealed a major weakness of the executive structure. The federal constitution strictly limits the number of councillors and ministries to seven. The creation of a specialized ministry for European affairs, for instance, would not be possible without a constitutional amendment. As a consequence, most councillors are in charge of several policy areas. The federal councillor of the interior, for example, combines responsibilities for social affairs, environment, culture, education and other issues. This reflects the chronic overload of a government that is too small in size to handle the complexities of modern politics. Plans for a reorganization of government existed long before European integration became an essential issue in Swiss politics. The burden of the EEA negotiations and other international activities accelerated efforts for institutional reform of the federal government. In 1992, a group of experts was commissioned to submit proposals for a reorganization. The various models had to be tested in view of a future Swiss membership in the EEA and the EU respectively. In 1994, the Federal Council introduced a bill to increase the number of secretaries of state from three to ten. Comparable to a junior minister, a secretary of state can fully represent the Federal Council in international negotiations. With seven senior and ten junior ministers, the capacity of the Swiss government to engage in international affairs and to participate in the busy agenda of European integration would have increased significantly. Yet a coalition of conservative parties and interest groups was strongly opposed to inflating the federal administration and launched a referendum against the bill. In June 1996, the Swiss voters rejected this reform of government by a vast majority. Constitutional provisions and popular veto thus set narrow limits to the adaptation of the structures of Swiss governance.

Administration

In view of the structural limitations of the executive, the federal administration plays an important role in European integration. The leading agency is the Integration Office, a joint agency of the foreign ministry and the Ministry of Economy, which was established in the 1960s. It consists of some fifteen public servants. The number has not been increased since the EEA negotiations. Occasionally, staff from the sectoral ministries are temporarily assigned to the Integration Office. In the other ministries, no specialized units for European affairs have been created. With the growing importance of international cooperation, most branches of the administration, however, have established an international section that deals, among other things, with EU affairs. Legal sections also have to deal with EU legislation. Before drafting a law or issuing an administrative act, most departments assess the 'Eurocompatibility' of the measure. Several sectoral ministries and offices were directly involved in the EEA negotiations, namely agriculture, education, health, labour, social security and transport. In the current bilateral talks, the respective directors of the sectoral offices are the leading negotiators on the Swiss side. Hence, each department has to gather information and expertise on the EU. The main source is the Integration Office or the Swiss Permanent Mission to the EU.

The Swiss Permanent Mission to the EU in Brussels plays an important role in the policy process. It is headed by a career-diplomat. Most of the staff are drawn from the foreign ministry. The Federal Office of Foreign Trade and the Ministry of Finance also have their representatives in Brussels. While the preparation of dossiers and administrative coordination remains the prerogative of the national bureaucracy, the views of the mission carry some weight in determining strategy. The mission serves as an early warning system and provides insights into the thinking of EU institutions and member-states. With the growing direct involvement of sectoral ministries, the influence of the permanent mission has decreased. Thus, over the past years, a decentralization of responsibilities has taken place. Yet no expansion of the bureaucracy can be observed. The Swiss administration adapted to the challenges of European integration by shifting, not building up, resources. This can be explained by a ceiling on the number of federal employees forced upon the government by the Parliament in the late 1980s.

Coordination within the ministries follows hierarchical lines. The secretaries-general of the ministries and the personal advisers to the federal councillors play an influential role. For interministerial coordination, the same procedures apply as in other policy areas. There is a written co-reporting procedure (*Mitberichtsverfahren*) which allows the ministries to review important drafts and policy papers before the Federal Council takes a decision. Three federal councillors, those responsible for foreign affairs, economy and justice, form a steering committee on European affairs at the executive level. Chief coordinator and negotiator is the secretary of state in the foreign ministry who reports directly to the Federal Council. Several interdepartmental working groups coordinate the activities of the agencies involved. The small size of the government apparatus also allows for informal consultation and initiatives by individuals and agencies (Klöti and von Dosenrode, 1995: 279). Government and administration are thus gradually adjusting structures and coordination procedures to the EU. More important changes can be observed in the relationship between the federal government and other institutional actors. The authorities have developed new methods to consult the Parliament, political parties, interest groups and cantons.

Parliament

The Swiss Federal Assembly consists of two chambers, the National Council and the Council of the States. Each chamber has a standing committee on foreign affairs consisting of 30 parliamentarians altogether. The committees are supported by a small staff in the foreign affairs section of the Parliament's secretariat. The federal government's foreign policy is under much less parliamentary scrutiny than its domestic affairs. Until recently, the Parliament played only a limited role in the formulation of Swiss integration policy. International affairs remained in the realm of the executive. With the growing internationalization of traditional domestic policy areas, the legislature started to take a greater interest in foreign affairs in the 1980s. The negotiations of and the referendum on the EEA were the turning point in executive–legislative relations (Sciarini, 1991). The EEA agreement formed a tight international legal framework which the Parliament had to translate into a package of national laws, the so-called Eurolex programme. Thus the law-makers had a strong interest in participating in the process that defines the international framework of Swiss federal legislation. During the EEA negotiations, the members of the two standing committees on foreign affairs were briefed regularly.

The growing involvement of the Parliament in foreign and integration policy resulted in a redefinition of the division of labour between the executive and legislative in the bill on parliamentary reform passed in 1991 and partially adopted by the Swiss people in a 1992 referendum. The revised Law on Inter-Institutional Relations gives the Parliament a greater input in Swiss foreign policy. It states that 'in negotiations in international organizations resulting in decisions, which establish or will establish new legislation affecting Switzerland, the Federal Council will consult the foreign affairs committees on the guidelines and the negotiation mandate before it takes decisions or makes adjustments'. This new consultation and co-decision procedure is now being applied in the bilateral negotiations with the EU. The Parliament is consulted on a regular basis. The 1995 draft constitution also contains a provision on inter-institutional cooperation and establishes a general parliamentary overview over foreign affairs. Foreign policy, and particularly integration policy, have thus become a shared competency between Federal Council and Federal Assembly.

However, for several reasons, the capacity of the law-makers to counterbalance the executive and to influence integration policy remains relatively weak. First, there is no consensus or clear majority in Parliament on European affairs. The legislature is as deeply split on integration policy as the population. Second, the Parliament and its foreign affairs committees have a very weak infrastructure. The law-makers do not employ a personal staff. The committees have little access to independent expertise and are thus highly dependent on information provided by the administration. And third, the capacity to respond quickly to developments in the negotiation process is rather limited given the fact that the Parliament meets only four to five times a year. In light of traditional Swiss foreign policy-making, the shift of power from government to Parliament is nevertheless remarkable.

Political parties and organized interests

In Switzerland, political parties, organized interests and cantons are heard before every major decision. There are two forms of participation. First, the Federal Council nominates a study group which will examine important projects of legislation. In order to include a broad spectrum of interests, the composition of these committees is as representative as possible. This process gives organized interests, which might otherwise call for a referendum, the chance to voice their opinions or to negotiate a compromise. Second, the constitution establishes a written consultation procedure (*Vernehmlassung*) which is also applicable to European affairs. The first draft of a bill is circulated among the political parties, relevant interest groups and cantons. When evaluating the results of this consultation, the federal administration is likely to adjust proposals that did not find sufficient support. Linder describes it as a cooperative process, mainly involving economic interest groups in the preparliamentary phase and political parties in the governmental and parliamentary arena (Linder, 1994: 124). This procedure usually takes several months and is too slow to be effective in international negotiations or European integration. New consultation methods were introduced in order to reach a faster decision. Hearings and informal consultation have replaced the traditional decision-shaping routine. During the EEA debate, the Federal Council also considered the creation of a consultative body which would facilitate and accelerate the dialogue between government and organized interests on integration issues.

In the EEA negotiations and currently in the bilateral negotiations, the major interest groups and other organizations are consulted on a regular basis, namely on the issues of direct concern such as free movement of labour, transport and research. Federal and cantonal governments and administrations also frequently draw on the EU expertise of business and labour organizations. Occasionally, business representatives directly take part in negotiation rounds. The main leverage of these interest groups is either their economic weight or their power to organize a referendum. Compared with other countries, the influence of the trade unions is relatively low, while business circles traditionally play an important role. Nevertheless, the federal government has had difficulties in mobilizing and sustaining support for its integration policy. Political parties and interest groups continue to voice their veto during and after international negotiations.

The role of the cantons

As in other federal states, the Swiss cantons are directly affected by European integration. Several policy areas addressed in the Swiss–EC free-trade agreement, the EEA Treaty and the current bilateral negotiations fall under the competence of the cantonal governments. This includes education, health, culture, infrastructure, public procurement, police and justice. Traditionally, the federal government assumed responsibility for foreign relations. With the intensification of crossborder cooperation and the creation of Euroregions along the Swiss borders, some cantons started to pursur a 'small foreign policy' and to promote micro-integration on their own. Articles 9 and 10 of the constitution entitle cantonal governments to conclude agreements within their competence with neighbouring regions.

With the beginning of the EEA negotiations in 1989, the federal and cantonal governments agreed to intensify information exchange and consultation. The Contact Committee, established in 1978 and used predominantly by the federal authorities for providing information for and pursuing coordination with the cantons in domestic affairs, served as a platform. It is chaired by the federal councillor in charge of justice and includes a minister of each canton. During the EEA negotiations, the Contact Committee met almost bi-monthly. In addition, several inter-cantonal ministerial conferences and working groups prepared programmes for adjusting cantonal legislation to EEA standards. Several cantonal ministers directly participated in the EEA negotiations as representatives of these inter-cantonal conferences. During the EEA process, most cantons reinforced their administration with permanent delegates for European affairs. Their main task is to follow EU developments, to coordinate cantonal integration activities, to provide expertise and to study the implications of integration on cantonal policies. They constitute an important focal point within the cantonal administrations. The cantonal delegates also meet on a regular basis and form an inter-cantonal network. After the failure of the EEA, however, several cantons downgraded or dissolved this office. In 1990, the cantonal governments also agreed to send an observer to Brussels in order to establish a direct line of communication with the EU.

The cantons were obviously not entirely satisfied with the consultation procedure during negotiations of the EEA and other international agreements. Coordination between cantons and federal government and among the cantons remained on an *ad hoc* basis, not institutionalized and without constitutional guarantees. Thus it was agreed to include a provision regarding the role of the cantons in the integration process in the package of constitutional and legal adaptations to the EEA. Article 21 of the 1992 transitional provisions to the federal constitution establishes the cantons' right to be informed, consulted and involved in the implementation of EEA legislation. This important constitutional amendment, however, was rejected with the entire EEA package in the 1992 referendum.

In the 1990s, Swiss federalism experienced two crises of internationalization. First, as a concession to the EU in view of EEA membership, Switzerland signed an agreement on trans-Alpine road transit on 2 May 1992, the very same day that the EEA Treaty was signed. In the agreement, Switzerland guaranteed free access for trucks up to 28 tons, a non-discriminatory policy on transit traffic and the improvement of two transit routes. On 27 September 1992, the Swiss population voted in favour of improving the rail infrastructure, the so-called New Alpine Transit Route (NEAT). Despite the negative vote on the EEA, the Federal Council upheld its international commitments. Yet the previous consensus on transport policy fell apart. Namely, the Alpine cantons changed their position. Fearing a huge increase in EU road traffic through Switzerland, a coalition of ecologists, political parties and politicians from the Alpine cantons most affected by road traffic pollution launched a constitutional initiative on the protection of the Alpine area. Among other provisions, the constitutional amendment (Art. 36 sexies) included a stop of trans-Alpine road construction and a complete prohibition of truck transits on the road by the year 2004. Several of the cantonal governments complained that they were not sufficiently involved in the negotiations on the transit agreement. Thus they had to resort to the *ultima ratio* of a constitutional initiative. This strategy was in clear contradiction of the Federal Council's policy and in open violation of international law as agreed in the transit treaty (Germann, 1995). On 20 February 1994, 51.9 per cent of the population and sixteen of the cantons voted in favour of the constitutional amendment.

Second, a coalition of Alpine cantons criticized the federal government for not including them in the negotiations on the Alpine convention and its protocols. The convention is a framework agreement among the seven countries concerned, including the EU, on the use and protection of the Alpine area. The protocols include guidelines on sustainable development, tourism, agriculture and other aspects. In the protocol on transport, the EU and the Alpine countries try to formulate a mid-term policy on trans-Alpine traffic. In 1995, the cantons prevented the Federal Council from signing the convention on the grounds that they were not sufficiently consulted in the process and that the protocols were unbalanced (Kux, 1994). Both developments illustrate that the traditional federal–cantonal consultation procedures were insufficient to deal with the growing internationalization of Swiss domestic politics. Swiss federalism experienced a crisis of adaptation.

In the meantime, the cantons have further institutionalized their cooperation and reaffirmed their demand for better consultation in integration policy. In 1993, a new inter-cantonal consultation body was established. The Conference of Cantonal Governments (Konferenz der Kantonsregierungen) unites the heads of cantonal governments. It provides a political framework to the sectoral conferences of the cantonal ministers. The conference includes several committees and working groups which try to coordinate cantonal policies in specific areas. The Committee on European Affairs elaborates recommendations and prepares common positions on European integration and cross-border cooperation. In contrast to the Contact Committee under federal control, the Conference of the Cantons is better institutionalized and allows independent horizontal coordination without participation of federal authorities. Moreover, the Federal Council and the cantonal governments agreed in 1993 to place a representative of the cantons in the Integration Bureau. Thus the cantons have representatives in Brussels and Berne providing timely, independent information and asserting that the interests of the cantons are taken into consideration.

The 1995 draft constitution suggests including an additional article calling on the federal authorities to respect the competencies of the cantons and to represent their interests in foreign affairs. Namely, the federal authorities have to provide the cantons with timely and comprehensive information, to consult them and to involve them in the preparation of decisions on foreign affairs. The cantons in turn have to guarantee the timely implementation of international commitments. This article is more comprehensive than Article 21 of the transitional provisions to the federal constitution which limits consultation and participation to the EEA and only to those areas that relate to the cantonal competencies. The draft constitution also reasserts the right of the cantons to conduct their 'small foreign policy' and to conclude international agreements in the field of their competencies as long as the federal authorities are not acting and the treaties do not contradict federal commitments (Art. 45).

The cantons are gradually waking up to the realities of European cooperation. They are beginning to formulate policies in a broader European context and to advocate their interests in a more assertive way. In the course of European integration, the consultation and co-decision procedures between federal government and cantons have changed radically. A Europeanization of Swiss federalism can be observed. There are, however, three caveats. First, there is a clear difference between the interests and attitudes of the border regions and the internal regions, the German-speaking and French-speaking cantons. The cantons will find it difficult to agree on a common position in regard to European integration. Second, micro-integration cannot substitute macro-integration. As long as Switzerland makes little progress toward European integration, the cantons face obstacles in cross-border and inter-regional cooperation. Third, in comparison to the seven Austrian or sixteen German Länder, the Swiss cantons are very small. Not all cantons have the resources and the expertise to engage in international affairs. Most cantonal administrations do not even have a European affairs section. Few cantonal constitutions include provisions on foreign relations or European integration. Improvement of horizontal coordination and division of labour among the cantons is necessary in order to avoid overburdening the cantonal governments. One measure would be the appointment of two 'speakers' representing all the cantons. This form of collective representation would resemble the rotating chairmanship (*Vorort*) of the pre-1848 Swiss confederation. This division of labour would allow the cantons to follow the process of Swiss integration closely and to respond quickly to the twists and turns of international negotiations.

Direct democracy and European integration

According to the Swiss constitution, both Parliament and people form the legislature. In Swiss direct democracy, voters can influence policy through initiative and referendum. The veto power of the people (i.e. the political parties and organized interests) is an important feature in domestic affairs and becomes increasingly relevant to the conduct of foreign policy (see Brunetti and Straubhaar, 1991; Dirksen, 1995.) As the 'no' to the EEA Treaty on 6 December 1992 demonstrated, Swiss integration policy not only has to pass the hurdle of parliamentary approval, but it must also face a popular vote. If the government plans to join a supranational organization or a system of collective security, the referendum is obligatory – otherwise 50,000 citizens can demand an optional referendum. Bilateral treaties with the EU or agreements with the WTO are subject to an optional referendum, whereas EU membership is subject to an obligatory referendum. The EEA was a border case. The Federal Council decided to submit the agreement to an obligatory vote since it would have had far-reaching consequences for the Swiss political and legal system. In the case of an obligatory referendum, a simple majority of the popular vote will not suffice – a majority of the cantons is also required. Theoretically, 30 per cent of popular votes, coming from the 12 small cantons, are enough to block a majority decision. In the EEA referendum, 50.3 per cent of the population and 17 of the 23 cantons voted against the treaty. Thus the compounded majority was missed by only 0.4 per cent of the popular vote, but by 6 cantons. A strong majority of 55–60 per cent of the people would be necessary to reach a minimum majority of 12 cantons (Linder, 1994: 75).

The main question is whether the Swiss system of direct democracy has to be adapted to European integration. Since EU and international law take precedence over national legislation, direct democratic systems have to find ways and means to deal with initiatives that contradict existing international commitments and referenda blocking their implementation. Since 1874, roughly 150 initiatives from political bodies and approximately 120 popular initiatives have been launched, most of them in the post-war period. As several studies show, only a very few would have led to a conflict with the EEA, the EU or other international agreements (Schindler, 1990). The Alpine initiative, for instance, would have violated the EC principle of non-discrimination and contradicted EC transport policy. Other important popular initiatives in recent years, however, would not have conflicted with EEA or EU rules. In case of a conflict between direct democracy and international agreements, the federal Parliament could annul an initiative or a referendum based on its violation of international law; or, the federal authorities could submit a compatible counter-proposal, or adjust conflicting provisions in the course of implementation. Altern-atively, the Swiss government could take the initiative to adjust European policies to the demands of direct democracy. In the worst case, the government would probably be prepared to risk a negative ruling by an international court or to face sanctions induced by a violation of international commitments. The draft constitu-tion contains provisions that would restrict initiatives and referenda if they violate international law and other commitments (Art. 119, 166 bis). Other proposals for the reform of the political system call for stricter restrictions or even the abolition of direct democracy (Germann, 1994; Dirksen, 1996). The federal government, however, would rather withdraw from international negotiations than restrict direct democracy. The government's current strategy is to conclude treaties below the threshold requiring an obligatory referendum. The bilateral negotiations, for in-stance, aim at agreements that are only subject to an optional referendum. The advantage would be that only a simple majority of the popular vote, but not a majority of the states, is required to pass the package of bilateral treaties.

Political adaptation

Policy toward the EU is one of the most contested and divisive issues upsetting a long tradition of consensus and low level of conflict in Swiss politics. National interests are not perceived as being co-defined by European policy. Political decision-makers and officials have not internalized European integration in domestic policy-making. The Federal Council is divided over integration policy. Since unanimity is required on important issues, the council frequently finds itself in a deadlock. Non-integration and neutrality have been and continue to be successful strategies for preserving the cohesion both among the population, within the ruling party coalition and in the Federal Council. The four governing parties are also deeply divided over the future course of integration policy. During most of the post-war period, Swiss political parties were not at all interested in foreign and integration policy (Saint-Ouen, 1989). Beyond standard references to Swiss neutrality and independence, the party programmes did not address international issues. Foreign policy was essentially absent from domestic politics. Since the late 1980s, especially during and after the EEA debate, European integration started to figure prominently on the political agenda. In an increasingly polarized political environment, the major parties are forced to take a clear position. In most cases, the orientation process is difficult and conflictive, since most large, popular parties include pro- and anti-integration constituencies.

The Social Democrats – in alliance with the trade unions – were the first to speak out in favour of the EEA and later the EU. The Radical Democratic Party, a neo-liberal, free-market and business orientated force was more divided. While the federal party supported EEA membership, several cantonal party branches were opposed. The party also had substantial difficulties in agreeing that EU membership should be Switzerland's 'strategic goal', the official position of the Federal Council. Currently, the Christian People's Party is debating the pros and cons of various models of limited integration. The Swiss People's Party, led by National Councillor Christoph Blocher, is opposed to most sectoral agreements, EEA and EU membership. Again, several cantonal party branches are contradicting the federal party and speak out in favour of economic integration. Among the non-governing parties, only the Green Party and the Workers' Party are in favour of EU membership. Several right-wing parties, the Freedom Party (formerly the Automobile Party), the Lega dei Ticinesi and the Swiss Democrats, for example, are strictly opposed to more integration and are thus potential allies of the People's Party. There is a clear division between the attitudes of party members in the French- and the German-speaking parts. The dispute over European integration has thus not only resulted in cleavages between the parties, but also within the parties. In formulating integration policy and nego-tiation positions, the federal government must therefore take into consideration the contradictory positions of the ruling parties and try to find a compromise between the opposing views.

A new trend in the Swiss political system is the emergence of influential extra-parliamentary movements which oppose or support European integration. The most articulate of these is Christoph Blocher's Action for an Independent and Neutral Switzerland (AUNS), founded in 1986 as a movement opposing Swiss member-ship in the UN. AUNS was the decisive force in preventing Switzerland's participa-tion in the EEA in 1992. The movement opposes almost any step toward closer relations with the EU, based on the grounds that it would undermine Switzerland's sovereignty and neutrality. It threatens to use the direct democratic instruments of constitutional initiative and referendum in order to block the federal government's integration strategy. The movement has strong local branches, is well financed and can mobilize approximately 500,000 members, more than most of the major political parties. AUNS also provides the platform for an informal alliance among the anti-integrationist, conservative and right-wing parties. The movement allows anti-integration leaders such as Christoph Blocher, member of Parliament for the Swiss People's Party, to participate in the governing coalition on the one hand, while attacking the very same government for its pro-integration policy on the other. The pro-integration movements are much weaker and less homogenous. The leading organization, the European Movement Switzerland (EBS), was founded in the 1960s and continues to advocate EU membership. The youth movement 'Born on 7 December' emerged out of protest against the 'no' vote on 6 December 1992. The strategy of the pro-integration movements is to put the federal government under constant pressure by launching constitutional initiatives in favour of EEA and EU membership respectively. The emergence of these para-party structures means that political conflicts can no longer be resolved within the traditional institutions, but are decided at the ballot.

Most interest groups are equally divided over integration issues. The only organization that takes a very clear stance on European integration is the Swiss Federation of Trade Unions (SGB) and its branch organizations. In line with the Social Democrats, the trade unions push for full EU membership. The Swiss Trade and Industrial Association (Vorort) advocates free trade and supports participation in the EEA. The association is less outspoken on the issue of EU membership. Just like other business organizations and the economy in general, the Vorort is paralysed by the opposing interests of its members, namely large versus small- and medium-sized firms, and export-orientated versus protectionist enterprises. While the export-orientated enterprises and the services industry generally support full membership, domestic enterprises, small trade and agriculture try to maintain protection from foreign competition and to defend cartels, regulations and other technical barriers to trade. This cleavage reflects the split nature of Switzerland's small-state economy as described by Peter Katzenstein (1984; 1985). A strongly export-orientated, pro-integration economy coexists next to a protectionist, anti-integration economy. As Wolf Linder assumes, in future the Swiss economy will not be able to have it both ways (Linder, 1994: 129). European integration would have a strong influence on the opening up of protected sectors of the Swiss economy. An important prerequisite of integration is, however, that business organizations make up their minds and state their priorities. As the example of Austria's EEA and EU phasing-in demonstrates, business organizations and trade unions are important transmission belts which can play a decisive role in mobilizing a majority in favour of integration among the population.

Thus the domestic arena is very 'noisy'. Conflicts over foreign policy and integration issues are no longer resolved within the traditional institutions, but are decided at the ballot. There has been a shift from representative to direct democratic decision-making in European affairs. The federal government has little domestic leeway for policy formation and coordination in European affairs. Swiss integration policy is increasingly influenced by the 'shadow of the popular veto'. Government and administration are losing legitimacy. Minor adjustments in Switzerland's position in the bilateral talks are immediately discussed, criticized and rejected in public. In a climate of mistrust, even purely technical issues are politicized. In this two-level game, the federal government has very restricted room for active policy-making. Meanwhile, Switzerland pursues a non-controversial policy of participation without integration. EU legislation is adopted unilaterally. New laws or administrative acts are examined on the basis of whether or not they are 'Eurocompatible'. Hence European integration is taken into account in daily policy-making. Since Switzerland is not part of common policy, these adjustments are voluntary and non-binding. Formal autonomy is thus preserved. There is, however, a growing awareness that important issues such as access to the European markets or trans-Alpine transport can only be resolved in cooperation with the EU.

By contrast to the adjustments in domestic policy-making, there are few changes in Switzerland's pattern of international interaction as a consequence of European integration. The federal government and administration have established regular contacts and institutionalized coordination procedures with neighbouring countries and EU institutions. Trilateral ministerial meetings take place on a regular basis, addressing issues such as the environment (Austria, Germany, Switzerland), transport (Germany, Italy, Switzerland) and interior affairs (France, Germany, Switzerland). These good neighbourly contacts have a long-standing tradition. Increasingly, the meetings focus on European integration issues, namely trans-Alpine transport and freedom of labour. The federal government tries to instrumentalize these networks for gaining support and influencing the negotiation positions of the EU member-states in the bilateral talks.

The administration has also expanded contacts with its counterparts in the neighbouring states. What used to be the privilege of the foreign ministry is now standard practice of the sectoral ministries. Occasionally federal officials are invited to take part as observers in some of the EU committees, expert meetings and working groups. This exposure to European affairs, however, is restricted to the few sectors where a bilateral agreement is under negotiation or has already been concluded. Not more than 150 'Eurocrats' – or approximately 3 per cent of the administration – are involved in EU affairs on a regular basis. In the German federal administration, more than 25 per cent of the higher officials are regularly involved in the EU policy process (Wessels, 1992: 46). In comparison with the administrations of EU or EEA member countries, the 'Europeanization' of the Swiss administration in terms of activities, contacts and expertise is thus still very modest. As long as Switzerland does not participate in the commitology of the EU or the administrative coordination of the EEA, exposure of Swiss officials to the administrative system of the EU will remain limited.

Strategic adaptation

The current strategy of participation without integration suggests that Switzerland is more of a taker than a giver in European integration. While it profits from free trade with the European partners, it is more reluctant to bear the negative consequences of integration and to contribute to cohesion, structural aid and social security. Switzerland was instrumental in shaping the EEA Agreement and has taken the initiative in the bilateral talks on several occasions. Its integration strategy, however, is reactive rather than pro-active. As a non-member, the country is not participating in the widening and deepening of the EU. It lags behind and contributes little to European integration. In international relations, Switzerland is in an outsider position. Since Berne is not a member of the EU, the UN, NATO or other multilateral organizations, it does not participate in an institutionalized coalition or alliance of states. The long-standing ties within the group of neutral and non-aligned countries (N+N group) including Austria, Finland, former Yugoslavia and Sweden, have also come to a halt. Traditionally, the Swiss have relied on coordination and coalition with Austria, France, Germany and Italy. In negotiations with the EU, these neighbours, however, are sitting on the other side of the table. Support by these states depends on the issue area. On transport questions, Austria pursues very similar interests to Switzerland. The two Alpine republics form a natural coalition. On the freedom of labour, in turn, Switzerland has to face the opposition of all fifteen EU states. During the multilateral EEA negotiations, the coalition of EFTA states was in a good bargaining position and could yield major concessions from the EU. After EU enlargement, the EFTA coalition has lost its importance. In the bilateral talks, Switzerland is on its own. The difficult, conflictive and protracted nature of these technical negotiations suggests that the EU is less interested and Switzerland has less leverage than in the EEA. Thus the country is in a weak bargaining position and is marginalized as a non-member-state.

Moreover, because of internal divisions, Switzerland has difficulties in speaking with one voice. The Swiss government is thus confronted with the difficult task of satisfying the expectations of its European neighbours and the opposition of powerful domestic constituencies. Given the pay-off structure of this two-level game, the federal authorities have to develop strategies that allow them to assert their interests and to preserve their sovereignty. The Swiss government has made it clear that it prefers the failure of negotiations in Brussels rather than risk a negative vote by the Swiss population. Thus there is a clearly articulated exit option. Especially in regard to trans-Alpine transport, the country has a strategic advantage. The threat of non-cooperation or non-implementation provides bargaining leverage, but also has a high political price. Switzerland risks turning from a reliable international partner into a cause of trouble. Relying on nuisance value is the strategy of a weak actor with limited resources and few allies in the international system. The current strategy of participation without integration reconciles these conflicting objectives. Switzerland unilaterally adopts EU policies. It is a semi-autonomous state, implementing legislation that has been decided by others. A margin of independence remains, allowing Switzerland to conduct an autonomous policy in areas such as the environment or transport. Autonomy has its limits, as the negative repercussions of the Alpine initiative have illustrated. As a small state surrounded by a large union, Switzerland is no longer able to act unilaterally.

Conclusion

The pattern of institutional adaptation observed in the case of Switzerland seems to suggest that the European nation-states manage to maintain their executive and administrative individuality and institutional identity in the context of economic and political integration. While international and supranational decision-making pose challenges to the efficiency of the Swiss political system, there is no need for fundamental reforms threatening the institutional autonomy of the country *per se*. The pragmatic, incremental improvements of governmental structures and procedures over the last years are proof of the institutional capacity to adapt. Efficient adaptation can also be considered as a compensation for non-membership. Widely considered as one of the major political failures in Swiss history, the EEA process offered a window of opportunity for institutional adjustment and had a profound impact on Switzerland's political system. The separated domestic and foreign policy decision-making processes are increasingly fused together. A little noticed, gradual 'Europeanization' of government, party politics, federalism and organized interests can be observed. Institutional phasing-in has made progress, and 'integration by stealth' proceeds.

In government and administration, institutional capacities have been built up. No fundamental adjustments have been made in the structures and procedures of government. Standard operating procedures for intra- and interministerial coordination have been retained. Thus there is less adaptation in government and administration than expected. Significant changes can be observed in the consultation of other foreign policy actors. The role of the Parliament in international affairs has increased, the cantons are consulted on a regular basis and the government takes into account the veto power of political parties, anti-integration movements and organized interests. Surprisingly, it is not the government and the administration that have been strengthened in the process of institutional adaptation, but Parliament, federalism and direct democracy. Policy formation, policy coordination and preparation of negotiations have thus changed considerably. Many of these changes are included in the 1995 draft constitution. It is difficult, however, to point out which adaptations were a consequence of developments in the EU and which other changes were simply in line with the more general process of administrative modernization and internationalization. As long as Switzerland is not a member of the EEA or the EU, pressures for adaptation remain weak. In comparison with the institutional set-up of more integrated states, the Swiss government and administrative system is not yet capable of meeting the challenges of intergovernmental and supranational decision-shaping and decision-making processes in a European context.

Switzerland also experienced substantial political adaptation. The improved Participation of parliament, political parties, interest groups and cantons in policy formation results in a democratization of Swiss foreign affairs. The growing importance of the pre-parliamentary stage and the emergence of powerful paraparty organizations results in a de-institutionalization and fragmentation of the policy process. Consultation and coordination increasingly take place on an *ad hoc* basis, outside the traditional institutions. The federal government is losing its traditional role as integration policy-maker and has difficulties in mobilizing and sustaining support for a particular integration strategy. Confronted with the twists and turns of domestic politics, Berne is seriously constrained in bilateral negotiations with the EU. Proposals of the EU are evaluated in terms of domestic politics. The shadow of the referendum defines Switzerland's bargaining strategy. Once the two sides reach an agreement, the Swiss authorities have to overcome strong domestic opposition against ratification and implementation. Switzerland's integration policy is thus poorly organized and highly vulnerable to domestic pressures. It is an internally divided, weak and wavering actor on the European stage.

Recent developments have illustrated that the direct democratic, federal and multi-ethnic state is coming under increasing pressure. Incremental adaptation is probably not sufficient to manage the unresolved conflicts and to bridge the widening cleavages within the Swiss polity. A more fundamental change may be required. Three scenarios are feasible:

1 *Emergence of a new consensus* The Swiss political system will find a new equilibrium without major adjustments in political alignments or adaptation of institutions. Confronted with the realities of European integration and encouraged by the results of the bilateral negotiations, a new consensus, first on joining the EEA, then on EU membership, will gradually build up as a result of the protracted tug-of-war between the opposing interests.

2 *Realignment of political forces* The Swiss political system will only adjust to European integration after a major realignment of political forces, parties and interest groups. A 'great coalition' consisting of the reform-orientated centre, the political left, pro-integration cantons and various interest groups will shift the correlation of forces in favour of EEA or EU membership. The four-party governing coalition will be replaced by a three-party majority block. This could include a switch from consociational to competitive government. Cleavages within the centrist parties, between the French-speaking and German-speaking party branches and within business organizations may result in a profound transformation of the party political landscape, affect institutions and influence policy style. Linder refers to the possibility of a realignment of the Swiss party system into three main forces: a new, populist national conservative party drawing anti-integration members from all governmental parties; a centre force consisting of liberal Christian democrats and radicals; and a moderate left including the social democrats and the Greens (Linder, 1994: 176).

3 *Fundamental reform of political institutions* Bold institutional and constitutional reforms will result in a fundamental transformation of the entire political system. Switzerland will switch from a consensus to a mixed, more competitive system. Direct democracy will be limited to essential questions of state organization and integration. Executive consociationalism will be replaced by a broader political and social dialogue, including stronger federalist and neo-corporatist elements.

The outcome will probably be a combination of the three scenarios. A quantum leap in the organization of the Swiss political system comparable to the one from the Swiss confederation to the federation in 1848 or the Fourth to the Fifth French Republic is rather unlikely. Incremental adaptation is characteristic for the development of the Swiss political system. Switzerland will move closer to the mixed-system type of Austria or Germany. Politics will become more competitive, just as it was during the inter-war period. Institutional and substantial reforms are necessary with or without integration. Consensus democracy has its political price. After decades of complacency, compromise and compensation, Switzerland is facing a wealth of unresolved problems. Agriculture, employment, education, health, transport, public expenditures and social security are critical policy areas in need of reforms. Despite its rejection, the EEA project helped to identify the problems and to mobilize reform-orientated forces. Small states seem to have more difficulties in adjusting to external changes than do medium and large states. The question is whether reform can be realized without integration or whether integration forms the leverage of reform. Integration was instrumentalized to justify reforms, for instance, in France in the 1950s and in Austria and Sweden in the 1990s. Reform through integration could also be an attractive strategy for Switzerland.

Inside and outside pressure for adaptation and integration will continue. The issue is timing and phasing. EU membership can hardly be achieved in one step but only through gradual adaptation in several intermediate steps. The next step in the integration of Switzerland is the conclusion of bilateral agreements, probably leading to the resumption of negotiations on EEA membership. Yet Switzerland may be running out of time. The radical change in the European agenda, the transformation of institutional roles and the emergence of a new group of active small states on the political map of Europe have all contributed to the growing marginalization of the country and have brought an end to the *Sonderfall Schweiz*. The country's non-participation in the EU, UN, NATO and other international institutions has not only resulted in an increasing self-isolation but also projects a negative image of an egoistic free-rider refusing cooperation and solidarity with the community of European states (Riklin, 1995). Moreover, Switzerland is increasingly becoming a divided, polarized country. The traditional consensus has been shaken, not only on European integration, but also on macroeconomic and social issues. For Switzerland, the alternative to institutional adaptation and integration is probably stagnation and disintegration. Arend Lijphart's model democracy is facing a prolonged period of conflict and uncertainty.

References

Brunetti, A. and Straubhaar, T. (1991) Internationalisierung und direkte Demokratie, *Schweizerisches Jahrbuch für Politische Wissenschaft*, 31 (Berne: Paul Haupt), pp. 237–56.

Dirksen, R-G. (1995) Die direkte Demokratie im aussenpolitischen Kontext. Ein Beitrag zur Staatsreform-Diskussion in der Schweiz. In Thomas Ellwein, Dieter Grimm, Joachim Jens Hesse and Gunnar Folke Schuppert (eds), *Jahrbuch zur Staats- und Verwaltungswissenschaft*, vol. 8 (Baden-Baden: Nomos), pp. 177–201.

Dirksen, R-G. (1996) Der Zusammenhang zwischen Verfassungs- und Europafrage. Die Grenzen einer Verfassungsreform in der Schweiz, *Zeitschrift für öffentliches Recht*, pp. 27ff.

Germann, R.E. (1994) *Staatsreform. Der Übergang zur Konkurrenzdemokratie*, vol. 50, no. 2 (Berne: Paul Haupt).

Germann, R.E. (1995) Die bilateralen Verhandlungen mit der EU und die Steuerung der direkten Demokratie, *Swiss Political Science Review*, vol. 1, nos 2–3, pp. 35–60.

Goetschel, L. (1994) *Zwischen Effizienz und Akzeptanz. Die Information der Schweizer Behörden im Hinblick auf die Volksabstimmung über den EWR-Vertrag vom 6. Dezember 1992* (Berne: Paul Haupt).

Huth, P. (1996) *Europäisierung oder 'Entschweizung'? Der Abstimmung der Schweiz um den Beitritt zum Europäischen Wirtschaftsraum* (Berne: Peter Lang).

Katzenstein, P.J. (1984) *Corporatism and Change: Austria, Switzerland and the Politics of Industry* (Ithaca, NY: Cornell University Press).

Katzenstein, P.J. (1985) *Small States in World Markets: Industrial Policy in Europe* (Ithaca, NY: Cornell University Press).

Klöti, U. and S. von Dosenrode (1995) Adaptation to European integration: changes in the administration of four small states, *Australian Journal of Public Administration*, vol. 54, no. 2, pp. 273–81.

Kreis, G. (1995) *Der lange Weg des Staatsvertragsreferendums. Schweizerische Aussenpolitik zwischen indirekter und direkter Demokratie*, Basler Schriften zur europäischen Integration Nr. 12 (Basle: Europainstitut).

Kux, S. (1994) *Subsidiarity and the Environment: Implementing International Agreements*, Basler Schrift zur Europäischen Integration Nr. 9 (Basle: Europainstitut).

Linder, W. (1994) *Swiss Democracy: Possible Solutions to Conflict in Multicultural Societies* (Houndmills: Macmillan).

Riklin, A. (1995) Isolierte Schweiz. Eine europa- und innenpolitische Lagebeurteilung, *Swiss Political Science Review*, vol. 1, nos 2–3, pp. 11–34.

Saint-Ouen, F. (1989) Les partis politiques face à l'intégration européenne. In Roland Ruffieux (ed.), *La Suisse et son avenir européen* (Lausanne: Payot), pp. 217–25.

Schindler, D. (1990) *Auswirkungen der EG auf die schweizerische Staatsstruktur*, Wirtschaftspolitische Mitteilungen, vol. 46, no. 2 (Zürich: Wirtschaftsförderung).

Sciarini, P. (1991) Le rôle et la position de l'Assemblée fédérale dans les relations avec la Communauté européenne depuis 1972. In Services du Parlement (ed.), *Le Parlement – 'Autorité suprême de la Confédération'?* (Berne: Paul Haupt), pp. 403–23.

Sciarini, P. (1992) La Suisse dans la négociation sur l'Espace économique européen: de la rupture à l'apprentissage, *Schweizerisches Jahrbuch für Politische Wissenschaft*, 32 (Berne: Paul Haupt), pp. 297–322.

Wessels, W. (1992) Staat und (westeuropäische) Integration. Die Fusionsthese, *Politische Vieteljahresschrift*, Sonderheft 23 (Opladen: Westdeutscher Verlag).

Chapter 12

Conclusion: The Nature of National Adaptation to European Integration

BEN SOETENDORP AND KENNETH HANF

In this concluding chapter we will try to make some generalizable points regarding the nature of institutional adaptation in general, and the experience that the individual smaller member-states of the EU have had with respect to the process of Europeanization. As was indicated in the introductory chapter, the aim of this volume has been to examine how the political institutions in eight small member-states and two non-members have responded to the internal and external demands springing from EC/EU membership. For that purpose we will organize our observations around the three dimensions of adaptation that we have highlighted: governmental, political and strategic. However, since the greater part of the previous chapters deals with governmental adaptation, we will treat this aspect in more detail.

Governmental adaptation

The essential conclusion we draw has to do with our expectation that joining the EC/EU would affect the political and administrative institutions of the smaller member-states in many ways, as the political leadership and the bureaucracy seeks to cope with a considerably larger and more complex political environment. In this respect we also assumed that there could be a significant difference between those countries that were members of the EC from the beginning, and those countries that joined an ongoing organization that made rather radical demands on their adaptive capacity. Whereas the older members (the Netherlands and Belgium) had participated in the design and development of the rules of the game, the later members (Denmark, Ireland, Greece and Spain) and especially the most recent newcomers (Sweden and Austria) joined an ongoing game. On the basis of the individual country studies we have to conclude that there seems to have been no radical shift or change in the way that things were done before and after EU membership. That is to say, the governmental adjustments were made in an incremental way, building upon traditions and arrangements that were already in place. Nor do these studies point to any significant difference between the four sets of countries, with regard to the point of time when they entered the EC/EU.

The empirical evidence in the previous chapters clearly indicates that in handling the new requirements of EC/EU membership, governmental adaptation was a series of *ad hoc* responses to emerging problems and demands. It appears that even the intensification of joint policy-making and the broadening of the range of national policies that fall under the EC/EU competence, following the signing of the Single European Act and the Treaty on European Union, have not triggered any kind of systematic, centrally directed adjustment to the demands of further Europeanization. While the process of European policy-making has become increasingly complex over the years, as more and more ministries as well as other domestic actors have become involved, none of the smaller member-states considered major organizational adjustments at the level of central government to meet the new challenges. No country examined, for example, the option of a special ministry for European affairs. Instead, the new tasks deriving from growing Europeanization were just added to the existing tasks of each department. At the most, a new European section was created within the present ministry to deal with intradepartmental and interministerial coordination. These observations apply to the older as well as the new small member-states. The Netherlands, which has recently gone through a complete reorganization of its foreign ministry, has actually kept the procedures and structure of European policy-making the way they had been set up in the late 1950s. During the many years of membership only incremental adjustments have taken place to accommodate the demands of EC/EU membership. For example, the overall responsibility for the formulation of a Dutch negotiation position in COREPER and the Council was transferred from the Ministry of Economic Affairs to the Ministry of Foreign Affairs, and special interministerial committees were established to evaluate new proposals of the European Commission and to monitor the implementation of decisions taken by the Council.

Also in the cases of Ireland and Denmark, Europeanization was more a process of gradual adaptation instead of a dramatic break with the past. Expanding Europeanization has led in Denmark, according to von Dosenrode, to increased interdepartmental coordination but has not caused fundamental structural changes. Or as Laffan and Tannam noted in Chapter 5, membership has imposed a severe burden on the Irish administration, which was ill-prepared for all that was demanded by involvement in the intense negotiating process in Brussels. However, EC/EU matters were, and still are, dealt with in the same manner as purely domestic issues. A similar observation could be made for Greece and Spain, who joined the EC/EU in subsequent enlargement rounds. Even the initial administrative planning for EU membership in Sweden, a newcomer who could learn from the experience of former accessions, was based on the prediction that membership would not fundamentally affect the Swedish model of governance. Ekengren and Sundelius have pointed out in Chapter 9 that this expectation of no basic change had to be reconsidered after the first year of working within the EU. But, as they suggest, this may simply result in a redistribution of human resources from the large to the relatively small ministries.

The only exception to these general observations seems to be Belgium, where successive and fundamental state reforms resulted in some basic changes in European policy-making at the national level. Yet, as Kerremans and Beyers have stressed in Chapter 2, the administrative adaptations that took place were rather the consequence of the state reforms that took place between 1980 and 1993. Whenever Europe was a reason to adapt the structures, the adaptation occurred on an *ad hoc* basis. There was certainly no general Belgian policy to adapt to the challenges and requirements of the 'new' Europe. The inclusion of two non-member-states in this study was quite enlightening. As the cases of Norway and Switzerland clearly illustrate, even non-members have to cope with the challenges of European integration. Sverdrup points out clearly that the Norwegian political system, like the member-states, also responded to the process of Europeanization of public policy-making through a process of a step-by-step adaptation rather than the inventing of radical new solutions. Switzerland, where not only EU membership but even accession to the European Economic Area was rejected, pursued a strategy of administrative adaptation as well. But as Kux illustrates in Chapter 11, constitutional provisions and popular veto have set narrow limits to the adaptation of the structures of Swiss governance to European integration. Consequently, cooperation between the federal government and the cantons regarding European integration has not been institutionalized and remained on an *ad hoc* basis.

Although the small member-states have not made significant changes in the organization and style of policy-making in response to the Europeanization of public policy, they have had to organize the input of their national bureaucracies into the multi-level and multiple arenas that characterize EU policy-making. Each new member learned very quickly that the EU was not just another international organization, where the foreign ministry could simply act as a mediator between the relevant national ministries and the specific international organization. Almost daily some national officials from the relevant leading department have to present a national position on a specific dossier in one of the many working groups set up by the Council of Ministers to discuss proposals for European common policies initiated by the Commission. Each member-state also has to prepare a number of national negotiation positions regarding various dossiers for the weekly meetings of the Permanent Representatives and their deputies, and to formulate final national positions for the regular Council meetings of the foreign ministers as well as the other sectoral ministers. Consequently, the member-states have found it necessary to make some arrangements for their interaction with the other member-states at the European level. This means that they have adapted the national system of public policy-making and the national standard operating procedures to existing structures and procedures of policy-making at the EC/EU level and the modification introduced by the SEA and the TEU. In the various contributions to this volume, we have seen that each member-state has created some kind of an overall coordination system to structure its national input into the European decision-making system which follows, in general lines, the cycle of policy-making at the European level.

However, as Laffan and Tannam argue, the nature and extent of the EU influence depends on endogenous factors in the member-states which affect their capacity to adapt. The different country studies demonstrate that the existing administrative traditions and domestic structures in the various smaller member-states have clearly set limits to the way that the individual members have organized the overall coordination of their input into the European decision-making process. Adaptation has not been a simple rational process of mounting the appropriate response to the problem of coordination and presenting a cohesive national position in the different EU decision-making fora. The coordination mechanisms and procedures are actually shaped by a number of contextual factors and are limited by institutional or political constraints. For example, the principle of departmental autonomy, which prevails in almost every small state discussed in this volume, restricts the primary responsibility of the Ministry of Foreign Affairs for the day-to-day management of the European policy process. It is usually the ministry that has the main competence in a specific matter, not the foreign ministry that actually formulates the initial position presented in the Council working groups. Only at the level of COREPER does the foreign ministry usually regain its principal responsibility for interministerial coordination and the preparation of the national negotiation position in the COREPER meetings as well as the Council meetings. The extent to which the prime minister is involved in determining the final negotiation position in the relevant Council, as we have seen, varies per member-state, depending on the unique political culture and the particular style of public policy-making.

The same observation also applies to the degree to which the Parliament in the various smaller member-states can intervene in the definition of such a negotiation position or the extent to which regional authorities and interest groups participate in the formulation of that position. In this respect the prime ministers in Ireland, Spain and Greece have much more control over the negotiating strategies of their country than their counterparts in the other smaller member-states. In Denmark, Austria and Sweden, more consideration is given to a proper exchange of views between Parliament and government preceding decision-making in the various Council of Ministers. The unique federal constitutions in Belgium and Austria, which regulate the participation of the Belgian regional governments and the Austrian provinces in determining the national negotiation position in the Council, clearly give the regional authorities much more influence in the formulation of national EU policies than in the other member-states dealt with in this volume.

Political and strategic adaptation

Despite the awareness among the smaller member-states of the fact and significance of the Europeanization of policy and policy-making, we have seen in the countries discussed within this volume a great diversity regarding political adaptation. Not all the political decision-makers in these member-states have been willing to change their behaviour to meet the new demands. But there is a clear distinction with respect to the extent to which the EC/EU dimension has been internalized in domestic policy-making between the member-states that have been present at the creation of the Community, and the countries that joined at a later stage. Belgium and the Netherlands are clearly committed to the value and institutionalization of European integration as such. Belgium, Kerremans and Beyers argue, can be considered 'more European than the European Union itself' and is certainly the most radical in its pro-European rhetoric. The construction of the EU on a federal basis has always been and still is a priority of Belgium's foreign policy. Also the Netherlands has always been in favour of the strengthening of EU institutions and the reinforcement of a federal mode of decision-making, although Chapter 3 draws attention to some moderation in the orthodox pro-European attitude of the Netherlands.

Notwithstanding the support for the goal of European integration in the smaller member-states that joined the EC/EU later, European integration is less strongly perceived in these countries as some kind of a higher normative goal. The approach to European integration is much more pragmatic. There is a consensus at the élite level on the need to join the EC/EU and the advantages expected from such a membership. Laffan and Tannam conclude in their chapter that Irish civil servants are socialized into the norms and values of Community policy. They have internalized EU business as part of the routine of their work, and see the EU as a legitimate arena of public policy-making. The existence of a generally favourable public opinion makes Irish policy-makers less constrained in their dealings with Brussels, apart from in relation to issues touching on security and public morality. The political élite in Spain and a newcomer like Austria also lacks any kind of inbuilt resistance to EU involvement in a wide range of policy sectors, provided that EU decisions take account of Spanish or Austrian interests.

However, even in critical member-states like Denmark and Sweden, the political élite is clearly aware that Europeanization, whether one likes it or not, is a given fact of contemporary political life, defining the context within and the possibilities for the pursuance of national policy objectives. In Chapter 4, von Dosenrode maintains that the Danish ministers dealing with EU affairs are generally 'pro-Europe'. They are embedded in a European environment and interact regularly with their European counterparts in EU Council meetings. But the critical domestic attitude regarding the EU prevents them from internalizing EU policies in domestic policies. He clearly demonstrates that, as European policy-making increasingly touches upon more and more domestic issue areas, one can notice a steady decline in the general public support for the EU. The margins in favour of EU membership in Denmark are very small and the population is actually divided into two almost equal large blocks of opponents to and proponents of further Danish involvement in European integration. A major reason for the Danish to approve the TEU was the fear of the economic disadvantages if the country were left outside the Union, rather than support for the European idea as such.

Although EU membership has made radical demands on the capacity of Sweden to adapt politically to the process of European integration, the political élite in the country was willing to take on board a rather extensive legislative programme already in place and to join institutional arrangements as well as to participate in both formal and informal procedures or ways of doing business that were already established. Ekengren and Sundelius have pointed out in Chapter 9 that the Swedish government developed an accommodating style prior to its application for membership. Its ambition was to make Sweden a more fully integrated state, even before entry, than many members had achieved after years within the Community. In that way the Swedish government hoped to belong to the inner core instead of having a marginal position as one of the many peripheral members. But, as in the Danish case, while there seems to have been a quick adaptation at the governmental level, public opinion rejection of the EU has increased. The record of Swedish adaptation to European integration indicates, according to Ekengren and Sundelius, that state and society appear to be out of touch with each other on the issue of European integration. Whereas the Swedish state moved towards adaptation at the governmental level almost a decade ago, only parts of Swedish society have done so after accession.

More recently, Norway and Switzerland are two other examples of the leadership being too far out in front of the general public with regard to the benefits of EU membership. The rejection of EU membership by a majority of the Norwegian population, while the Norwegian government already participated in the EU meetings in Brussels as a potential member, indicates how deep the gap has been between the politico-administrative establishment and the rest of society.

For the political leaders in some small member-states the EU clearly offers an opportunity to achieve domestic political goals. Ekengren and Sundelius claim that an important pro-membership argument was that active participation in European policy-making was necessary to shape future domestic conditions in Sweden. The political élite in Sweden believed that only through membership could Sweden gain influence on the formation of those EU policies that would influence developments inside the country. Moreover, the government hoped that the EU would adapt to the progressive values of Swedish society and expected Sweden to play a pivotal role in turning the EU into a progressive force in world affairs. Other political leaders in the smaller European states have less ambitious goals. The EU could simply help to reinforce their position in the domestic political scene. The best way for a Belgian politician to prove that he is a statesman, Kerremans and Beyers say in Chapter 2, is to present himself as a European leader.

As mentioned in the introduction, with regard to the EU the proof of the pudding is also in the implementing of EU policy. Effective execution of European legislation continues to be a serious problem. The references to the implementation problems in the country chapters illustrates the concern with this issue, which is not, of course, limited to the small member-states. The declaration of the leaders of the member-states appended to the Maastricht Treaty underscores the political concern with the issue of effective implementation. However, a poor national record on implementing EU directives is not necessarily a sign of lack of political commitment to the idea of integration or an indication that a country does not take its commitments as a member-state seriously. Although much has been written regarding the possibility of recouping positions lost in the formulation of EU policy by purposefully dragging one's feet, or indeed introducing substantive changes during the implementation phase, there is little evidence of this kind of obstructionist behaviour. As Luif suggests in Chapter 8, being a 'good European' in terms of implementing EU directives depends more on the institutional structure of a country than on the general public support for European integration. In some cases, like the Netherlands, the formal procedures involved in transposing EU directives into national law are long and time-consuming. Problems of coordination among different national actors with regard to the formal implementation of EU legislation can also lead to delays and lack of decisive action. The relations between national and other institutional actors in the country can also be a cause of 'poor implementation'. For example, the implementation record of the EU directives concerning the internal market of the member-states (as of 15 May 1996) shows that federal states like Belgium and Austria are at the bottom of this list. Federal states apparently have particular problems in implementing EU rules because more than one level of government is involved.

The studies in this volume indicate that all the countries discussed were aware of the fact of a new strategic context within which national governments need to act.

Laffan and Tannam point out that European policy-making is not simply a vertical interaction between Brussels and the member-states. National officials are no longer just agents of their national government. They are participants in an evolving polity which provides opportunities for political action but also imposes constraints on their freedom of action. The evidence from the country chapters does suggest that the small member-states are slowly learning that a keen understanding of the dynamics of complex negotiations in the Union and the attitude of one's partners and EU institutions is as important as technical competence in the policy area. Nevertheless, no government has had a strategic plan to make the country more effective in pursuing national objectives and preferences at the European level.

It has been argued that small member-states, in particular, if they are to play this game effectively, will need to have a capacity for developing coherent, well-reasoned national positions on the policy issues up for decision. They will have to be able to present and defend convincingly these stands in the different arenas of negotiation and decision-making. All the country chapters in this volume indicate that, in this regard, the primary strategic response of the member-states to joint policy-making at the European level was the development of some kind of a coordination mechanism. The presentation of one homogenous position in the negotiations in the Council and its preparatory fora was considered to be a satisfactory instrument for effective behaviour in Brussels. As we have seen, departmental autonomy nevertheless forms a great hindrance to almost every country speaking in Brussels with one voice. Interesting in this connection is the attempt of a newcomer such as Sweden to respond effectively to the difficulty of central coordination in the EU context by means of the formation of 'common national outlooks' across the many policy sectors of EU relations that can guide Swedish representatives in the complex and decentralized European policy-making process.

The chapters in this volume also demonstrate that the modifications in the functioning of the EC/EU, introduced by the SEA and the TEU, have required the smaller member-states to adopt a more strategic approach to EU membership. For example, the extension of qualified majority voting to an increased number of policy areas has made the need for coalition-building crucial, especially for the smaller member-states. This has made new demands on the smaller members. Many domestic ministries had to engage in transnational contacts with their counterparts in the other European capitals. They had to be informed about what is going on in other EU countries, to avoid isolation during negotiations, and to be aware of potential coalitions with other members. Some smaller members still behave in a reactive manner, while other small members are more pro-active. The more active members, like Belgium, the Netherlands, Spain or Sweden, try to form *ad hoc* coalitions with the larger states, while the smaller states, like Ireland or Greece, wait and see what the outcome is before settling for a compromise in exchange for some rewards. At the same time, Spain is not adverse to working with other, smaller member-states, which share similar concerns and problems of economic development. Quite surprisingly, there are no stable coalitions among the smaller member-states. A potential coalition between like-minded states such as the Nordic members and the Benelux is almost non-existent.

New smaller members also had great difficulty in adapting to the decision-making style and the negotiating methods in the EU. Sweden, for instance, had problems with the legalistic and hierarchic–administrative culture within the Commission and the Council secretariat. The short deadlines and the high pressure under which decision-making in the Council takes place has created great difficulties for the strong tradition of consensus-building in these countries. Because of the short preparation time for Council meetings and the need to compromise during such a meeting, national representatives have no time to secure wide support at home for positions taken independently in Council meetings. Austria learned very soon after its entry to the EU that tight instruction for negotiations in the Council left no leeway for negotiations, and actually weakened the bargaining power of the Austrian minister.

It is not surprising that the small member-states examined in the country studies in this volume have indeed recognized the new strategic context within which they must act in both the definition and pursuit of national interests under conditions of Europeanization. Being a member of the EU forces institutional actors, both public and private, at all levels, to confront the need to learn how to participate effectively in this multi-level European policy process. While the nation-state may remain a central actor in this process, it can only continue to do so if its institutional capacity can be developed to meet the challenges of membership in the emerging European Union. In all the countries discussed in this book there are strong signs that important governmental adaptations have taken place in this direction.

At the same time, there are equally strong indications that there is a danger that the governmental leaders may be too far in front of both the general public and other institutional and societal actors. In some cases this has led to rude awakenings with regard to plans for formal membership. In other instances, there are signs of growing disillusion with the results or pay-offs of membership. Especially in some of the new members, but even in the case of older members, the ideological – or principled – commitment to European integration as such has weakened, or was absent from the beginning. The legitimacy of membership – and the justification for the efforts to adapt and for the disruption of some traditional ways of doing things – is seen in the pragmatic calculation of economic benefits and the contribution to national problem-solving of EU policy products. The danger here is that when, as can be seen in some of the countries examined, disappointment with these results sets in, this can lead to disillusionment with the idea of membership. There is perhaps no immediate danger of a mass exodus of smaller member-states. Nevertheless, the possibility of a 'political credibility' gap between the political and government leaders and officials whose jobs bring them in daily contact with their counterparts in the different decision arenas, suggest that more attention should be paid to avoiding a situation where the leaders have lost their followers.

Many observers have argued that the small states in particular can reap advantages from membership of the EU. Here they can exert more influence and achieve more of what they seek than if they were forced to compete on their own in the 'international political market' with the larger powers. The formal institutions and procedures of the EU, in this view, provide both opportunities for being heard and protection against being overwhelmed by the larger members. Within the EU small states have to be taken seriously – at least more seriously than outside. If this is so, one would expect these states to be particularly conscious of the need to adapt to changes in the institutional context within which they act at the European level. While this is in fact the case with regard to governmental and political adaptation, there is less indication of strategic adaptation. In this regard the lesson we may draw from this study is that the smaller member-states, which do not have the ability to control the policy-making process in the EU, still have a long way to go in developing a capacity to approach the overall development of European integration in terms of the role of the smaller states in general and the appropriate strategy for their own countries in particular.

Index

Note: users are advised to look for subjects under countries as well as under general entries.